Dispatches from the Peninsula

Six Years in South Korea

Praise for Dispatches from the Peninsula

Tharp is like some punk-rock Huck Finn, as aware and humane as he is blithely non-PC, drama springing up around him with every choice he makes: another country, another drink, another thought he maybe should have kept to himself—but his brain is bigger than his mouth, and *Dispatches from the Peninsula* gives us the whole show. And somehow, amid all its intelligence and humor, the book packs a deeper wallop too, as a serious meditation on the lifelong experiment of growing up.

Lawrence Krauser, author of *Lemon*, *The Joy of Google*, and *The Day in Question*

Tough and true is Tharp's journey in South Korea. I found myself back there, welcoming anew Korea's wonder, her wrangle, the distinct spirit of the peninsula and her people. All along the way, Tharp is an observant and steady companion.

Cullen Thomas, author of *Brother One Cell*

Chris's descriptions of life as an expat in Korea show us a part of the world Americans know little about, other than crazy leader Kim Jong-il and a vague recollection that there was a war there long ago. Tharp's writing is a mix of the sensitive and the whimsical, with a strong human touch, and I smiled as I read his stories, wondering what my own life would have been like had I followed in his path and ventured off to Korea. *Dispatches from the Peninsula* is like a bowl of spicy travel kimchee for the curious mind. Savor every drop!

Michael Luongo, travel writer and winner of NATJA's Grand Prize in Travel Journalism Award 2010

Dispatches from the Peninsula

Six Years in South Korea

by

Chris Tharp

SIGNAL8PRESS

Hong Kong

Dispatches from the Peninsula

Six Years in South Korea

By Chris Tharp

Published by Signal 8 Press

An imprint of Typhoon Media Ltd

ISBN: 978-988-15161-1-4

eISBN: 978-988-15161-5-2

Typhoon Media Ltd: Signal 8 Press | BookCyclone

Hong Kong

www.typhoon-media.com

www.bookcyclone.com

www.signal8press.com

Cover design: Clarence Choi

Cover and author photos: Will Jackson

CONTENTS

For Chaunce and Glo

CHAPTER 1

NEON CROSSES

THE first thing I noticed was the crosses—red, lit-up crosses—attached to the steeples of the city's many churches, floating in the darkness of the early August evening. They popped out in contrast to all the restaurant and shop signs in the blocky circles, squares, and right angles of the Korean script known as *Hangul*. There were churches everywhere, each displaying its own garish cross, reminding you of Christ's sacrifice with a burning, neon fervor. Despite my agnosticism, I found all this incandescent evidence of Christianity somehow reassuring: *At least some of them worship the same God as us.* This assuaged my Western anxiety, and—in my mind—reduced the likelihood of me being maimed, killed, or eaten.

The bus I traveled on was a "limousine bus," though there was neither a wet bar nor a sunroof (not to mention any smooth surfaces off of which you could snort cocaine), and it wasn't stretched out longer than any bus I'd ridden on before. It was nice, but unless you're a touring rock band, there are very few ways you can dress up a bus. This bus simply served as transportation from the airport to several key points in the city of Busan, South Korea's largest seaport and second biggest metropolis... and my new home. Calling the bus a "limousine" was fine with me: I could imagine I that was riding in style and forget the fact that, despite having traveled over the world's largest ocean to a country where I didn't even know the word for *hello*, no one had bothered to pick me up at the airport.

The bus careened through the car-clogged city at obscene speeds, only to jerk to a stop within minuscule distances, sending bags sliding and causing my head to slam into the seat in front of me. Despite the trappings of affluence on the road—shiny new cars, high-definition digital reader boards, working traffic lights, a pothole-free surface—Korean bus drivers drove Third-World style. Later I would find that the drivers of the blue and orange city buses are worse: they pilot with even more violence, and the smashed-together payloads of standing passengers just endure the jostling without complaint. At least I had the privilege to sit, though I'm sure my fingers left divots in the plastic armrests as the driver barreled through the crowded streets. He smoked skinny cigarettes and loudly sang along with Korean *trot* music, its mournful vibratos and Casio keyboard cha-cha beats blaring from the speakers. Korean bus drivers, it seemed, were culturally mandated to drive like meth addicts on their way to a score.

As we shot up the highway, over the Nakdong River and away from the airport, I took in the approaching skyline. A ridge of medium-sized skyscrapers reached up in front of an imposing mountain. I took this to be the core of the city, the downtown. Of course I soon realized that these weren't skyscrapers as I knew them, but rather a cluster of apartment blocks, and that we were still deep in the suburbs. This first visible line of urbanization was merely a sliver of a disconcertingly long city that snaked its way along the coast, up valleys, and between rises of ancient fortress-topped mountains. Korea is an extremely mountainous country, with only about thirty percent of its land suitable for building. The cramped panorama of apartment towers that jutted in front of me served as a testament to this. Every bit of available space was utilized—people were literally stacked on top of each other—so it was *crowded.* With the exception of the crosses, this was Asia as I had imagined it. I was in Korea, and it was already weird.

Jimmy, my local contact, didn't want to come pick me up at the airport. Something about traffic, he had muttered in halting English a few days before, over a trans-Pacific phone connection. We had spoken one last time before I boarded the plane to fly over and work in the language school where he served as vice-director. Like many Koreans who speak any English, he had adopted an English nickname, drawing out the second syllable as he spoke it: "Hello, this is Jimeeeeee." I had called him from the airport, deftly navigating the forlorn payphone (Korea has one of the highest rates of cell phone ownership on the planet; it's amazing that payphones even exist) and receiving instructions on which bus to catch. I was to get off at the Marriott Hotel in Busan's famous Haeundae Beach, porter my bags (a year's worth of shit) to the nearest payphone, give him a call, and wait for his arrival. Upon stepping off the plane, *this* was the warm embrace I was wrapped in.

After over an hour of blazing through the city, the limousine bus arrived at Haeundae Beach, a one-and-a-half-kilometer stretch of imported sand, hotels, and raw fish restaurants that is one of Korea's most popular tourist attractions. In the summer, the hordes descend southward from Seoul, fleeing the choking combination of smog and humidity that smothers that city during the hottest months, turning the beach into a wall of bodies and parasols. As we pulled up to the Marriott, I took in the surrounding buildings: most were brightly-lit love motels, with motifs of palm trees, sexy girls, and ocean waves plastered on the side. One architectural monstrosity loomed prominent: it housed a Bennigans, TGI Fridays, and Starbucks. Sixteen hours of traveling and here it was, the mysterious Orient, splayed out before me in its very Western glory. Perhaps I wasn't as far from home as I thought.

Unlike most Koreans, Jimmy drove an economy-sized car. Koreans are smallish people living in a smallish country, but the cars they drive don't reflect this. Most drive large, Korean-made, four-door sedans—with the odd SUV, even. But Jimmy rolled up in a Hyundai Tico, the Korean equivalent of the old Geo Metro or AMC Gremlin. When he got out to help me with my bags, I saw that he was shockingly tall and thin as a famine victim, with small glasses and a very reasonable haircut in the style of most East Asian middle managers.

"Hello… welcome to the Korea. The flight was… uh… okay?"

We weakly shook hands. He held his left hand to the middle of his right arm while we shook, a display of respect in this still-very-Confucian culture.

"It was fine."

"It was very long?"

"About eleven hours from Seattle to Tokyo, a small layover, and then about two hours to here." I didn't mention the bottle of duty-free Jameson that I had dipped into somewhere around the Alaskan coast, which made the time melt away like ice cream in a hot car.

"Good. Good." He beamed an extra-forced smile and nodded enthusiastically.

"I met a Japanese student on the plane. He gave me this for good luck." I displayed the tiny owl on a string that the kid next to me had given me as a gift. It was one of those charms that you attach to your cell phone. Jimmy sucked through his teeth and eyed it suspiciously.

"As you may know… we Koreans do not like the Japanese."

After a slight pause, he gave a gummy laugh, cueing me to do the same. The tension broken, we got into the car and he started the engine.

"So this is the main beach?" I said, gesturing toward the darkness beyond the hotel as we pulled out.

"Yes, yes. Haeundae," he replied, lighting a skinny cigarette. I was soon to find out that Korean men are a nation of Virginia Slims fans.

"*Hyundai*, like the car company?"

"No… no… *Hae-oon-dae.* It is not same."

"Hae-oon-dae."

"Yes… yes. This place is very famous. Now is beach season. Girls are many. Sometimes wearing bikini." He smiled again and gave me the thumbs-up sign, nervously chuckling through his coffee-stained teeth.

Jimmy made more small talk as he drove me to my new apartment, provided gratis by the school. His English was decent, and though his accent was heavy, I could easily make out most everything he said. But I got the impression that conducting a conversation required his complete concentration, as if every word was chosen after an excruciating search. This is the case with a lot of Koreans who study English for years in school but have little experience using it in actual conversation. They have a large bank of vocabulary words and a grammar framework in which to put them; it's just the retrieval system that runs slowly. Having made some strides in learning Korean, I can now sympathize with their predicament.

Jimmy escorted me to my new digs and unlocked the door. We slipped off our shoes and walked into the tenth-floor *one-room*, as they're locally known. It was in a new building and actually quite a nice little studio apartment. *Little* is the operative word here, but I was very happy to have a place of my own, after many months of semi-nomadic wanderings back home. I had done a lot of crashing around while figuring what step two of my life would be, and here I was in the first moments of the new phase. My expectations were exceeded, especially after reading about other teachers who had been put up in microscopic hotel rooms that smelled of stale cigarette smoke and semen. I was more than pleased. I took a quick visual inventory: twin bed, television, air conditioner, basic kitchen with a bar/countertop that divided it from the rest of the room, bathroom with actual toilet and glass-enclosed *real* shower (a luxury of which I knew nothing at the time).

"Okay, Chris. Here are keys." He actually pronounced my name "Kuh-rees-uh." Koreans, like the Japanese, tend to put vowels between English consonant pairings, transforming the mono- into polysyllabic.

After a three-minute tour of my one-room, we took the elevator down, and he walked me to the school, which was located in a building just one minute on foot from the main door of mine. Everywhere I looked were blazing neon signs, bolted to the sides of the buildings, often stacked three or four high. I felt as if I was wandering through a pinball machine, and thought, *The sign makers must be minting cash.*

"Here is our academy." He pointed upwards toward the shiny side of the ten-story silver building. "Go to third floor. Tomorrow. 9:30… in morning. Okay?"

"Okay."

"Okay okay okay." He accentuated each one with a pat on the shoulder.

Nine-thirty? This was less than twelve hours away. I was hoping for a day or two to get my bearings. It seemed I would be afforded no decompression, no time to recover from jet lag. I'd be getting straight into the classroom with no training or prep, doing the thing that I'd come to Busan to do.

And what *was* that thing, really?

By the mid-'90s, Koreans had decided that the best way to get a leg up in the competitive global marketplace was to train the coming generation to become fluent in English. It became a national directive, embraced with a nearly fanatical passion in their already education-obsessed society. You could say that the country went English-crazy, with private language academies (known as *hagwons)* popping up faster than acne on an adolescent's face. Learning English became the order of the day, and soon—taking a cue from the Japanese (who had been at it since the '80s)—Korea started importing large numbers of native-speaker English teachers from abroad. Most of these teachers came from North America and tended to be young, fresh-out-of-college sorts, looking to travel, save some money, or pay off onerous student debt. The bar wasn't set too high, either: *Come to Korea and teach. All you need is a degree and a pulse.* This derisive saying, whispered around and within the English teacher community itself, wasn't always (and still isn't) far off the mark. The main requirements for teaching in the country are a four-year degree and a passport from one of seven designated English-speaking countries. Being white, attractive, and young helps, but the reality is that Immigration isn't turning too many people away at the door. The demand is simply too great.

One can imagine the pull this opportunity has for the masses of slackers with liberal arts degrees and little career advancement back home. After all, your employers in Korea pay for your flight; you are given gainful employment, health insurance, and an end-of-contract bonus; and best of all, you don't have to pay rent.

For me, that alone was worth the flight over.

I fit the profile for an ESL teacher in many, many ways. While I didn't possess a liberal arts degree, I did possess a *fine arts* degree, which is even more useless for securing a proper job in the pecking order of practical college educations. I definitely had a thirst for travel and adventure, and had reached a point in my life where I needed a serious change of not just scenery, but makeup, costume, lighting, and script. I had spent much of the '90s and early '00s in Seattle and then L.A., plunging into the world of improv comedy and fringe theater. I graduated from the Professional Actor's Training Program at Seattle's Cornish College of the Arts in 1995, and immediately poured myself into the then-burgeoning performance scene.

I had been active in the music scene before that, playing in a number of loser bands, trying to ride the rising tide of the grunge explosion. Lacking a band with looks, talent, or non-awful songs, this phase fizzled, and it was only after graduation that things got serious with acting and comedy. I started a performance troupe called Piece of Meat Theatre with some fellow Cornish alumns, and we became notorious in both the theater and music scenes for our testosterone-driven theatrical shows, which often featured gallons of blood, chainsaws, and giant stunt cocks.

In the meantime, I was donning the anarchic trappings of a self-styled revolutionary theater artist, working a shopping list of nowhere day jobs and ingesting most every nasty drug I could get into my lungs, nostrils, or veins. At the end of 1999, just after the infamous WTO riots (a going-away party of sorts), I, along with the Piece of Meat boys, relocated to perpetually sunny L.A., in the grand quest for a development deal, or at least a screenplay that would guarantee us a lunch table at Spago and Ben Stiller on speed dial. Our cult status in the underground of Seattle had gone to our heads. We had developed an inflated sense of showbiz destiny. We did have a good run of it, cranking out pages of scripts and performing in dingy theaters all throughout Hollywood—glad-handing bottom-feeder agents and chatting up C-list celebrities at parties—but after three years, the City of Angels had worn me down.

I inauspiciously bowed out, fleeing back to Seattle and even doing a stint as a guitarist for a washed-up industrial band in Chicago. By 2004 I was back in my hometown of Olympia, staying with my parents—who were just entering into a long slide into ill health—and seriously contemplating borrowing frightening amounts of cash to finance a couple of years of graduate school.

So there I was: a failed actor, over thirty, broke, with no girl, shitty prospects, and even shittier credit. I had taken to spending my days dodging white-belted hipsters on the streets of Olympia, poring over grad school applications, and scouring the pages of Craigslist for a gig to lift me out of my funk. What was I to do? One day I found it:

> *Have you ever wanted to get to know a foreign culture? Do you want a taste of adventure? Come teach English in South Korea.*

I had known a couple of people who, straight out of school, had come to Asia to teach. Both had spent short stints in South Korea and hated it, but I was in no position to be choosy. So I answered the ad, and within a week I interviewed on the phone. Two weeks later I had a contract and a work visa and was 30,000 feet over the Pacific en route to Busan, wherever that was.

What the hell did I know about Korea?

Well, I knew it was a rocky peninsula sandwiched between two often-hostile neighbors who had seen fit to invade and subjugate it much of the time. I knew something about the Korean War through some reading and films (along with *MASH*; Hawkeye was a sage)—but only from the American perspective. I knew that they made crappy cars that weren't considered so crappy anymore. I also knew that their national dish was *kimchee*, but only had a vague idea that this was some sort of pickled vegetable that was considered either the height of flavor or something that tasted as if it had been strained through a homeless man's underpants, depending on who you talked to. And, other than the name, I knew nothing about Samsung. I actually thought the company was Japanese, something I've still never admitted to a Korean, out of fear for my personal safety.

What about the people? Surely I could have gleaned something from them. Growing up, I had come into contact with many Koreans, but I really had no understanding of their culture, traditions, or thinking, aside from the fact that they usually worked harder than three of us and universally hated Japan. They consisted of a handful of quiet and studious kids I had gone to school with—none of whom was my friend—along with countless convenience store owners who had sold me candy bars, and later beer and smokes. I had also known some American army brats who had spent time in the country with their families, but most of these had always been confined to the cocoon of the base, and knew next to nothing of the world outside of the protective walls of the compound. They weren't so different from me, in this regard.

So, yes, with the exception of a few general things, I didn't know shit about this country I had impulsively decided to move to. I didn't even bother to learn a single word of the language, despite the fact that I had always enjoyed studying languages and managed to become nearly-fluent in Spanish. Granted, I didn't have much time to study, since I left in a whirlwind, but this blindness was intentional, as—arguably out of laziness—I convinced myself that I wanted to hit the ground as green as possible. And in this, I succeeded.

Jimmy left me back at my apartment, where I stood, looking at the lights of the neighborhood below. Again, more crosses. I opened the window and poked my head out, gazing down at the activity on the sidewalk below. It was humming. People sat at plastic tables outside of a convenience store. They drank from cans of beer, ate from a communal tray in the middle, laughed loudly, and talked. The timbre of their voices echoed up from the streets, intermingling with the sounds of car engines and delivery scooters. It was early August and hot, even well into the night. The humidity stuck to my skin; I began to sweat and closed the window. Jimmy had shown me the air-conditioning unit, bolted to the wall above the television. He had even given me a brief tutorial on how to work it with the white remote. I picked up the remote, which had only slightly fewer buttons than a controller for a DVD player. I fumbled over the buttons with my big white clumsy hands, attempting to decipher the alien characters inscribed upon it, suddenly self-conscious about my lack of grace and understanding—a crystal-ball vision for my future in this country. Finally, the machine hummed and the long mechanical lip of the thing's mouth opened up, pouring out cool, cool air. As I felt it blow over my damp torso, I was interrupted by the jarring, computerized tones of Beethoven's "Für Elise":

> *Duh-Dee duh-Dee duh-Dee duh-Dee-duh-Dee! duh-Dee duh-Dee! duh-Dee duh-Dee! duh-Dee-duh-Dee duh-Dee duh-Dee-duh-Dee!*

Repeat.

I frantically searched for its origin, then realized that it was coming from the direction of my door. *Ah, yes, the doorbell!* As I approached, I noticed that the screen next to it was lit up bright grey. I could make out the figures of several people standing. I had visitors.

When I opened the door, I stood face-to-face with three white foreigners.

"You must be Chris. We'll be working with you. Wanna get a bite and a drink?"

Laura was a blonde girl from the hinterlands of Saskatchewan, and looked the part. She was strong and sturdy and could probably buck the hell out of a bale of hay. Rick was from Georgia, and Jillian was from Toronto. They all taught at the hagwon where I had been hired, which was called the Bayridge Language School—or as the Koreans pronounced it, "Bae-ree-juh."

They took me to an area of restaurants very near my apartment, which is redundant, really, since everywhere in the city seemed to be an area of restaurants. I had never seen so many places to eat in my life. Everywhere you looked, people were serving up food. These particular eateries were located in a square of sorts—a place blocked off from the city's ubiquitous cars—a rarity in this pedestrian-beware town, as I was to find out later. We took a seat at an outdoor table with a grill in the middle and checked out the one menu, which, of course, was written in Korean.

Rick opened it up and Jillian leaned in, poring over the entries and scrunching her nose. "Do you eat meat? I thought that I'd ask, because I'm a vegetarian, and I hate it when people just assume I eat meat. This is a fucked-up country to be vegetarian in. They do eat a lot of vegetables, but they tend to put meat in everything. It's disgusting." She took out of pack of Dunhill Lights and lit up.

"Yeah… I eat meat… these days." I didn't know whether to be proud or ashamed.

The owner came out, wiping sweat from his forehead. It was obvious that he knew my three companions from before.

"Hello hello hello!"

Rick replied with the standard Korean greeting, "*Annyeong hasseyo*?"

"CHRIS—IS—A—NEW—TEA—CHER—AT—OUR—SCHOOL." Laura bawled at the guy as if he was a retarded four-year-old.

"Okay okay okay okay okay." He nodded enthusiastically and attempted a smile. Whether he understood or just wanted to get our order is debatable. Rick rattled out our order in nimble Korean, and before long the owner's smiling wife brought out a large silver tray, on which were some small dishes containing unidentifiable vegetables, a basket of lettuce leaves, garlic cloves, sliced mushrooms, and a plate of thick pork slices that resembled cuts of bacon. Also included were two large bottles of cold beer, with glasses.

Soon the beer was opened and the pork strips thrown on the grill. The cold lager cooled me down in the night heat, and the smell of the pork awakened my stomach, which was still full of salty airline food.

"What is this?" I asked, pointing to the meat.

"It's called *sam gyeop sal*," Rick chimed in. "It's pretty much the same as bacon, only uncured. The Koreans eat the shit out of it. So do I."

Jillian shook her head and put some mushrooms on, far out of range of the growing pool of pork grease.

"Ya ever had kimchee?" Laura gestured to one of the mystery dishes filled with what looked like sliced cabbage, covered in a glistening red sauce.

I had been to a lot of Asian restaurants, but mainly Thai, Japanese, Indian, and Chinese. Only one time could I remember eating proper Korean fare, and even then I don't recall trying kimchee. So I gripped my unwieldy metal chopsticks and dove in: pungent, salty, sour, and a bit spicy. The texture was firm and slightly crunchy: strange, but also compelling. My mouth was alive and electric—I could feel my taste buds firing at full capacity. This really was a new taste, and quickly I hit the dish again, trying to figure out just what it was I was eating. After that I hit it again. And again.

I was already hooked.

"Fermented cabbage and *gochujang,* which is Korea's red pepper paste. They use it in everything. Traditional Korean cuisine uses a lot of fermented stuff—it's how they'd preserve it for the winter before refrigeration came around." Rick was obviously the expert on all things Korean at the table.

Jillian raised her eyebrows. "I can't eat it, because they also use anchovy paste."

The grilled pork was succulent and delicious, especially when wrapped in leaves and topped with a bit of *dwoenjang*, a brown bean-paste common in Korean cooking. We also cooked the garlic in the pork grease, which like much of the meal, was a first for me. After we finished the food, my three compatriots lit cigarettes.

"Do you smoke?"

I didn't at the time. I had quit four months earlier and had enjoyed the self-congratulatory state of being a non-smoker. But as I took in my surroundings—brightly-lit restaurant signs, scores of people eating, drinking, and conversing—I was overcome with a desire to embrace this new situation for all it was worth.

"How much are cigarettes here?"

"Less than two bucks a pack."

"At that price, it's too cheap not to smoke." With that, I bummed one, lit up, and inhaled, immediately feeling relaxed, if not just a bit groggy from the flight.

Just then, at an outdoor table at the restaurant directly across from us, I heard an explosion of machine-gun Korean. This was met with a return volley of shouting, and immediately two men at neighboring tables stood up and faced off. They bellowed at each other, each verbal assault punctuated by loud "*Ya!*"s. The first man wore a black suit, and his friend grabbed him and attempted to drag him back into his chair, which served only to pour gas onto the fire. Now both parties—four sets of couples—were on their feet, lunging at one another in a drunk, enraged dance. The women joined in, screeching, raving, and pointing. At one point a metal ashtray was hurled, followed by more yelling. Despite all of this high drama, no one was actually throwing punches.

"Welcome to Busan," Rick joked. "The people here are notoriously hot-tempered. They're known throughout the country for it. And the guy in the black suit may be a gangster."

"They have them here." Jillian took a long drag from her cigarette.

Soon, tempers slightly cooled, and the guy in the black suit's party paid their bill to the mitigating owner and staggered off, as he shouted parting shots over his back into the dark.

"This is what *soju* does to people."

Soju is the green-bottled vodka-like alcohol found everywhere in Korea. It is cheap and strong and gets people psychotically wasted.

We laughed at Laura's remark and decided to order one more round of beer before calling it a night. They asked me about Seattle and my pre-Korean life, which I filled them in on as honestly as I could. Just when Rick was refilling my glass, I saw the man in the black suit running back out of the dark, toward the offending table. He carried a metal rod and was followed by his friends, who were shouting after him. The other table noticed him just in time to stand up before he turned his rod on their table, smashing the bottles, plates, and glasses and then kicking it over. At this point a few punches were thrown, but again the two main combatants were held back by their more sensible friends.

"Holy fuck."

Soon a police car drove up and two very young-looking cops emerged, placing themselves between the warring groups. They did their best to defuse the situation, coolly talking to both sides, trying to calm everyone down. I was amazed at their show of diplomacy. In America, they would likely rush in and tackle whomever they perceived as guilty to the ground. But my shock was amplified when the man in the black suit turned on the young cops, spat out a litany of abuse, and proceeded to *shove* them. Incredibly, the cops didn't push back. They didn't bust out their clubs and split his head. They didn't Taser him. They just gently tried to talk him down.

"I can't believe what I'm seeing…"

"The police are younger than this guy," Rick explained. "In this culture, respect for elders is the most important thing."

"Even if your elders are total assholes," Jillian snorted.

"Yeah, but they still have to show him some respect." Laura shrugged and sipped while Jillian shook her head.

Eventually, with the insistence of the restaurant owner, the cops managed to convince the man in the black suit to get into their car and drove off. The rest of the people involved walked away, the only thing lost being face, which is everything in East Asia. We finished our beers and split up our more peaceful meeting, knowing that we'd see each other in the morning, at the hagwon.

****

I awoke to a three-second panic: *Where am I?* We've all experienced this when coming to in strange environs, but this time it hit me with an extra-strength wallop, especially when my toxic-steamed head sorted out the answer: *Oh, yeah. Korea.*

I looked at the clock: it was just a bit past 6 a.m. Jet lag. I had done some traveling in Europe before and had known the effect, but this was my first time experiencing it going in the opposite direction. After all, I had gained a day. The only time I was ever awake at six was when I was going fishing or had neglected to sleep the night before—not unheard-of in my amphetamine-fueled earlier days. But sleep was now out of the question, so I got up, stretched, and looked out my window.

So this is what Korea looks like.

Brand-new buildings mixed with traditional-looking red brick houses; church steeples loomed, the cross lights now turned off. Despite the homogeneity of colors and shapes, there was an incongruity to the surroundings. Unlike back home, stringent zoning codes have yet to make their way to the peninsula. A dark wood Japanese restaurant might exist next door to a sleek modern medical center, across from which is a preschool in the shape of a pink and blue mushroom. But turn the corner and there may be a group of nearly identical, featureless industrial workshops. The dense city ran for several blocks and then stopped at the base of a mountain—*Jangsan*, as it's known locally. The top of the mountain was enveloped in low-lying cloud that growled with summertime thunder.

I decided to kill the time before work by wandering around the neighborhood and hunting down some breakfast. Bacon and eggs sounded ideal, but I'd settle for the local version, whatever that was. Soon I was dressed and out the door, walking into the misty, humid morning. Even at this early hour, there was a lot of activity on the street. Outside of my apartment was a short, tough looking middle-aged woman, known throughout the peninsula as an *ajumma*. She wore white gloves, a yellow vest, and a matching visor over her tight perm, and stood sentry alongside an ice-chest on wheels containing nothing but small cartons of milk and even smaller packets of liquid-yogurt. A few other permed and visored ajummas approached her and purchased the said products. This was my first introduction to the micro-specialty that is small business in Korea.

Across the way I saw a market. I crossed and entered, seduced by the colors and smells. The edge of the market was dominated by ajummas selling fruits and vegetables—watermelon seemed especially prominent—which came as a surprise to me. I had always associated watermelon with the long, hot American summers. It was entirely steeped in our tradition—at least in my eyes. To see these hardened-looking Korean women hawking fat watermelons was a seismic incongruity. I passed further into the market, past stalls stacked with pots and pans, towels and linens, colorful traditional Korean clothing known as *hanbok*, meat, live seafood, dead seafood, and ready-to-eat street cuisine. All this food made me hungry, but I was ignorant of what anything was. Eventually I passed a one-room restaurant, in which were seated several grizzled locals. They sipped soup from bowls, along with side dishes of kimchee, bean sprouts, and fried, whole fish. There was a menu on the wall which I couldn't read. But I could identify the food from at least three of the other customers' plates, so I grabbed a table and waited to be served.

A beaming ajumma approached me. She was dark-skinned, and deep lines cut into her dried-fruit face. She addressed me in raw Korean. I shrugged, looked to the older guy sitting next to me, and just pointed at his half-consumed food.

Within minutes I was served the same and went at it with vigor. I was used to wooden chopsticks back home, but the Koreans use much heavier, metal chopsticks, and this took some adapting to. After a minute I managed to get the hang of it, albeit clumsily. What I did notice was that all the other patrons were eating the rice with spoons. I had known of the Japanese custom of lifting the rice bowl to your mouth and shoveling in the rice with chopsticks, but the Koreans were having none of it: the bowls stayed on the table, and spoons were employed. It seemed very sensible to me, so I aped them accordingly. At one point the ajumma approached me and rattled off what seemed to be a barrage of questions. She motioned toward my chopsticks, perhaps congratulating me on my skills, and growled more Korean my way. I just laughed and shook my head, which was contagious. She laughed, and then seemingly made a joke at my expense, and suddenly all the other patrons in the place (about six or seven people) were laughing as well—hearty, deep laughter, the laughter of the poor. I joined in, somewhat reveling in the attention, and then pointed to my rice bowl:

"This. What is this? How… do…. you… say…. this?"

She looked confused. I pointed once again.

"*Bap*," she replied.

"*Bap*?"

"*Nae, bap.*"

"*Bap*," I confirmed. "Bap."

I had just learned my first Korean word. My education had begun, and I had yet to teach a single class.

CHAPTER 2

GORILLA TEACHER

MOST everyone who comes to Korea to teach English starts at a hagwon. This is where the entry-level positions are: they have the greatest demand for teachers, and are, as a result, less selective than other institutions. Hagwons are study factories, short on long-term vision and obsessed with immediate results. They are also desperate for foreigners. Hagwons go so far as to fly people across the world on the basis of visa qualification, a photo (very important), and a very brief phone interview, with almost no further vetting. This tells us something: having at least one foreigner on staff is essential for business. Contact with native speakers is considered to be the quickest path to English mastery by the legions of fickle Korean moms planning and paying for their children's extracurricular education. Never mind if the foreigner in question has a P.E. degree from a third-tier school, no teaching experience, and a chronic drinking problem. Fliers with a few nice photos featuring attractive Western teachers translate into more students. More students mean more money, and money is what it's all about.

Most Korean students attend hagwons after their regular school hours. If they're lucky they go home, maybe grab a bite, and then are stuffed into vans, off to one of tens of thousands of hagwons around the country. English hagwons make up only a small percentage of these after-school academies: there are math hagwons, science hagwons, music hagwons, art hagwons, Korean language and literature hagwons. Most operate late into the night. Nine or ten o'clock is standard for English academies, though it's not unheard-of for students to get out of hagwons at eleven or even twelve. There are stories of some operating all the way to one in the morning. Recent legislation is said to ban this practice, drawing the line at eleven p.m., but Korea is a country of many laws and selective enforcement. A few white envelopes passed into the right hands could give little Min-woo a couple more hours to master the present perfect tense every night.

When I first learned of this system, of what I was being paid to participate in, this simple question crossed my mind: *How much would it suck to have to go to school after school? These poor, poor kids.*

The most alarming thing about hagwons is the variation in quality. Despite some recent attempts by the government, it is essentially an unregulated industry, resulting in a Darwinian swamp of greedy operators doing whatever it takes to lure Mom's *won*. Some are well-equipped and well-staffed, with quality classrooms, plentiful books, and other materials. Others are fly-by-night outfits with shady owners only in it to grab the cash and run. I've been in hagwons that were unheated in the coldest winter months, with the students sitting in tiny rooms around rickety tables wearing parkas, their breath visible as they attempted to master English prepositions. These are the hagwons for teachers to look out for: perpetually understaffed, and even more importantly, underfunded. There are volumes of horror stories about teachers being paid late or not at all, being put up in filthy hovels, and being cheated out of their taxes, pension, bonuses, and airline tickets.

The reality is that in a hagwon, education doesn't rank first. This honor goes to profit-making. If the mommies start complaining and pulling their kids, radical changes in curriculum and policy will be instituted overnight. After all, there is always the competition across the street. Just the slightest complaint from one mother is taken with utmost gravity by the hagwon director, and the orders are passed down the food chain in order to pacify the unhappy customer. What the directors usually don't realize, though, is that overreacting to one mother's criticism often ruffles the feathers of the other hens in the brood, causing a counter-reaction. You can't please everyone.

Many new teachers fail to understand this fundamental truth about what they're getting into. They want to come and teach and be effective. They want to make a difference. But what they actually *make* is the mistake of setting high standards and being strict with their students, believing themselves to be educators, rather than mascots. Such is the highway to teaching suicide, and academy directors show no affection for the newly arrived Westerner who wishes to inspire his or her students through regimentation and tough love. This is a sure way for a high-minded teacher to get canned. Aside from providing examples of perfect pronunciation, foreigners are not brought into the hagwon to teach, really. That duty is reserved for the Korean teachers, who give homework, mete out discipline, and instruct the kids in grammar and writing. Foreign teachers are there to keep enrollment up, impress the mothers, and above all, *entertain.*

I got a lucky draw. I blindly took the first job that was offered to me and was fortunate on that first day to walk into a modern, clean, and well-funded school. The Bayridge Language School was owned and operated by the Daekyo Corporation, one of the largest educational service companies in South Korea. The building itself (also the property of Daekyo) contained office space, too, as well as three other hagwons specializing in non-English subjects. When I walked into Bayridge, it was clear that the boys in the main office had invested some money in the school. A large, shiny red logo hung behind the front desk, behind which sat a very pretty young Korean woman (demure smile; tasteful makeup; straight, glossy black hair). Jimmy greeted me from the communal teachers' office and gave me a tour. The school occupied two floors of the building and came complete with fully stocked classrooms (whiteboards, chairs, tables, desks); a science room (microscopes, model of the small/large intestine, take-apart human brain); a computer lab that was home to about twenty PCs and a digital overhead projector; and a shared staff room stocked with books, teaching aids, and games. As far as facilities went, this was top-notch, and I can't imagine any new teacher strolling through the door and being underwhelmed. Judging by both my apartment and school, I had gotten lucky.

After introducing me to the non-English speaking director—a devout Christian woman with the English name Brenda, who spent a lot of time alone in her office praying (*Please Lord, I beseech Thee, more students!*)—Jimmy led me upstairs to a classroom, in which sat six women in their thirties and forties. This was the school's "housewife class." Many hagwons offer a once- or twice-a-week class for housewives who wish to improve their English, and this was to be the first trial-by-fire of my ESL teaching career. Jimmy gave me a fifteen-second introduction in Korean, handed me the attendance folder and textbook I was to use, and unceremoniously walked out of the classroom as they tepidly applauded, shutting the door behind him. The clapping immediately ceased, and I took in the housewives, whose eyes looked like those of livestock about to be slaughtered.

"Good morning!" Despite my jet-lag-dizzy head, I did my best to inject the proceedings with some good ol' fashioned Yankee enthusiasm.

Silence.

I tried it again. "Hello!"

One of them waved very weakly. I waved back.

"Good morning! It's okay… you can talk back... hello?"

A pause. I cleared my throat.

"Hello?"

"… Hel-lo…," one of them murmured as her face turned into a ripe tomato.

And thus it began. I had been warned about some Asians' pathological shyness when it comes to speaking English in front of native speakers, but I figured that anyone who signs up for a class would have already overcome such a barrier, that they would be ready and willing to talk away, even if imperfectly. But here I was, confronted with the reality of a group of women who had paid to speak English with a real, living foreigner, but were too terrified to actually vocalize any words. It was going to be a long fifty minutes.

What about me? What teaching methods could I have employed to open them up, to break the ice and get these ladies talking some English? Surely there is an arsenal of tricks useful for getting new students to open up. The truth is that I had none. Jimmy had led me into the bear cave without even a pep talk; he just opened the door and chucked me in like the proverbial Christian to the lions. There was no prep, no orientation, no discussion of syllabus and/or methodology. And aside from some drama workshops and improv classes that I had presided over back in Seattle, I had almost no practical teaching experience at all, especially when it came to ESL. I was a complete neophyte, and if not for the textbook that I clutched like a Gucci handbag, I might have flung myself out of the fourth story window, right then and there.

I managed to make it through the class relatively unscathed, relying on the exercises in the book to make up for my utter lack of preparation or knowledge of what to do. Soon enough the bell rang, and Jimmy led me by the sleeve back downstairs, the school's other wing, the real money-maker. It was only my second class, yet time for me to hit the front line of children's ESL education: *morning kindy*.

Bayridge was one of many schools that specialized in kindergarten English immersion. Five- and six-year-olds would come to the school every weekday to do basic kindergarten, almost exclusively in English. These are perhaps the most successful of all the English language programs in Korea, because they are catching kids at the perfect age for language acquisition, throwing them into the sea of a new tongue and letting them swim. These programs are also some of the most lucrative for any institution, since the tots spend several hours a day under the school's care, and the parents are billed accordingly.

The bell rang, and I watched as the other teachers scurried to their rooms: Pavlov's dogs carrying plastic baskets full of books, photocopied worksheets, board markers, and colorful flash cards. Jimmy escorted me into my kindergarten class, where I met my Korean counterpart, an emaciated, bug-eyed Korean girl named Lisa, who many of the children snarkily referred to as "Gollum Teacher," a nod to her resemblance to the tortured creature from *Lord of the Rings*. Yes, the kids were ruthless.

After the requisite introductions, I found myself attempting to stare down twelve lethally cute six-year-olds dressed in identical yellow sweat suits, on which the company logo was prominently displayed. Children of this age are universally adorable, but the Korean variety of kindergartner occupies what may be the highest plane of cuteness. Black bowl cuts, pigtails, and matching uniforms, accompanied by their tiny dimensions: this was cute concentrate, enough to practically paralyze me. I'd never seen anything quite like it.

I figured I'd again hit them with enthusiasm.

"Good morning!"

In unison: "GOOD MORNING, TEACHER!"

They showed almost none of the shyness of the housewives. These little imps had been conditioned.

One of the boys pointed at me and screamed in laughter, which lit like white magnesium around the classroom. Suddenly all dozen of them were pointing and screeching: East Asian groupthink at work.

I figured I'd try a new line on a boy nearest to me. "How are you?"

His eyes rolled back in his head and he convulsed with laughter, his body possessed by an entity of pure chaos.

I tried the saucer-eyed girl next to him. "How are you?"

She stood up and belted out, "I FINE THANK YOU!", then jumped up and down like a miniature demon, clapping her hands.

I repeated the line to another girl—the only shy one of the bunch—who just stared ahead, refusing to utter a word. When I asked the boy next to her "How are you?" he replied:

"ME SPIDERMAN!"

He leapt out of his chair, pretending to shoot webs from the palms of his hands. This served as a cue for the rest of the boys to bolt from their seats, resulting in a spontaneous superhero mêlée. One girl joined them and proceeded to wrap herself around the lower part of my left leg. A boy with bleached streaks in his hair got on top of the table and shouted:

"I'M *UNG-GA*!" He squatted down and mimed shitting on the table. This move was repeated by two thirds of the other students, who squealed with poo-poo/pee-pee joke bliss.

Just then two of the girls were at the white board, scribbling maniacally with the board markers in red and black. As I bent down to try and intervene, I felt a sharp poke near the center of my ass. Bleached hair *UNG-GA* boy had hit me with the most practiced weapon in the Korean kid's arsenal: the dreaded *ddong chim.*

I remember a similar thing from those two years of misery in my life which was known as middle school. Sometimes, when bent over at a locker or desk, one of those awful thick-necked boys who already had a moustache would poke you in the ass and say "Ha! Just checkin' yer oil!" He'd then saunter off, looking for another weakling to call "fag" or menace with a wedgie.

The *ddong chim* (which translates as *poop needle*) is the Korean student's version of the North American *oil check*, yet it is far more pervasive. Boys and girls of young ages practice it with abandon, with the tacit support of the Korean teachers—who, when faced with an angry foreigner who objects to such a thing, just laugh and say, "Oh, he is doing the joke."

They think it's cute. I don't. It is a finger in my ass, and such privileges are not even extended to my girlfriend.

But things had already gone too far for me to put my foot down. In the course of one hundred and twenty seconds, I had completely lost control of the class. I yelled and tried to act harsh, but it had no effect. It was obvious that these kindy kiddies just saw me as a huge stupid white clown. Kids can smell fear, it is true. This group had sniffed it out like a pack of starving, feral dogs, and they were ripping off large mouthfuls of my teaching confidence. But this was just the opening salvo, so I gathered myself, and did what any self-respecting *morning kindy* teacher would do on the first day:

I pretended to be a wild gorilla and ran amuck.

Channeling my best inner silverback, I went at them. Where this came from remains a mystery, but some primal voice inside me was chanting, *Gorilla! Gorilla! Gorilla!* I pounded my chest like an enraged King Kong, howled, and charged—grabbing tykes under my arms as I passed, with the intention of taking them back to my den to be devoured (this gorilla craved flesh). I snarled and barked, all the while terrifying the living hell out of my miniature torturers, who scattered like roaches under a turned-on light. I was now in control. The gorilla could not be stopped! At least until Gollum Teacher came back to restore order.

She opened the door and entered with total authority, her bulging eyes aflame with indignation. She opened her mouth and a jet-engine voice rumbled from a place deep within, filling every crevice of the small classroom and even frightening me. The children were back in their seats within three seconds, backs erect, hands on their heads, and staring straight ahead like tiny soldiers. Silence was observed. An air of absolute solemnity descended upon the room. Gollum Teacher then, drill-instructor-like, rattled off a litany of questions, to each of which the students answered, as a group, *Nae*! (Korean for *yes*). After the last question, she scanned the kiddies, who were still at attention, gave me a quarter smile and a shallow bow, and strode out of the room.

They listen to their fellow Koreans. I don't even enter into it. This is good to know.

****

I knew very little of what to expect before actually arriving in Korea, but by the end of my first two weeks on the ground, I knew I wasn't going back to the States anytime soon. During my brief time in the country I had managed to procure:

- One good, secure job with a company that was sure to pay me on time;
- An apartment, near work, nice;
- A set of friends, brand-new;
- A fascinating, unknown place and culture to explore;
- One girlfriend—Korean, and hot.

It's as if, when entering the country, at Immigration, I'd been handed a magic bag containing a *brand new life*. It was like being in witness protection or passing into an alternate universe. I was ecstatic, and began regularly having nightmares where I found myself back in America.

Sometimes I was stuck there for good, and other times I would realize that I had to be at work first thing in the morning. In Korea. On several occasions I literally awoke with a slamming chest and sweat pouring over my body. This was anxiety of the highest order. I had stumbled onto something good and I didn't want to lose it.

When you're over 30 and broke back home, coming to teach in Asia can be a sort of paradise. This is especially true if you take to teaching, which I did. I enjoyed my classroom time. I'm a big kid at heart—a real goofball—so I'd just teach some and play more. That seemed to do the trick, since if the kids were happy, so were their mothers and by extension, my bosses. And it wasn't just the job that I enjoyed. I was fascinated with living in Asia, with being surrounded by newness. I explored the restaurants on my own, going in solo and pointing at random selections. I'd wander the markets and try the street food, marveling at the strange ocean life being sold: cuttlefish, octopuses, orange sea squirts, and pink worms resembling huge, flaccid penises. It was all amazing to me and I couldn't believe that I hadn't come to Asia sooner.

Yes, it was a honeymoon period. Novelty is exciting and those first few months were no exception. But strip away the novelty and I was still enjoying the hell out of my new circumstances. I was teaching thirty hours a week at Bayridge, which as far as teaching goes is a grind, but I barely noticed it. I had worked some shitty jobs in my day: dishwasher, truck loader, laborer, courier driver, temp office drone, fishmonger. I had even once been paid to *poison a lake* (invasive weed control). I had done some awful, low-paying, soul-destroying, ball-busting gigs. Compared to most any of those, teaching kids how to say "The eraser is under the desk" was the easiest thing I'd ever been paid to do. It was cake.

My new friend Sam agreed. He was a 6'4" sinew of a guy from Boise, Idaho—a cynical, whip-smart, no-bullshit fellow Northwesterner whom I immediately bonded with.

"Dude, you wanna know what I was doin' for a living before this? I was pouring concrete. Have you ever poured concrete?"

I shook my head in the negative.

"It fucking *sucks*."

As much as it initially surprised me, I soon found out that not everyone was so enthusiastic when it came to teaching here. I immediately started meeting scores of people who hated their lives in Korea, people who counted the days until the end of their contracts, people who incessantly moaned about every inconvenience, perceived affront, or cultural difficulty. These folks weren't just the odd whiners, either. They were everywhere.

At Bayridge were two such champion Korea-complainers. They were a couple from Texas, Jeff and Renee. They had moved to Busan together and were both hired to work at the hagwon. They had been there for a several months by the time I arrived and bitched about their jobs and the country at seemingly every chance possible.

"Koreans never tell you the truth. Jimmy tells us one thing but tells the kids' mothers something else. I just can't deal with all of this dishonesty."

"You know we can't play CDs in the classroom anymore? One of the moms complained, saying that she can just do that at home and that we should be teaching more? What does she know about teaching English."

"They keep changing the curriculum. It's so unprofessional."

"The air's so bad here."

"Koreans are so rude. Just yesterday an old woman elbowed me out of the way and took the last empty seat on the subway."

"Jimmy's always smoking in the back room and it stinks. I can't believe they smoke so much here. They're dirty."

The telling point with this couple came when their vacation time rolled around. It was their first real break since arriving. They were given a week off, and rather than spend it at some exotic Asian locale just a few hours away by plane, they instead elected to fly back to Houston. They had been in Korea less than a year, but evidently really needed that fix of Americana. In fact, after returning to Busan, they both incessantly talked about the highlight of their journey: a trip to Sonic Burger for some *real* fast food. How they had missed good ol' Sonic Burger.

I hung my American head in shame.

It wasn't too long after that they explained to us, their fellow teachers—over a pitcher of beer—that they had decided to pull what's called a *midnight run.*

"We're going to Japan. In the morning. We haven't told Jimmy. I mean, it's just so much better there. The people are nicer. They're not all liars and alcoholics. They don't spit in the street. The food isn't all spicy and inedible. They treat foreigners well in Japan. Not like here. Yeah, we're going to Japan."

With that, they were gone, and the rest of us were all given extra hours—with the same pay—to cover until a new teacher could be found. Thanks, guys.

To be fair, they were young, fresh out of school, and not just a little bit naïve. They probably would have been better served to stay back in America and have daily access to their beloved Sonic Burger. They probably would have been happier in a place where smoking is strictly regulated and public spitting is almost nonexistent. Regardless, they did teach me one thing: most of the people who come to Korea and hate it are just people whose lives haven't sucked enough back at home yet.

CHAPTER 3

SAFE IN A WAR ZONE

WHEN I told my friends and extended acquaintances that I was going away to live and teach in Korea, many people were concerned:

"Is it *safe there*?"

"Aren't you afraid of *terrorists*?"

"Are you sure that this is the best time to be living outside of the USA?"

Most Americans are untraveled, internationally. This is reflected by the fact that, according to the State Department, only one in four of us own passports, a point much-derided by the many Canadians and Europeans that I've met abroad. For many Americans, anywhere outside of the huge womb of our country is strangely dangerous, swarming with anti-American mobs and prone to terrorist attacks. This attitude was especially prevalent in the years following the 9/11 attacks—when I came to Korea—during the reign of our most untraveled President, George W. Bush. Bush's "pre-emptive" wars and go-it-alone cowboy diplomacy caused our country to become deeply reviled throughout much of the globe, and stories filtered their way back home of a heightened level of hostility toward Americans everywhere we went. Also, most Americans knew close to nothing about Korea—other than that at some point we were in a war there—so I could understand some of their concern.

It turned out that Busan is one of the safest places I could possibly be. It is certainly safer than any city in the States. There is pretty much zero street crime. You can walk (or even stagger) down a dark street at four a.m. and no one will bother you. I have never heard of someone getting mugged in Busan. Sure, there is a lot of petty theft—bikes, motorcycle, and bags frequently disappear—and, like almost anywhere, women need to exercise caution when alone. But terrorism? No way. There is a big difference between Busan and, say, Mogadishu. But many people back home seemed unable to make the distinction. Baghdad, Kabul, Karachi, Busan: all the same place, a sordid, violent place where good Americans got kidnapped and their heads turned up in ditches, complete with a set of bloody nuts in the mouth. These are all places where the people are all vaguely... *brown.* One must watch out. Too much caution is not possible.

Okay, maybe I'm being unduly harsh. People's concern for my safety abroad generally came from a good place. It's because they cared about me and loved me, right? I could have said, "Hey, guess what, I'm going to volunteer in an ebola hospital in the Congo," and my friends could have said, "Seize the day!" I could have been secretly hated and universally wished harmed. But that's not the case. People were worried. They were so concerned that many, poker-faced, would ask me:

"Are you going to teach in *North Korea*?"

"You guessed it. Not only that, I'm defecting. I've received a personal invitation from Kim Jong Il. We're going to swap hair tips."

This concern really illustrates the American character. It shows that one: we're really nice people at heart; and two: we don't know shit about the rest of the world.

Yes, there was a war. There was a really nasty war. Over thirty thousand Americans died, along with hundreds of thousands of Chinese, and two to three *million* Koreans. In fact, the war never ended. A peace treaty was never signed—just an armistice. So, technically, I was living in a war zone, and it was the safest place I'd ever been. I'd lived in rough neighborhoods in Seattle, Los Angeles, and Chicago. Believe me, this was nothing. However, all it would have taken was one soldier, hothead, drunk, or worse yet, a rogue general (*à la* Doctor Strangelove) to start taking potshots across the DMZ, and the shit could've all kicked off again, and I'd have been practicing my breaststroke all the way to Japan.

The prospect of me teaching in North Korea was and is absurd. But North Korea does loom in our minds as some sort of hellmouth, out of which springs part of the world's extremism and bizarre aggression. After all, weren't they part of Bush's infamous Axis of Evil? Aren't they our sworn enemy? The North Korean government has one of the worst reputations of earth—a reputation that, honestly speaking, didn't spring out of a vacuum. They have often been up to some very nasty stuff. Aside from oppressing their own people through executions, slave-labor camps, starvation, and pure brutality, they have, over the years, employed sabotage and outright terrorist tactics to destabilize the Southern regime and further their own ends. They have sent commando teams south, most famously in 1968 in an attempt to attack the Blue House and assassinate then-President Park Chung-hee. They blew up a Korean Air jetliner in 1987, and in 1983 murdered 17 South Koreans—including four government ministers—in a terrorist bombing in Rangoon, Burma. There have been numerous naval incursions and skirmishes, including one in 1999 that resulted in the deaths of over 30 northern sailors. In March of 2010 the South Korean Navy vessel *Cheonan* was sunk by what an international team of investigators claims was a North Korean torpedo, resulting in the deaths of 46 sailors. This event increased tensions on the peninsula to their worst point in decades. Over the years, the North Koreans have also abducted a number of South Korean and Japanese citizens, some of whom still live in the Stalinist state. The Cold War never ended on the peninsula. In fact, less than two months before finishing this book, North Korea let loose a full artillery barrage on the civilian-occupied South Korean island of Yeonpyeong-do, killing two residents along with two soldiers. This was an international incident that brought the peninsula to the brink of all-out-war. This place is, in some ways, an ideological time warp, so perhaps my American friends' worries weren't so unfounded.

Abducted!

Abduction can be an effective tool to achieve your ends, but we would be mistaken to believe that it's just the North that has a monopoly on abductions. The Southerners are adept at it too, as I was to find out one night in my second week there.

Those first two weeks were really hot, accompanied by a steam-bath humidity that, as a West Coast native, I was completely unaccustomed to. Humid places stay hot at night, and this particular night was no exception. I was sweaty and restless and wanted a beer—maybe even two or three. So I went down to the convenience store of my building, bought a couple of beers, and (being bored with my little apartment) sat down at the little plastic table in front of the store, and proceeded to drink. Korea, like many evolved, non-police-state countries, has no laws against public drinking. It's not really encouraged, but it's accepted. If you want, you can sit outside and sip a beer. No hassle. No cops. No nothing. In these small ways, the country is much freer than the Land of the Free, where so much seems hyper-regulated by the finger-wagging nanny state. Try walking the streets of most any American town while sipping a beer and you'll see exactly what I mean.

Picture this scene: as I sip on my nice, satisfyingly cold beer, two Korean businessmen and a woman sit down at the table next to me. The men have obviously just gotten off work, as evidenced by their rumpled white shirts and ties. The woman is casually dressed in jeans and a tight shirt: strictly non-professional attire. The three of them begin to drink beer as well, and at one point, the woman notices me sitting alone, and turns to talk to me, as best as she can. Koreans are often anxious to try out their English, especially when a bit of alcohol dampens their debilitating initial shyness. She introduces me to the businessmen, *Mr. Park* and *Mr. Young*. (Park, Cho, Young, Kim, and Lee are the dominant surnames on the peninsula.) She tells me her name, which I immediately forget. I'll refer to her here as Margaret Cho, due to her resemblance to the well-known Korean-American comedienne.

Suddenly, my new Korean friends get up from their table. Margaret Cho gestures to me to come with her palm down. This is initially confusing, since it quite resembles the Western gesture for *get the fuck out of here.* I stand up and walk toward her. She grabs me by the arm and pulls me into a taxi. Then we're off…

"You... want... gae-bah?" she says. "Gae-bah?"

"What?"

"You know… gae-bah?"

The men are behind, following in another cab. She holds my arm and pulls me closer.

"Gae-bah?"

Rapid-fire Korean to the cab driver. Gestures, voices increasing in volume. Laughing. Then shouting. Are they now arguing? Busan people are known for their loud and rough demeanor. They often sound like they're ready to stab each other when in fact they're only talking about the weather.

The two taxis pull off into a busy area by the beach. We get out. Margaret Cho again glues herself to my arm and we go into a nondescript building, climbing three flights of stairs. I am then led into an empty nightclub bathed in blue neon. The place is immaculate and designed with the utmost economy. Silver, white, and black are the dominant colors. Nothing superfluous exists. Sleek minimalism reigns.

We sit at a bar facing the dance floor and are immediately joined by two striking Asian transsexuals: tall, sleek, elegant, and gorgeous. Gloved hands are extended.

"He-lllllllo."

Demure looks, lingering hands.

My hosts give some orders and soon there is a spread on the counter consisting of a beautiful platter of fresh fruit; a dried, flattened cuttlefish with various dipping sauces; several glistening bottles of beer; cans of juice and cold tea; and two large bottles of whiskey. We get right to it, eating and drinking communally, as is the custom. In Korea specifically, it's considered the height of greed and rudeness to pour your own drink or to sip from an individual bottle. One bottle is always opened and used to fill everyone's glass, usually from eldest to youngest, though a foreign guest may trump even an old man. So the whiskey starts flowing, followed by beer, bits of cuttlefish, and more whiskey.

My hosts then gesture to me, to one our hostesses, and to the karaoke machine that sits at the head of the dance floor.

"You go. You go."

A karaoke book is thrust into my lap. The selection is dizzying, with thousands of songs in Korean, English, and Japanese. I settle on the Eagles' "Desperado," and am led to the machine.

As I belt out the ballad, one of our hostesses dances to the slow beat of the song. She is a good six feet tall in heels and wears a form-fitting red dress. She performs a serpentine writhe as I give it my all. Applause. Ovations. More whiskey. Margaret Cho gives me the eye—with a certain unmistakable glint.

Our hostesses sit across from us and make conversation, flirt, and put ice cubes in our glasses. They imbibe as well. Their English is good. We are then joined by a third hostess, a stunning beauty wearing all white. I get up and dance with her and make small talk; she tells me that she is a real woman. I want to believe her and do. The others, despite their beauty, are still quite tall and a bit too angular to be the genuine thing. I look for a prominent Adam's apple, a giveaway for a man. I see none. I ask my hosts.

"Yes, she girl."

"My *sister*," says Mr. Young.

I step back up to the karaoke machine and Mr. Park joins me for a song. I choose the Sex Pistols' "Anarchy in the UK."

"I am the Antichrist… I am an anarchist!"

Mr. Park yells it out with me in full punk-rock glory. He is a bit pudgy, with glasses and a now-loosened tie: an Asian businessman straight out of Central Casting. Sweat beads up on his forehead as he hits each note with a quivering vibrato. It's a Tuesday night. Where am I?

We stagger away from the "gae-bah" toward a Japanese-style restaurant/ drinking establishment. Koreans never just drink. They always eat while drinking and drink while eating. The food is brought out quickly—some hot soup and a pan full of tiny octopuses in red pepper sauce known as *nakji bokum*, searing in its spiciness. Bottles of soju appear and our shot glasses are continually filled. I follow none of the conversation and laugh when they laugh, which is often. My tongue is burning. We are all getting very drunk. Mr. Park suddenly becomes worried about me. Perhaps he's never drunk with a foreigner before and doubts my tolerance.

"You okay? You okay?"

"Sure, I'm fine!"

"Too much drink, no?"

I *am* fine, my head turning to jelly and the packed wooden restaurant now taking on a glimmering, crystalline look. I keep drinking with fervor, my face now steaming red from the booze and spice.

Margaret Cho looks at me longingly. Mr. Park gets up and goes to the restroom. Mr. Young knowingly nudges me.

"You like? You like?"

He openly points to Margaret Cho. She feigns embarrassment, shooting me looks in between.

"She like you. You go… You go her home?"

Mr. Park returns to the table. He senses something afoot.

He looks to Margaret and then locks eyes with me.

"She my girlfriend. She... she... my girlfriend."

He knows the score and defines the terms. He then pays the bill.

We stagger outside. Margaret Cho takes my arm. I slither out of her hold.

"She my girlfriend. She my girlfriend." Mr. Park forces himself between us, much to my relief. There are times when I welcome the cock block.

She looks at me. Mr. Park grabs her upper arm and barks at her in Korean.

I then make my escape, running into the dark and taking in the sea air.

Sweating It Out

I awoke the next morning to a shrieking alarm clock. As I opened my eyes, the morning light poured through the window and stabbed at my receptors, blurring the images in the room that were attempting to spin into focus. My mouth felt as if every molecule of moisture had been seared away with a hair-dryer; my insides were swollen and aching dully; my head hissed and my throat felt like it was filled with biting ants. This was the beginning of a soju hangover, which must be among the most brutal in the world.

I slithered into work and staggered through two hours of kindergarten classes, barely able to focus. I could feel the alcohol steaming through my pores, burning the skin on the way out. I gulped down countless cups of water and sipped green tea, in vain attempts to alleviate my misery. At one point in the class, shortly after singing "The Rabbit Song," I slumped into a chair and just gave up, letting the kiddies run around and play. The mild physical exertion put forth in "The Rabbit Song" (it involves various hand gestures and jumping about) left the inside of my head cracking, and I successfully waited out the last part of the class without getting caught. I was lucky enough to work at one of the few hagwons that had yet to place surveillance cameras in every classroom.

I knew that I reeked of booze and so did the kids (after all, most of their fathers were Korean businessmen), who commented on it freely: "Oh, teacher, *sul nemsae!*" (*Alcohol smell!*) Jimmy picked up on it soon enough, as well. On a break between classes, he walked up, grinning, and holding the paper cup of machine super-sweet instant coffee that he was always sipping from, said:

"Oh… Chris Teacher. Last night you were many drinking?"

I smiled and shrugged. There was no denying it. Busted.

Jimmy chuckled to himself and patted me on the shoulder. "You must be careful not to miss the class at the Bayridge Language School."

"Of course, Jimmy."

"After work you must go to sah-oo-na."

"Where?"

"Sah-oo-na."

"Sah… What?"

"SAH-OO-NA. The public bathroom."

"Oh, you mean the *sauna.*"

"Yes. Go to sah-oo-na. There is across the street. There!" He pointed out the window to a large building with a red logo that seemed to be a symbol for hot water. "You go tonight. First sah-oo-na, and then *jjim-jil bang.*"

"What's the *jjim-jil bang*?"

"It is kind of resting room. You must go. Very refreshing!"

The idea of going to a Korean public bath intrigued me, though I have to say I viewed the prospect with some trepidation. While a hot soak and steam sounded ideal, I was still not thrilled about going and hanging out in a room with a bunch of other naked men. I've never been too keen to get naked with strangers. Perhaps this comes from my childhood, when my grandfather used to take me to the swimming pool at the local Elks Club, where he was a member. Attached to the swimming pool, were a locker room and a sauna. The locker room was always full of old naked guys just *hanging out.* These old boys would just stand around and talk to each other—business, family life, whatever—while their bits and pieces dangled for everyone to see. These were wrinkly, saggy old men, with swollen grey nut sacks that hung down to mid-thigh, like a couple of oranges wrapped in a baby elephant's ear. I saw up close and personal the effect of forty years of steak and martini lunches on a man's body.

Reservations aside, I decided to give the sauna a go. While my hangover had lessened by the time I ground out that last hour of class, it still possessed me like a malevolent spirit, and the only way to banish it from my body would be through heat and sweat. So after work I walked straight over to the building, entered through the door, and approached the front desk, which was staffed by two pretty young women. I paid six thousand won (US$6.00) for both the sauna and jjim-jil bang, and was handed a numbered key attached a semi-elastic band, as well as a shirt and pair of shorts. I thanked them and walked toward the elevator, only to be stopped by one of the women's voice shouting after me: "Shoes! Shoes!" She pointed to my shoes and then gestured to the rows of small lockers in front of the elevators.

Ashamed to play the part of the uncouth Westerner, I bashfully waved back and removed my shoes, opening the locker with the key I had been given.

The elevator brought me up to the fourth floor, where the men's sauna and locker room were located. I entered the locker room and searched for my number. There were hundreds of large wooden lockers in the warm, brightly-lit space. This locker room had none of the dank smell of man-sweat, like a place back home. It was clean and welcoming. Men congregated near a television set showing the evening's baseball game. Some were nude, while others wore the shorts and shirts provided for them to wear in the jjim-jil bang. Their eyes were fixed on the game, while a few munched on hard-baked eggs that sat out in a wooden bowl on the seating platform. An attendant was seated behind a desk and greeted me as I walked in. A commercial refrigerator sold soft drinks and cans of coffee. A door led into what looked like a tiny barber shop. I quickly located my locker, stripped down, took a deep breath, and headed toward the entrance of the main sauna.

In the West, when we say "sauna," we usually mean "steam room." A Korean sauna contains steam rooms, soaking pools, as well as showers and personal cleaning stations. This is what I first made out as I sauntered into the main area. Steam hung in the air, and the place echoed with the sound of jetting water and men's distorted voices. It was not a particularly quiet place. A few eyes darted my way as I came in, but for the most part I was ignored. I soaped up and rinsed off under one of the countless shower nozzles, and then went to check out the actual baths. There were three hot baths to choose from: I slipped into the largest one and let the hot water envelop me.

Immediately I felt the talons of my hangover loosen their grasp; my body relaxed as I loudly exhaled. As I opened my eyes, I saw a young boy sitting across from me, next to his father. The boy's eyes were transfixed, as if he could not believe the vision of a real live foreigner relaxing in front of him. I closed my eyes once again. When I reopened them, I saw that his stare had not abated. He was just a curious kid, but I was beginning to feel like a zoo animal and couldn't help but be annoyed. As I looked away from the boy, I saw an older man—perhaps in his mid-50s—enter the pool and look my way. He smiled. I politely returned the smile. He waved. I nodded. He then waded across the bath and approached me.

Oh no, please.

He sat next to me and began to talk: "Hello!"

"Uhm… hello."

"Where are you from?"

"I'm… uh… I'm from the USA."

"Oh, America? Yes, yes, I know. I've visited America several times…"

The man spoke English well and no doubt wished to practice. I had already experienced this several times, so I wasn't surprised. What caused me to recoil was the fact that he grabbed my arm and touched me as he spoke.

A naked man touching me while I, too, am naked. No.

Call it homophobia, but the idea of a nude guy touching me ANYWHERE while I also lack clothes just scrapes against the grain.

Is this some old pervert hitting on me in what seems to be an otherwise respectable public bath? Or is he just being friendly?

As I scrambled for some sort of cultural bearing, I saw at once that my meters were out of whack. They needed some serious recalibration. Even so, I extricated myself from the pool as quickly and politely as possible, and jumped into the cold bath, which cooled me off and immediately cleared my head. My skin contracted and my thoughts sharpened. The sensation of going from faint-headed hot to bracingly cold is one of my favorites in life. I couldn't imagine the sauna without a cold pool. It's the best part, really. I knelt in the waist-deep water and looked out onto the scene playing out in front of me. Korean men—all black-haired and yellowish-brown-skinned—walked and bathed and washed in the white-tiled room. Their uniformity made me self-conscious. I was big, pink, and different. Many of them were seated on small stools in front of cleaning stations, where they went at themselves with vigor. I saw a father lay his son over his knee while he scrubbed the dead skin off the kid's back with a rough red exfoliating cloth.

This sort of father-son grooming is very common in the saunas of Korea, and no doubt helps to strengthen an already-deep bond. Such a thing is much rarer back home. My father was a very warm and emotionally-generous man, but aside from when I was an infant, he never washed my naked body and surely never wanted to. This contact I took in was not just limited toward relatives, either. I saw two teenage boys—friends, it seemed—showering next to one another. At one point, one boy scrubbed the other's back. I've seen such a thing on many occasions since, an exchange that would be unthinkable in the West.

This was my first lesson in the fact that Korean men are much more physically intimate with each other than many of us foreigners. They often touch when talking (even in the sauna, as I found out), and after drinking, many older men will even walk hand in hand. There's nothing sexual about it: they just happen to be a lot less hung-up about physical contact than, say, we Americans are. I view this as a generally a good thing, a reflection of a certain warmth and camaraderie that we lack in our personal-space-valuing culture back home.

Some things in the sauna didn't strike such a sentimental chord with me, however. One older Korean man (known as an *ajosshi*) viewed the sauna as not just a place to soak and sweat, but also as a gym of sorts. He took the opportunity to do his daily stretches, *au naturale*. He lunged and bounced and placed his naked body at all sorts of strange and demanding angles—at one point even doing several toe-touches, which, when viewed from behind, was acid to the eyes. Also, a few other ajosshis evidently viewed the sauna as an appropriate place to clear their throats and sinuses of a week's worth of stored-up snot and phlegm, blowing and hawking up loogies that seemed to come from the deepest recesses of their bodies. These mucous evacuations were shot and spat straight onto the floor, the same floor that the rest of us were walking on, *barefoot*. The fact that the floor was regularly rinsed with water did nothing to dispel my gnawing annoyance at such wickedly nasty behavior.

I emerged from the sauna soothed and spotless and changed into the jjim-jil bang pajamas given to me by the woman at the front desk. The actual jjim-jil bang was up on the fifth floor, so I walked up the stairs and explored the space. The Koreans refer to a jjim-jil bang as a "relaxing room," and it is just that, though it's actually made up of several rooms, rather than just the one. As I entered the main room, I saw many people sitting or lying on blankets on the floor, watching a comedy program on a large-screen TV. The TV show consisted of a team of men running around and screaming at each other, accompanied by endless instant replays of them falling down or getting hit in the balls with foam baseball bats. While it was silly and obviously entertaining for a lot of people in the room, it was noisy as hell and anything but *relaxing*.

Next to this common room was a snack bar, selling drinks and *cup ramyen* (ramen noodles). A bored-looking ajumma stood behind the counter, her eyes fixed to the smaller TV blaring above the bar. I noticed many young couples milling around the jjim-jil bang: boys in blue, girls in pink. I made my way past a room where people were just sleeping, and then opened the door to a small, dark room. The floor was made of little grey stones, which soaked up the heat radiating outward from the heat source. I wrapped the towel around my head and lay down on the hot stones, forming a sort of gravel angel with my arms and legs as I settled in. In no time I was sweating, soaking my shirt and towel, expelling the remnants of my crazy abduction drinking session the night before. After about twenty minutes I had all I could take, and stepped into the cooler environs of the main room, where I bought a cold drink from the woman.

I was now relaxed and felt purged, as if a host of toxins had been flushed from my body. I walked around and tried out the several other rooms which made up the complex, sweating some more and letting go of tension that had been stored up from years of stress. It was nice, and nothing like I had ever experienced before—literally clean and wholesome fun.

I could get used to this place.

That night I had my best sleep in months.

CHAPTER 4

TERRIBLE CHILDREN

WHEN I first decided to come to Korea—when I answered the ad, secured a visa and decided to make the plunge—I figured I had it made. Teaching in Asia? Nothing to it. It couldn't be like teaching in America, with all of those rude, disrespectful kids. I'd be going to an ancient Confucian society that valued education, a place where teachers were truly esteemed.

I remember envisioning tidy classrooms full of obedient, disciplined, and well-behaved students, who sat at immaculate desks arranged in straight, precise rows. I imagined them bowing in unison when I entered the room, and sitting erect, soaking up every English word that fell onto them from on high. I would be respected and deferred to. My lofty position would be untouchable, my decisions beyond reproach. I would be an *honored teacher.*

My first hint that things may be otherwise came during my phone interview. Scott, the head teacher at the hagwon (and later close friend), was asking me some basic questions about my background and why I wanted to work abroad. When he was finished, he asked if I had any questions.

"Yes," I said. "How about the students? Are they disciplined? Are they well-behaved?"

There was a slight pause as Scott—being a very polite Canadian—struggled to choose his words. In the end, he let out a brief sigh and just said, "Not really."

****

It can be said that I'm a permissive teacher. I let my children get away with a lot in class. I figured out early on that this was the best way to operate at a Korean hagwon. If you start cracking down hard and being a fascist, it's just going to cause you a bigger headache. It will only serve to generate complaints from the mothers, which is kryptonite to any English teacher. And as I mentioned earlier, these kids in question go to regular school all day and then have to come to the hagwon for a couple more hours: school after school. It must fill their little hearts with joy. I suppose you could say that I sympathize with their plight, that I have no interest in being Mr. Hardass, that I want them to learn English, but that I want it to be fun. As long as they're practicing English, I let them get away with a lot. They can yell, they can hit me, they can call me names… whatever. It just has to be done in ENGLISH.

Case in point: My favorite class at the Bayridge Language School was in the afternoon and consisted of only three kids—two boys and one girl. Like all my students, they had English nicknames: Peter, Louis, and Marie. They were my most advanced class. The kids were firecrackers, as smart as it gets. However, these kids, like all kids, could at times be truly regrettable, awful little organisms. Every day, I started the class with an informal English conversation. This is known as *free talking*, a kind of warm-up before we opened the book. I would ask them very some basic questions and they, in turn, would answer. Early on I noticed that these kids had a morbid streak, that they entertained dark fantasies of death, carnage, and destruction. Maybe this was a subconscious manifestation of living in a country that has always faced the specter of total war. Maybe they watched too many violent movies or played too many gory computer games. While I can't be really sure about the root cause, what I do know is that it didn't take long before I became the central figure in these fantasies. Before long it evolved into a daily ritual. Every day, one by one, the kids would go up to the white board, and tell me, with the aid of an improvised diagram made with markers, *how they would kill me.*

Let me recount a few of the scenarios from a typical day:

Little Peter always went first. On this day said that he would pack me into a box filled with dynamite and drop me out of a plane into Iraq.

Little Louis was simpler in his plan, which basically involved kicking me off the top of a very tall mountain and me landing on dynamite. However, after the fatal explosion, as my spirit ascended into the heavens, I was set upon by a gang of angels wielding sharp swords, thereby assuring the complete destruction of my soul. I was killed *twice*—both on Earth and in the afterlife.

Little Marie's were (she had two) the most elaborate, as usual, since she was always the leading candidate for the Most Evil Child in Class award. I didn't quite understand the first one, though it incorporated her shooting some sort of projectile at me that ended in dismemberment. The second fantasy resembled Peter's in that I was dropped out of a plane, only instead of Iraq I landed in "Aprika" [sic], where I was boiled in a pot by a bone-through-his-nose native. She employed the old-style African native on more than a few occasions. I don't know where she got it, but Korea's still behind the curve when it comes to progressive views of black folks and Africa. Comedy skits employing blackface and Afro wigs are still quite common on their TV variety shows, and some of the depictions of black people I've seen in children's textbooks look like they came straight out of the minstrel show.

Marie was the star of the Let's Kill Chris game, since she really invented it. Her scenarios usually ended in cannibalism, where I'd be served in soup, over rice, or as "Chris-gogi" (*gogi* is Korean for *meat*).

Peter's were the most explosive and often employed advanced technology. They usually involved dynamite or bombs. One time, a flying robotic dragon dropped me into a dynamite-filled volcano.

Louis liked to employ animals. I have been eaten by both tigers and lions, as well as bitten by hundreds of deadly snakes. Once I was bitten by snakes after being cut into pieces by scores of knives. Another time he drew what looked like a clawed animal paw and, without a hint of emotion, stated:

"You are crushed by bear hand."

The Nicknames

"Grasopor."

Some of the kids began calling me Grasshopper. This is just a variation of Christopher, my full first name. They are syllabically similar, so I guess the leap wasn't so hard to make.

Officially, I was known as Chris Teacher. Some of the more respectful students even addressed me as Mr. Chris. This led to another nickname:

"*Miss-teol* Christin."

Miss-teol is a play on the word *mister.* The clever little fucker who invented this one succeeded in both calling me a girl (*Miss*) and ridiculing my arm hair (*teol*, which is Korean for *body hair.*) Korean children are obsessed with my arm hair, which is light to moderate at best. They constantly stare at it, pull at it, stroke it, and uncontrollably laugh at it.

Christin, of course, is a play on Chris, and turns me into a girl TWICE. This was an endless well of glee for the little hellspawn.

"Cow."

The children in one class began calling me Cow. This was only after I forbade the use of the word *pig. Pig* is a very mean word to use in English, though the children fling it around like a fifty-cent Frisbee, both in English and Korean (the Korean word is *dwaeji).* They even used it to describe a teacher named Brian, who was six three and nothing but bone and sinew. One time a nefarious little fucker told him that he was "100% fat." I pity the truly fat in this country. The abuse must be an endless torrent.

"Super Dung Man."

The same group of children mentioned above used to call me Super Dung Man, but only on Fridays. This emanated from a white board drawing one of them did of me in which I was composed entirely of feces, complete with ravenous flies circling my poo-ey form. Korean children—boys and girls alike—are obsessed with poo, and often kill the time by doodling endless piles of it, always in neat coils.

"Supercrazy Baboteacher."

I invented this one on my own. *Babo* basically means *dummy* or *fool* in Korean. The kids used it all the time. I think *babo* is a hilarious word. It just sounds like what it is: dumb.

"Super Gorilla."

Most of the kids already knew me as "Gorilla Teacher," because, from time to time I would act like a gorilla. "Super Gorilla" grew out of this. I used to sometimes play a card game with the kids called Crazy Eights. This game consists of a deck of cards split into categories. One of the categories is animals, and one of the cards is a gorilla, featuring a huge silverback ape. One student began referring to the card as "Super Gorilla." The idea of a Super Gorilla intrigued me, a gorilla even more savage and stupid than a regular gorilla. This eventually led to me channeling the Super Gorilla, which was just a more extreme version of my regular gorilla. From time to time I would burst into a class room shrieking and grunting, pounding my chest and attacking the furniture. It was cathartic: the kids would totally freak out. It was like giving all of them a giant whap of pure sugar in the jugular. You know how you can rev up a puppy, how you can just bombard it with frenetic energy until it starts running aimlessly, back and forth through the room, biting at the air and growling at the carpet? Well, you can do the same thing with children. They're basically just like puppies, only a lot meaner.

Killing My Dragonfly

About nine months into my first year, I helped some of the kids put up a spring mural in their classroom. We made construction paper flowers and grass. One of the kids made a sun and clouds. Another made a bee.

I made a dragonfly. The next time I came into class, I witnessed the following scene: the kids had attacked my dragonfly with pins, impaling its head and totally destroying one of its plastic eyes. They said that it was "very bad" and that they were "happy it is die."

The Baby Game

The reason I know children are truly terrible beings is from my experience playing the Baby Game with them. It started off in one kindergarten class, where a particularly spunky and malicious little girl would point to any given object and shout, "Teacher – baby!" I'd then take whatever object she pointed to—be it a book, an eraser, a pencil case, or even the clock on the wall—and stuff it under my shirt, as if pregnant. I'd make a popping sound with my mouth, and the baby would then be born. And what would happen next? The WHOLE CLASS would ATTACK THE BABY. They would all try to KILL THE BABY.

This game became so popular that I came up with two variations:

In the first, I'd stuff some tissue paper in my shirt and then pop it out. The class would then grab my "baby" out of my hands. They then would all look at me, giggle like SS leprechauns, and proceed to RIP MY BABY APART. I'd scream "Oh, my baby! My baby!" This only served to accelerate the pace and intensity of the laughter, as well as the ripping apart of my progeny.

The second variation was the most simple and most popular among the kindergartners. I'd stuff a ball under my shirt and say, "Look at my baby." The youngest and cutest girl in the class would then step forward and pound on my stomach with her fists, screaming in ecstasy like a half-formed harpy. This would continue until the baby was aborted or miscarried, and the fetus/ball would then invariably be thrown and kicked around the room.

I loved that first year of teaching in Korea. The students were beings of pure chaos, the very opposite of the obedient Asian student that I had expected to encounter before I came over. It was open field for imagination, even if I was the butt of most the jokes. Anything went, as long as the kids weren't harmed and the moms didn't complain. In fact, all of these sick games just made me more popular among the kids and the parents. I had a hard time really believing it, because if it had been America, I would have been fired after *two hours.*

INTERLUDE

FEBRUARY 2005
HO CHI MINH CITY, VIETNAM

I sit with Sam at the rooftop bar of the Rex Hotel, an old Saigon landmark. Another friend from Korea, Angry Steve, is here, along with his buddy Josh, a balding, neurotic Philadelphian who never can seem to apply either enough sunscreen or bug repellent. We sip cold beer and bask in the tropical night air. The city slithers underneath us, a flowing artery of motorcycles, infinite in number. From atop the building we can hear the wail of their horns as they make their way down the town's French-built boulevards—the cry of one huge, slinking organism. Sam and I rented our own bikes today. It was the first time I'd ridden in over fifteen years. We smoked a joint beforehand and immediately became separated in the vast gush of riders. Sam got hopelessly lost, ran out of gas, and had to be led back to our hotel by a Vietnamese Good Samaritan. He was visibly rattled and may have even cried.

It is just three days before Tet, the Lunar New Year, which brings to mind the famed offensive from 1968. Shadows of the war follow us everywhere in this intriguing land. Just today we scurried around the Cu Chi Tunnel complex and even took in a war-era propaganda film which castigated the American "bastards" and their South Vietnamese "lackeys." It didn't sound too different than the modern-day pronouncements being made north of the Korean DMZ. Everywhere I look, I imagine the barrels of Kalashnikovs and napalm blasts. Scenes from *Platoon*, *Full Metal Jacket*, and *Apocalypse Now* replay in my head. Vietnam has existed as a kind of specter my whole life, and now I'm finally here, drinking a bottle of beer and thinking about what I'll eat for breakfast in the morning…

Sam and I are here for just over a week, having managed to escape Korea during its own Lunar New Year celebrations. It was punishingly cold the morning we set out from Busan, with Siberian winds lashing the whole of the peninsula. Vietnam is scorching in the afternoon, but just about as perfect as it gets, come nighttime. We'll do a Mekong River Tour and then spend five days at the beach in Mui Ne, before jumping on a plane, donning our jackets, and returning to the land of spit, scowls, and elbows.

CHAPTER 5

THE SOUTH'S SECOND CITY

WHEN I was hooked up with my first job in Korea, my recruiter, via email, informed me that I'd be coming to Busan. She really tried to sell me on the job based on location, talking up the fact that I'd be living near the beach in a city with mild weather and, by urban Asian standards, pretty clean air. She made Busan sound like a nice place to live, a laid-back town whose rhythms would be easy to relax into, like a piece of California placed on the rocky Asian mainland. The truth is that I needed no convincing. I would have taken the first job thrown my way, whether it was in Seoul, Busan, Daegu, or some hellish rural outpost. I was eager to jump on a plane, earn some cash, and start the story that would be my new expat life. I just happened to get lucky.

Busan or *Pusan*? You see it spelled both ways. *Busan* is actually more correct, phonetically, and is the preferred choice these days, but *Pusan* was and still is in usage. I didn't know anything about Busan, but the word *Pusan* rang a bell. I had read about the Korean War and recalled the Pusan Perimeter, which refers to the last line of defense that South Korean and American troops made during the early months of fighting. The city never fell to Northern forces, mainly due to it being one of the southernmost cities in the country and cut off by the Nakdong River. Pusan was also known to me as one of those mysterious Asian ports visited by American Navy personnel. Surely my Uncle Bob—who had spent 25 years on a Navy submarine—had mentioned Pusan in one of his many stories whispered to my older brothers at family gatherings. These stories always involved shore leave, obscene amounts of liquor, and prostitutes doing unmentionable things with baby turtles and ping pong balls. Pusan definitely figured into this seedy mythology; this Pusan—the one of hooker bars, VD, and Navy brawls—contrasted sharply with the much gentler city described by my recruiter. It just sounded dirtier: *Pusan. I'm gonna get me some poon-tang in Pusan.*

When I arrived on the peninsula, I noticed at once that people—especially expats—were often asking the question: Seoul or Busan? And at first glance it seemed like a no-brainer. Seoul, with its 20-million-plus inhabitants, is *the* city of Korea. To many it seems like the only city in Korea. It's the national capital and the trend capital. It is cosmopolitan, suave, and sophisticated. It's international, and anything that happens in Korea has to happen in Seoul, right?

This is true in many ways. Seoul is where it's at, but if you glance at its massive shadow, you will see her little sister, Busan. Sometimes you feel sorry for Busan, since she is so often passed over, ignored in the presence of her more-glamorous sibling. She's a bit of a Cinderella—never asked to the prom. But like any second city, Busan has a distinct spirit and vitality. I love second cities for that reason. They can never compete with the inflated metropolitan egos of first cities, so they are forced to develop unique charms of their own. Chicago, Marseilles, Osaka, and Busan—these are all places with strong, down-to-earth identities. They've had to forge through on their terms, and are always far less pretentious than the bigger, more famous towns.

I found this immediately in Busan. I saw that Busan and Pusan existed at once, in the same place. The new and the old comingled in a way I had never seen before, and it didn't take me too long to fall in love.

Oiseo! Saiseo! Boiseo!

I thought I knew fish markets. After all, I had spent a few months working in one of the most famous fish stands at Seattle's Pike Place Market. I wasn't a very successful fishmonger (I was fired for general incompetence), but in that time I learned a thing or two about slinging seafood. I certainly was comfortable around fish. I had grown up near saltwater, in a family that loved to catch salmon, pot for crabs, dig clams, and eat all of them. I love getting down with most all manner of sea creatures. You could say that the taste is in my blood; it was just something I grew up with, and this appetite has increased throughout the years.

However, Western and East Asian seafood tastes are two different things, and this especially goes for Korea. The Western eater-of-seafood has nothing on a Korean. He is a quaking pansy compared to his Asian counterpart, who will eat almost any form of life that lives in the ocean, no matter how carbuncle-covered, slimy, or half-evolved. In fact, it often seems that the more bizarre and hideous-looking the creature, the more sought-after it is by the Korean seafood fiend. As far as I can tell, the only real criterion for inedibility is poison: if the particular sea being is likely to kill you after ingestion, then it usually is considered best to leave it be.

Usually is the operative word here. Case in point: the blowfish, one of the most venomous fish in the sea. The toxin from one fish alone can easily kill several men, yet it is widely eaten in restaurants around the country. I've had the soup on several occasions and have (luckily) lived to write about it, but you never know if that one bowl will be your last. It only takes one careless chef.

The first time I went to Jagalchi, Busan's famous fish market, was with my friend, co-worker, and original phone-interviewer, Scott. Jagalchi is located in Nampo-dong, Busan's harbor area and the oldest part of town. It's a massive complex, both outdoors and indoors, conveniently sitting next the dockside, eagerly taking in the boats' daily hauls.

Scott and I took the subway across town and got off near the market. The Nampo-dong area, despite undergoing a facelift in recent years, is still a bit hardscrabble. Much of it has a rougher feel than other, more gentrified parts of the city. It is the port, Busan's old gate to the world, and you can feel this as you walk its narrow alleys and side streets, which are crowded with shops selling T-shirts, ceramics, leather jackets, and bags of dried fish. Hulking Russian men can be seen sauntering through the markets, their peroxide-haired women in tow. Photo-snapping Japanese tourists mix with small groups of South Asian factory workers out shopping, and old Korean moneychangers sit in silence, biding their time for the next foreigner looking for that favorable rate.

As we approached Jagalchi, the selling of goods transformed in the selling of food. Raw fish restaurants, their unfortunate menu items forlornly housed in aquariums in front, lined the road to the main body of the market. At once it became very crowded, with waves of people heading there and away. Drivers honked as they tried to squeeze their cars through the people, who brushed by one another with not even a nod. The smell of raw fish mixed with the smell of grilled fish. People sat at plastic tables in front of the restaurants, slurping down oysters and grilled clams, drinking from clear shot glasses. Seagulls circled above. The place was buzzing, with an energy and chaos that I've only ever tasted in Asia.

We walked in silence into the main artery of the market, and let ourselves be led by the slipstream of people heading into its heart. On each side of us were countless stalls with their wares splayed out in front of us. At first it was mainly fish—cod, flounder, mackerel, and monkfish, along with the omnipresent *galchi*—long, thin, and bright silver—known as scabbard fish in English. These stalls were almost universally manned by tough old women in rubber boots, rubber gloves, and visors. These women sat on squat stools, bundled up against the slicing winds of early March, barking out prices to the river of passersby. The ground was wet and at times there were small puddles of muck: this market was a place for heavy shoes or boots, and I was thankful that I was appropriately shod.

"Check that out." Scott pointed to an old man in a straw hat who haphazardly manned a wheelbarrow containing the carcass of a huge shark.

To our left the fish stalls began to get more exotic in their inventories. Octopus was now the dominant feature, with huge specimens hanging from hooks. I stopped and clicked pictures, much to the annoyance of the old woman manning the booth, who brusquely waved me away. I ignored her for a short time, too fascinated by the jarring beauty and pure alien form of the cephalopods in front of us. As we walked further, we saw more octopuses, this time smaller and, moreover, alive. They were kept in buckets of seawater. At one point I saw a crafty fellow escape his prison and make a break for it, correctly heading in the direction of the sea. He made it about fifteen feet before his minder—another rubber-and-visor-adorned grandmother—noticed his attempt. She rose from her stool and tromped over to the octopus, grabbed it firmly by its head, and flung it back into the bucket. No gentle keeper, she punctuated this move with a barrage of verbal abuse delivered from the depths of her throat. There is no room for sentimentality at the fish market.

At one point Scott and I headed off of the main concourse, into one of Jagalchi's raw fish pavilions. This was a giant indoor space—a kind of warehouse. The women were now mainly replaced by men, who wore rubber bibs and manned seafood stations made up of multiple tanks, a prep area, as well as tables and chairs. The open-topped tanks housed not just fish, but shrimp, scallops, octopus, squid, bulbous orange specimens called *mongae* (sea squirt), and *gaebul* (long pinkish things that resembled huge, uncircumcised penises). The customers gathered around the stations and picked out their own goods, which were then dispatched, sliced up on the spot, and served raw. As we wandered through the gargantuan complex I was dizzied by the sheer number of workers and customers, not to mention the sea critters themselves. The building was bathed in fluorescent light, and the din of hundreds of Koreans eating and drinking echoed off of the structure's concrete pillars.

When Scott went to pee, I found myself standing alone, self-conscious as I felt the eyes of many patrons drawn to me, a lone foreigner who was clearly dazed by the pure force of Koreans digging into some crazy seafood. Four older men were sitting at a table near me and staring hard. One motioned for me to come over, a big grin over-taking his flushed-red face.

"Hello hello hello! Soju?"

He held up a bottle. The other guys erupted in noisy approval.

"Sure, why not?"

Old Korean men inviting me to join them for a few glasses of soju—this was a phenomenon that I would get very used to over the next several years. Drinks were poured and glasses clinked.

"*Gonbae!*"

I managed to get several glasses down—as well as a couple of slices of fish, before I saw Scott making his way back from the pisser. The liquor warmed my insides against the late-winter chill. I waved goodbye to my new friends and walked with Scott back out into the thick of the market.

Jagalchi has been around for over six hundred years, making it one of the oldest continuous seafood markets on the globe. It is its own unique place—the most purely "Busan" of any place in the city. Jagalchi is so distinct that it has its very own dialect—known as *saturi*—which is only spoken by the people who work there. This is reflected in the market's slogan: *Oiseo! Saiseo! Boiseo!* (Come! Buy! See!).

The deeper we got into Jagalchi, the weirder it became. We passed by a whole section dedicated to the eating of raw shark meat, which gave way to dolphin, then whale. Seafood no longer held exclusive rights, as I took in places selling frogs, live turtles, and a few severed pigs' heads. The crowd briefly split as a beggar made his way through their midst. He lay on his stomach, underneath which was a board on casters. In front of him was a donation box, as well as a car battery connected to a portable stereo, on which played a repetitive Buddhist chant, complete with knocking wood sounds. His legs were shriveled—useless it seemed—and covered by leggings made from tire rubber. He propelled himself by his arms—literally dragging himself over the wet and filthy pavement. He looked like a sad merman, and would be the first of several more I would see that day, a common sight throughout the old markets of Busan.

A bit taken back, we walked in silence, until Scott asked, "So, what do you want to eat? There's plenty to choose from."

"Hmmm…" I considered my options, which were intimidating in number. "Let's walk a bit more and see what grabs our eye."

As we continued, I noticed several places selling live eels, which swam and slithered in the display tanks. Men sat at in chairs, eating sliced bits of the things frying on tabletop gas stoves.

"That looks interesting."

An old woman working at one of the joints sensed our curiosity and shouted our way, urging us to come in and eat.

"*Mashisseoyo!*"

I recognized the word—it was one of the first I had learned: *delicious.* She scuttled out to where we stood and smiled, waving us in and pointing to one of the empty tables in her stall, where, before we knew it, we were seated next to a portable heater, sharing a bottle of soju and waiting for our pan of undulating chunks of eel.

Perhaps the most interesting—or horrifying—thing about Korean fried eel (known as *geom jang-eoh*) is its preparation. The eels are plucked from the tank, one at a time, and literally pinned to a wooden cutting board by the head. The cook then skins the thing alive and chops the wriggling body into easy-to-eat segments. These still-moving bits—which squirm for some time after death—are thrown onto some aluminum foil over a pan, and fried up with red pepper paste and a liberal amount of onions. They twitch and jerk until the heat of the pan finally renders them still, and are then wrapped in sesame leaves and eaten, along with some side dishes. This is almost always accompanied with soju. *Goem jang-eoh* is most popular with older men, who value the bony tail above all, for its alleged properties of stamina.

We were ignorant of the alleged sexual properties of fried eel that day, choosing it instead for its exoticism. While eel is eaten in many European countries, it is generally scoffed at in North America, where it's considered a low-quality fish—a scavenger—almost never sought-after as a meal. This probably has a lot to do with the fact that eels do resemble snakes, and this primal fear of snakes is more than enough to keep eels off the menu back home.

Scott and I took down our eel with fervor, though. The woman who ran the stand was tickled to have to these two very green foreigners giving it a try, laughing at our fascination with the dish, and thrilled to be letting us in on one of Busan's secrets. She didn't have to sell us too hard, though, because the meal was delicious. It was also aided by several bottles of soju, which helped to make the flow of the market melt into a happy blur. Jagalchi is both the heart and soul of Busan. To understand the market is to understand the city's history, and this first trip gave me a taste of the old city, which, while disappearing a bit more each day, will always be alive down at Jagalchi.

Take Me out to the Ballgame

The place was packed. Thirty thousand rowdy fans squeezed into Busan's Sajik Stadium to watch their beloved Lotte Giants take on rival Seoul's Doosan Bears. It was early May, and while much warmer than the previous few frigid months, the cold still lingered—especially after sundown. I had come to the game with my new friend Angry Steve, who was and is a consummate baseball fan. He was fully determined to turn me onto the sport that is not just America's pastime, but Korea's as well.

Baseball didn't really grab me until later in my life. As a kid I never played Little League and took the most remote interest in the travails of my local team, the Seattle Mariners, the then-perennial bottom-dwellers of the American League West. It wasn't until the late '90s—when the Mariners suddenly got hot—that I began to take real notice of the game. Call me a bandwagon jumper, but I caught the fever. This enthusiasm was short-lived, however, as the Mariners once again went into a freefall from which they have yet to really recover. I came to Korea with a whetted appetite, but was in no way not what you'd call a real fan.

Steve, on the other hand, was real. Though he grew up in Massachusetts, he was an avid Yankees fan. Like a lot of East Coast guys, Steve knew the game inside and out. He picked up on every nuance and watched the action like a manager from the dugout. Baseball was in his genes, it seemed. It coursed through his veins, and watching a game with him was always an education.

I knew that the Japanese were crazy about baseball, but Koreans? Well, it turns out that they too have embraced the game, nowhere with more passion and dedication than in Busan. People said that Busan fans were the most ardent in the country. They supported the team through all their ups and downs. An early-season sell-out stadium for a team just two slots from last confirmed this fact. The Giants had become a squad of losers, a team that usually falls short, but always plays with heart. This is what I was told, at least, and to see the masses of fans settle into their seats, or just lay some newspapers down on any available space and turn toward the field, only served to confirm this.

The Korean Baseball Association is made up of 8 teams, representing the largest cities in the Southern Republic. They are named for mascots which, more often than not, are versions of tried-and-true American staples: Bears, Tigers, Lions, Giants. Sometimes the mascots do get more creative, such as the Wyverns and the now-defunct Unicorns (really), but these are the exceptions. The real marketing genius behind the naming of Korean teams lies in the fact that instead of being called by the names of the cities they actually hail from, the teams carry the corporate titles of their conglomerate backers: Samsung, SK, Kia, Hyundai. The result is that rather than chanting "Busan" or even "Giants," thirty thousand ticket-buying fans instead shout and sing "Lotte!" in unison. This is in turn televised nightly. It's an epic scam. You couldn't ask for better PR.

As I made my way through the stadium with Steve, I was struck most by the anarchy of the surroundings. Unlike MLB games in the States, which are carefully controlled occasions to soak the fans for as much money as possible, this Korean game was a complete free-for-all. Aside from a closed-off area behind home plate, no seats were reserved. It was strictly first-come-first-sit, or, more accurately, first-come-first-put-as-much-shit-as-possible-over-any-available-seats-to-reserve-them-for-your-friends-who-will-come-later. People walked into the cement ball park with full coolers in tow, which in turn were stuffed with food and booze. Though *No Smoking* signs graced the stadium, men lit up openly, driving home the point that such signs are suggestions rather than rules in modern Korea.

Vendors walked freely through the stands, displaying no sort of official ID or licenses. They sold beer—both in cans and from back-pack taps—along with roasted chicken, fried chicken, pigs' feet, *kimbap* (rice and ham rolled in seaweed), hard-boiled eggs, rice wine, cuttlefish, boiled potatoes, water, milkshakes, coffee, tea, and ice cream. But unlike back home, the price wasn't hyper-inflated to gouge a captive audience. The pure competition kept everything more than reasonable. And if you didn't want to buy from a vendor, you could just walk down to the convenience store *inside the stadium* which contained all manner of goods, for the same price you'd pay on the outside. There was none of the corporate fascism we see so much at home—with its endless rules, profiteering, and overzealous security. An air of total permissiveness permeated the ballpark. Everyone was settling in to eat, drink, and watch some baseball. It was pure *fun.*

Eventually Steve and I found a couple of outfield seats. We bought few beers, along with a box of chicken (forget peanuts and Cracker Jacks, Korean baseball is all about chicken), and attached our eyes to the game unfolding on the field.

"You know, the level of play isn't bad here," Steve commented. "It's about on par with good minor league back at home. They flub a few catches, make an error or two, but hey, it's still pretty good. And at five bucks a seat, who's gonna complain?"

I took an interest in the game all the while talking with Steve. The cans of beer went down well and relaxed me into the atmosphere. As each Lotte Giants player went up to bat, the crowd got onto its feet and erupted into a song or chant composed for that player alone. I knew neither the players' names nor the words of encouragement, but that didn't stop me from taking to my feet and pretending to join in. It was contagious.

The music was nonstop. As the game went on, the crowd become drunker. Some lost interest in the game, turning to each other instead, pouring drinks, stuffing their mouths full of pork and chicken, and engaging in loud, red-faced conversations. This was less of a ball game and more of a complete, massive piss-up. The screen kept showing shots of the cheerleaders—slim, sleek-thighed girls with shiny, waist-long hair. They were led by a disturbingly enthusiastic man, who jumped and clapped and worked the crowd over a headphone mike.

"I'd like to bang every one of them," Steve quietly remarked, "except the guy."

I nodded in agreement.

The game was close and held our attention the whole time. There had only been one home run, and that was by Doosan in the 5th inning. By the bottom of the 9th, the Lotte Giants were down 3 runs to 2. As they went up to bat, all thirty thousand fans once again rose to their feet. By this time most everyone in the crowd was wearing orange trash bags on their heads. These are always handed out in the 7th inning for people to pack up with all of rubbish that's left over at the end of the game. Busan fans have taken to blowing them up and tying them around their heads. It's a tradition. Another tradition is the singing of "*Busan Galmaegi*" ("Busan Seagull"), a tune about lost love and longing that has come to signify the Lotte Giants. It's a mournful song, sad in that way that only old Korean music can be, and when thirty thousand people sing it in unison, I dare you not to get goosebumps.

The song must have worked its mojo, for the Giants managed to get runners to both first and second base, but now had two outs on the board. This was it. The batter stepped to the plate, feeling the eyes and hopes of the whole stadium upon him. At that moment, I noticed the Koreans next to me looking up and pointing. Our eyes followed, only to take in a lone, white crane flying just above the stadium. It swooped over, as if giving a sign. The players too looked up and a hush overcame the otherwise drunk and boisterous crowd. Finally, it passed, disappearing into the dark, above the range of light. Doosan's pitcher then hunkered down, stretched, and threw.

Lotte's batter slammed the ball. It arced over the shortstop and rolled past the center fielder, bouncing all the way to the wall, just in front of where we sat. Steve and I leapt to our feet. The runners sprinted for it as the Doosan player scrambled for the loose ball. The runner from second scored, and the man from first ran for all he was worth. The Doosan midfielder got hold of the ball and cannoned it full strength, but it was too late. The second runner ran across home plate, putting the Giants over the top—the most dramatic finish I've ever witnessed at a live baseball game. Angry Steve—along with the other thirty thousand people sitting in Sajik that day—slapped hands and hugged each other. The young Korean guy next to me threw his arms around me in crushing embrace. The place exploded incendiary hot with the kind of spontaneous joy that only sports can ignite. Fireworks shot up into the sky. I grabbed my beer and took down the last swallow, screaming with the crowd as I crushed it on my hand. This was baseball in Busan.

Kimchee on the Beach

It had sounded like a good idea, at least the day before. After all, it was late July and surface-of-Venus hot. I had been in Korea for almost a year, and I lived right next to the beach, so why not spend the day there? This is what Scott proposed over a fried rice omelet at our go-to lunch joint, Kimbap Village:

"You can just relax, read, take a swim, drink some beer, eat… whatever. Beat the heat."

"Sounds great." I dug into a small pile of kimchee and took his word for it.

So the next day I met Scott and his girlfriend, Hae-jin—a curvy Busan girl with plump lips and ink-black hair—along with Sam, with whom I had made countless glasses of beer disappear the night before at the Join Bar, a basement haunt near the beach that had become our local boozer. Sam's eyes were painfully red, looking as if he had just taken about six bong hits. His bloodshot veins were instead the result of his wicked hangover, and just looking at them gave me a headache as well. I could see his capillaries throb.

"What wrong Sam? Last night you is much drinking? I think maybe you go hospital or you is die!" Hae-jin teased.

Hae-jin's English was broken and error-strewn, but unlike most Koreans, she wasn't shy to speak it. She belted out her mangled sentences with the confidence of an opera diva. This was refreshing, actually, as it contrasted with the looks of horror that wrinkled into other Koreans' faces at the slightest chance of having to speak our tongue. Perhaps she should have been an ESL instructor: despite her mistakes, it was obvious to that she was doing something right.

We made our way toward the beach, down the side streets lined with pork restaurants, beer joints, and small stores hawking sun hats and beach balls. Old women manned street carts selling chicken skewers, tiny sea snails, and steaming bowls of silkworm pupas—known as *bondaegi*—whose clouds of noxious fumes caused me to gag as we passed by. Sam turned noticeably green. He had eaten a few *bondaegi* at a soju tent next to my apartment building just a few nights before and immediately vomited all over the gravel underneath our table. These outdoor tents, known as *pojang macha*, are often erected over such gravel, which is very convenient for covering up the evidence of late-night pukings. This is done on purpose, I'm sure. Sam proved to be a trooper: after spraying the contents of his stomach onto the small grey rocks, he buried the evidence with his feet, and within five minutes he was onto another beer. Such is drinking on the peninsula, though *pojang macha* are a dying breed these days. The government has long been eager to rid the land of such reminders of a rougher, poorer time, and they're now being replaced with whisky bars, fusion restaurants, and upscale coffee shops.

Like the fish market, I smelled the beach before I actually saw it. Only this smell was foul and unnatural, nothing of the clean air and salt that one usually associates with the seaside. What instead assaulted my nostrils was the reek of refuse, and, moreover, *people*. I could smell the mass of humanity that we at once walked into: a sea of people next to the actual, real sea. The beach was a pulsating mob of human beings—sitting, walking, talking, eating, drinking, bobbing in the shallows, and lying under countless parasols, which sprouted up from the sand like mushrooms in profusion. I had never seen so many people in one place at one time. It was overwhelming—frightening, even. How could this be enjoyable? I had seen photographs of Spain's Costa del Sol in the height of summer. I had spent a few years in southern California and passed days on Venice Beach during the most crowded of times, but nothing had prepared me for the sight which now writhed and bellowed before my eyes. It was unreal. We were on a stretch of sand with well over *half a million* other people. It was as if the whole state of Wyoming had decided to go swimming. This was Korea's idea of a relaxing day at the beach.

We rented a parasol from a couple of muscled-up guys working one of the stations that dotted Haeundae Beach. They looked hard and sported a few tattoos, adding credence to the rumor that the parasol/inner tube/sun bed rental racket was controlled by the local mafia. But for just five bucks, the price was right, and after some recon, we managed to find a bit of precious real estate on the scorching sand. Scott set up the parasol while Hae-jin threw down a beach blanket. Sam and I followed suit with our feeble towels, and after a moment we were settled into the chaos, attempting relaxation in the midst of the mob of shouting Koreans.

"Man, there's a shitload of people here," Sam remarked, shaking his head.

"It's the height of beach season," Scott replied. "Come the end of August. They'll all be gone back up to Seoul and we'll have the place to ourselves."

"Thank God," Sam sighed, opening his paperback.

Beach Season. Haeundae, along with other of the country's famous beaches, is only officially "open" from the beginning of July to the end of August. What "open" really means is anyone's guess, since you can go to the beach at any time of the year, though lifeguards and parasols are only present during the official season. But the Korean beach-going public is very aware of these official dates. The day before the beach "opens" can be gorgeous, with scalding temperatures and blue skies. Come then and you will see a semi-occupied beach, at best. There will be plenty of room for you to set up volleyball nets, play Frisbee, or swim unmolested. Come the next day, when the season officially begins, and the beach will be a sardine can, monitored by overzealous lifeguards who are almost North Korean in their enforcement of the rules. I found this out for myself.

"Fuck it. I'm going swimming."

With that, I kicked off my shoes, stripped off my shirt, and walked down the small path between the fields of parasols until I reached the actual water. Children, teens, and adults all frolicked in the sea, many floating on inner tubes, air mattresses, or wearing inflatable water wings around their arms. Most were fully clothed, skin and actual swimsuits being a rarity. The water was a sick brown color and disconcertingly warm. I thought at once of how much urine two hundred thousand kids could produce at one time. I could make out the outline of several plastic bags floating listlessly, like dead jellyfish. As I waded further out it cooled off, and I saw that there were almost no bathers out closer to the float-line that marked the boundary of the swimming area. I dove in and proceeded to swim toward the border, as far out of pee range as possible. When I came up I noticed something floating near my head: a chicken leg, with bits of meat and tendon still on the bone. *Nice.*

When I got to the float line I turned over on my back, looking up toward the hazy sky and burning July sun. I gently splashed in the water to keep myself afloat, imagining myself in more pristine surroundings.

After about thirty seconds, I heard the incessant chirp of a whistle cutting through the general roar. It kept on and on, and soon I changed positions to see where it was coming from. My feet reached the sandy bottom, while the water came up to the top of my stomach. As I turned toward the shore, I saw a red-clad lifeguard blowing for all he was worth, motioning for me to come in.

What's his problem? I'm inside the line.

I held up my hand and gave him an OK sign, but the whistling continued at the same frantic pace. He shook his head and waved at me with even more fervor. I put my hands on my hips and just stared back, hoping he'd tire of his chore and walk away, but my disobedience served only to incense him further. Finally I gave up and made my way in, while he eyed me like a raptor. His obvious sense of authority buzzed like radiation as he crossed his arms and faced me, mirrored sunglasses obscuring his eyes. When I was close enough, he opened his mouth and pointed toward the float line, screaming, in English:

"TOO DEEP! TOO DEEP!"

"What are you talking about? It wasn't even over my head." I pantomimed where the water line was on my body.

"NO! TOO DEEP!" He made an "X" sign with his forearms and then, sentry-like, turned and marched back to his observation platform.

Exasperated, I returned to the parasol, plopped back into the sand, and recounted my story for my friends to hear. Scott calmly endured my ranting and explained:

"Well, the truth is that most Koreans can't swim. A lot of people drown here each year, so the lifeguards just assume that no one is comfortable in the water. They don't understand the fact that most Westerners grow up swimming."

"Can you swim, Hae-jin?" Sam asked.

"I no fucking swimming, only the float," she replied, smiling.

As we sat through the afternoon, reading and napping, a stream of vendors walked past, selling bottled water, cans of beer, boxes of chicken, kimbap, ice cream, dried pressed fish, and the ubiquitous grilled cuttlefish. We grabbed a few beers and even chowed on some fried chicken, which, when looking around at the other hordes of beach hounds, seemed to be the pick of choice. Korean fried chicken is damned good and sold *en masse* at any big gathering. We made sure to put the bones back in the box, though, so as to spare any other swimmers the horror of coming face to face with a floating, half-eaten leg, wing, or thigh.

CHAPTER 6

YELLOW FEVER

IT is no secret that many of the Western men who move to East Asia quickly end up falling for the locals. Look at any of the countries and you will see the same: legions of expat men hooking up with beautiful Asian women. Sometimes they marry, and other times the relationships have much shorter lifespans—based more on curiosity than any kind of deep love—but you don't have to be on the ground to long to witness the phenomenon.

This is especially true in Korea, where, despite its Confucianism and somewhat prudish mores, mixed couples can be seen anywhere. Sometimes you will see Western women with Korean men, but nine out of ten times it's the other way around, and once the Western guy goes east, he seldom returns across the dateline—at least for a while, anyway. He gets bitten with a bug that is far more prevalent than SARS, avian, or swine flu will ever be: *Yellow Fever.*

Before moving to Korea, most of my girlfriends had been white. That wasn't necessarily because I preferred girls of any one race—I just happened to be around mostly Caucasians. I knew that Asian women could be stunningly beautiful, but my experience with any was limited to a couple of brief flings. Certainly they would grab my eye from time to time, but I never sought them out. I never favored them. I was indifferent, really. I in no way possessed an *Asian fetish.*

As for Korean girls, they almost never entered into my estimation. Like many Asians that I worked or studied with, they left little tangible impression. Most of the Asian kids I went to school with were somehow invisible to my friends and me, the result of their own shyness, nose-to-the-grindstone study ethic, and our innate racism, to be sure. If you were to have asked my opinion of Korean girls specifically, I would have probably given you a negative one. My brother had a beautiful Japanese-American sweetheart during high school, but when it came to Korean girls, I somehow remember them being hopelessly bland and frumpy. At least that's what I thought at the time, but once I actually set foot in South Korea, this old prejudice evaporated like water in a steam bath.

Once in the country, I was flabbergasted by the sheer number of gorgeous women. I had the added benefit of arriving in the summer, so the short shorts were out and skin was bared mightily. The streets of Busan—like many in Asia—are packed with people; some shopping areas are frequented exclusively by young women, a great majority of whom are stunning. Literally, everywhere you look, you see viciously pretty girls. It can actually be *annoying*—a kind of sensory overload.

But why is this? Why does the ratio of really attractive women seem to be much greater in Seoul, than, say, St. Louis? Genes surely play a large part, along with the relatively low-carb diet and non-sedentary lifestyle younger Koreans enjoy. These girls are *fit.* They're eating soup, veggies, and fish every day, and not jumping in an SUV every time they need to run to the store. They can be tall or short, skinny and curvy, but you don't see large numbers of really overweight women.

Korean women also take great pride in—or are obsessed with—their looks. The cosmetic industry alone is a multi-billion dollar business. They take skin care seriously here, with shops of pricey creams popping up on street corners and in subway stations. They're everywhere. Just turn on the TV and it's an endless parade of skin care commercials.

Plastic surgery is also big business, with Korea having one of the highest rates of surgery on the planet, perhaps second only to Venezuela in per-capita work done. A stroll around the area surrounding the Lotte Hotel and Department Store in Busan reveals countless "beauty clinics." Patients can be seen streaming out, eye and face patches concealing fresh double-eyelid and nose jobs. According to a recent article in the *New York Times*, over 30 percent of all Korean women between ages 20 and 50 have undergone some type of cosmetic surgery. Korean women are known throughout Asia for their looks and the meticulous effort they put forth to preserve them. Many times, when I'm in another Asian country and tell a woman that I'm from Korea, I get this response: "Oh... Korean women are so beautiful. They are the most beautiful in Asia."

I'm not sure if this is really true, since I've encountered plenty of hot women in all of my Asian travels. No country has a monopoly on beauty, but Korea certainly has gotten good at *marketing* it. This is mainly to do to what's known as *hallyu*, or the Korean Wave, which refers to the massive popularity that Korean movies, pop music, and (most importantly) TV dramas have achieved throughout East Asia. These entertainment exports have been gobbled up in countries such as Japan, China, Thailand, and the Philippines, and with that, a Korean beauty ideal as well. Suddenly Korean women have become *alpha-females*, the torch-bearers of the new Asian beauty standard. This is being emulated—for better or for worse—by hundreds of millions of other women in Asia, who go as far as bleaching their own skin in a desperate attempt to possess just a fraction of the beauty displayed by their Korean idols.

****

I had just been in the country three days when I met my first Korean girlfriend, who I'll refer to as Miss Kwon. My workmates at the Bayridge Language School had taken me to the Vinyl Underground, a club in the Kyungsung University area of the city, a district popular with college students and young expats looking to blow off some weekend steam. We hit the club after midnight, having spent the earlier portion of the evening downing pitchers of Cass beer at the Join Bar in Haeundae. After catching the end of a set by an expat rock band (I was pleasantly shocked to learn that playing loud music was both an acceptable and possible pastime), the DJs came on, and before you know it, I was getting down on the floor.

I met Miss Kwon outside, while escaping the sauna-like heat of the club and sucking down a cigarette. She was tall, with straight black hair, broad shoulders, and small eyes accentuated with blue eyeliner. She spoke passable English, but informed me that she had recently spent two years in Mexico City, working, studying, and learning Spanish. When I found this out, we quickly switched to the latter, which she spoke much better than English, it turned out. I had learned Spanish in school and had honed my skills over the years in a string of jobs where I worked with many Mexicans. Now that I was in Korea I wasn't sure when the opportunity to speak Spanish would again arise, so I was keen to practice. It also turned out to be our default tongue, providing the easiest way for us to communicate.

Miss Kwon was rare in that she was in her later 20s, unmarried, and didn't live with her parents. She instead inhabited a small one-room apartment near Pusan National University, from which she had graduated. This is unusual in Korea, where most children stay at their parents' homes until marriage, even if this lasts into their 30s… which is increasingly common these days. Miss Kwon shared her tiny apartment with an even tinier Dachshund puppy named Apo, whom she would tie to a line when she was away. Apo was the neediest, whiniest puppy I'd ever come across—absolutely desperate for any whiff of human attention. When I ever I came over, the little guy would get so excited that he would invariably lose bladder control and pee all over the place, squirting out urine with each frenetic wag of the tail.

It turns out that Miss Kwon had dated foreigners before, which neither surprised nor bothered me. She was one of a breed of modern Korean girls who is not just curious about foreigners, but is confident enough to go after them. She smoked cigarettes (still a taboo for women in Korea), drank cocktails, and liked to dance to hip-hop music. She spoke enough English to make foreign friends and meet Western men. Miss Kwon was both forward and assertive, displaying a chutzpah that I've come to expect in some Korean women who socialize with foreigners.

If Western men easily succumb to Yellow Fever, does it work the other way around? I would be lying if I were to state that a lot of Korean girls don't enjoy flirting with foreigners, but few have the confidence to do more than shoot demure glances followed by "Hello! Oh! Very handsome!" I suspect that pop culture is at play here, that a lifetime of watching Brad Pitt and Tom Cruise onscreen turns many of us into movie star facsimiles when they see us in person. It gets ridiculous at times. Korean women are notorious for telling even the most homely of Western men that they are the spitting image of some Hollywood hunk.

"You Brad Pitt. You Russell Crowe. You Johnny Depp!"

Yeah, maybe a half-bald, splotchy-skinned Johnny Depp after four years of Big Mac sets and binge drinking. I guess we just all look alike.

This does go to some of our heads, though. It's not that women throw themselves at foreigners here. They don't. But they, along with Koreans of all ages and sexes, shoot attention our way where ever we go. Any given subway journey subjects us to stares. Any walk down a crowded street is an excuse for groups of kids and teenagers to try out their best *Hello!*s, *How are you?*s, and *Where are you from?*s as we pass by. It is sometimes flattering, often annoying, but a reality of living in Korea. This sort of foreigners-as-zoo-animals mentality has lessened in recent years, as Korea has become more worldly and gotten more used to the fact that many non-Koreans do indeed live among these most homogenous of people. But the constant and unasked-for attention does still exist, and makes us often feel like some sort of freakish celebrities.

My first Korean relationship was a short one. Miss Kwon and I called it quits after only about two months. It was a fun time but the proverbial spark was never really there. We both realized this and broke it off amicably, over cold beer and a sausage plate at the White House, a palatial Korean-style drinking establishment, complete with blue lights, gothic pillars, and a five-piece Filipino cover band. We finished our drinks, shook hands, and walked out of each other's lives.

However, it didn't take long for me to meet a new girl. I was drinking one Saturday night at a dingy little bar aptly named the Box, run by a long-haired Korean hipster named Sang-ook. As I staggered out into the now-frigid November night air, two pretty Korean girls—one tall, one short—stood in front of me. The tall one spoke up:

"My friend think you handsome."

She gestured to the short girl, who stood there beaming a lippy smile and blinking her rather large, darkly made-up eyes. She wore a black coat, checkered skirt, and furry boots. She was adorable—painfully cute, really. There was no way I could resist such concentrated sweetness. So, I responded: "Well, I think she's very beautiful."

Her tall friend translated. The short girl smiled and blinked some more.

"Handsome," she said.

"Pretty," I replied.

I bent down and gave her peck on the lips.

And so I acquired my second Korean girlfriend.

Her name was Bo-ra, and in the several months we spent together, I learned very little about her. I knew that she lived with her sister near the university, and that she really liked dogs. She liked them so much that she once insisted on going to a dog café. This was an actual café that also doubled as a kennel. These are found throughout the country. You go there, admire and pet the pooches, and drink coffee and eat pizza, all the while taking in the sour aroma of dog shit. Not my idea of an appetizing time, but Bo-ra loved it. She was cute and she adored anything else that was cute.

I was reasonably happy at first with her, but there was just one little problem: she spoke no English. She knew a bit—some basic words and phrases—but actually carrying on a conversation was totally out of the question. This was only a few months into my first year and I was incapable of anything but the most rudimentary Korean, so it seemed I was in a pickle. I had gotten myself into a relationship with *someone I couldn't talk to.* All of that lying in bed with your girl and talking about your fears, your loves, your hopes, your dreams? That was all off the table, along with everything but physical contact.

This situation is not so rare with mixed relationships in Korea. Many times I hear guys on the phone with their Korean girls, bellowing at them in condescending baby talk: "You where? Home? You home?

Go sleep now? I with friends. Drinky-drinky. I go home soon. Taxi. TA-XI. Brrrrrrm Brrrrrrrrm Brrrrrrrm. I GO. SOON."

Brian Aylward, a Canadian standup comedian who spent three years in Seoul, describes it like this: "It's kind of like dating a hot retard." And he is right. (No doubt they feel the same way about us.)

I had nothing in common with this girl. She would come to my apartment and watch Korean TV programs, or spend the whole night exchanging text messages with her friends. Mostly she would just sleep, though. The only thing she liked more than dogs was sleeping.

Like many Korean girls, Bo-ra was a master of the text message. When tapping out a message, her fingers were the very model of dexterity. They would drum and whir over the touchpad, reminding me of Clark Kent typing at the speed of light in the original *Superman* film. She sent dozens to me a day. It was only after our first day that I received this one:

chris! i love you *(heart heart heart heart heart heart)*

I've been in relationships for nine months without ever uttering or writing those deadly three words, but that didn't stop me from reciprocating her message two minutes later. I was lying, yes, but I suspected that she was as well.

Her text messages were usually part English, part Korean, and part symbols, more often than not that strange mix of eyes and mouths known as emoticons. Korean girls are experts at employing the various symbols on a cell phone keyboard to create an amalgamation of moods and emotions.

chris, i miss you! *(heart heart heart spiral double triangle sad eyes)*

chris! *(happy-faced winking rabbit)* **How are you today?** *(Swirly cloud star star star heart star)*

i so sad not see u... *(crying U eyes and upside down hedgehog)*

Her messages employed more of these bizarre symbols as they went on. I began to get lost in them. It was like trying to decipher some strange Korean girl hieroglyphics without the text-message Rosetta stone.

The last message I got from her contained no symbols at all. It came in at five a.m. and contained just the following six words.

chris i sorry we have breakup

I tried calling for a whole week afterward, but she never picked up. She was ending it and that was that, my persistence be damned. Even if she chose to respond, I wouldn't have understood anyway, so perhaps it was for the best.

Live by the text message, die by the text message, I guess.

****

Though Confucianism began in China, it is the Koreans who have most strongly embraced its teachings in the modern age. Respect for authority, filial piety, and a certain social conservatism are all hallmarks of this philosophy. When it comes to sex and relationships, we see can see its imprint everywhere in contemporary Korea.

Though a stroll on Haeundae beach in the summer will reveal a handful of young Korean women sporting bikinis, it is still much more common to see both men and women, young and old, to go into the water *fully clothed.* Modesty is the rule, though it gets bent more and more as each year passes. Up until recently, Korea had a national law mandating a minimum skirt length for women. I've seen grandmothers publically dress down young women—strangers—whom they considered to be too scantily clad. For a young woman, just baring shoulders can earn her scowls and death glares from older folks. And public displays of affection are not only frowned upon, but sometimes met with vehement indignation. I've had adult students tell me how the sight of young people kissing in public fills them with rage, as if these punk kids are disrespecting generations that came before them. One time I was strolling on the beach with an English girl I was dating at the time. It was very warm, almost summer, and the day's last light was reflecting off the waves. I pulled her close and we kissed, caught up in the romance and seeming perfection of the moment. Just then I heard a loud screeching, a concentrated volley of angry Korean. When I looked down, I saw an elderly woman seated on a stool, selling coffee and fireworks to beachgoers. She hissed an endless stream of vitriol our way, wagging her finger and letting us know—in no uncertain terms—that we had just crossed the line.

Even seemingly liberated young Koreans are not free of Confucius's yoke. I've been out with women well into their thirties—educated women who have spent time abroad and speak English—who still must field interrogative phone calls from Mom at 12:30 a.m.

"Where are you?"

"Who are you with?"

"When are you coming home?"

They almost always lie, telling their mothers that they are just out with their Korean girlfriends, that they've had a bit to drink and will likely be staying at the aforementioned friend's family's home. Mother grumbles and hangs up, probably not believing her daughter, but fulfilling her duty nonetheless. Sometimes it seems that these exchanges are more ritualistic than anything else, that in a culture such as Korea, people are expected to play certain roles, and just going through these motions is enough.

But Korea is a schizophrenic place, where polar extremes exist together. Yes, Confucian morality is hard-wired into the culture, but capitalism and Western influence have transformed the country profoundly. Sex is everywhere. Look no further than the K-pop girl bands that are one of the nation's hottest commodities. Groups such as Wondergirls and Girls' Generation feature dead-hot young women in very revealing outfits, strutting and posing and grinding and doing all they can to *turn you on*. Overt sexual imagery is used in all advertising—from beer commercials to billboards for jeans. Celebrities such as Lee Hyo-ri are one-woman industries, built entirely on male fantasy. With her twinkling eyes, tiny waist, and ample breasts, Lee Hyo-ri uses raw sex appeal to sell movies, music, and those little green bottles of soju, suggesting that rather than a pounding headache and the dry heaves, a night drinking soju offers you the possibility of banging grade-A girls.

And what of the young people? Are they having sex? Marrying

a virgin is still considered optimally important for many traditional-minded Korean men, but hymen-intact brides are become harder and harder to find. Some women have found a way around this, though: they elect to undergo the cosmetic surgery operation known as hymenoplasty that promises to restore their "innocence," or at least give the appearance thereof to the concerned husband on the wedding night. This is only drives home the point that young folks are indeed getting busy. If purity weren't a rarity, there would be no demand for such procedures. And though most of them still live with Mom and Dad, there are venues where they can go and *do it*:

Love Motels

These cheap and plentiful motels are found everywhere, in clusters throughout the cities, and even in the countryside. Huge rubber blinds hang down in front of the parking area, shielding customers from outside eyes. In the city, the entrances are typically shrouded by large potted shrubbery. Often the receptionist cannot even be seen: you just speak through a darkened Plexiglas barrier, handing your money and receiving the key through a half-moon cut out at the bottom. Sometimes the beds are heart-shaped, and more often than not they vibrate. Lotions and creams are offered up gratis, and third-rate Korean and Japanese porn can usually be viewed on the TV. Some love motels even feature murals on the ceiling depicting breasty women in various states of undress. On certain holidays such as Valentine's Day or Christmas (seen as a couples' day in Korea), the nation's love motel rooms are booked solid, with millions of young couples getting it on.

DVD Rooms

These are even cheaper alternatives to the love motels. For about ten dollars, you pick a DVD from the collection in the lobby and get a private screening room, complete with a large, comfortable sofa-type seat. While some people do go there to actually view movies, true interest in cinema usually takes a back seat to other more primal needs.

An old Korean friend used to be a DVD room attendant during his last year in university. Aside from ringing up the customers, his main duty consisted of emptying the used-condom-filled trash containers.

Though not as overt as say, Thailand or the Philippines, prostitution is rife in Korea. It exists all over the country in just about every corner, on many different levels. The biggest consumers of prostitutes are obviously the nation's businessmen, who, after soju-fueled drinking and karaoke bouts with co-workers, will often end up in *room salons*, where hostesses pour drinks, chat with clients, and perform a host of other services, if the price is right. These establishments can be seen all throughout the cities, and are often advertised with flashing neon signs. They are pricey, however, and not really set up for the average Joe. Much of the money that is pumped into the room salons comes from company and corporate expense accounts. Entertaining employees and clients is seen as a basic cost of doing business in Korea, and companies set aside large funds for this exclusive purpose. But what is *entertainment*? Meals? Drinks? Karaoke rooms? Paying for sex with willing young women?

Prostitution is technically illegal in Korea, though this is spottily enforced, to say the least. It is widely participated in—and winked at, even. I've taught many businessmen who not only admit to, but proudly proclaim their love of, prostitutes. It's a certain mark of manhood. And it's not just the swanky room salons where this is going on. Proper red light districts exist in every city in the country—especially in areas near US Army bases. The most famous one is "Hooker Hill" in Itaewon, the foreigner district in Seoul. It is a hill packed with *juicy bars* and brothels, and has been around since the Korean War. One block away is "Homo Hill," which is the most visible gay district in the country. In Busan there are several backstreet brothels with red-light windows in which the girls sit on display, Amsterdam-style. Most will refuse Western clients, though a persistent foreigner will usually be able to get serviced. These are as close as one gets to open-air sex markets.

Lowest on the food chain are the old-school *dabangs*, which serve instant coffee, tea, and additional services, as well as the ubiquitous barber-pole rooms—massage parlors and sex joints, always marked by spinning barber poles. They're usually staffed by older women who have moved on from the higher-paying places, time having taken its toll on their marketability. If you want a cheap blow job performed by a lusty ajumma, you've found your place. And unlike some contend, the barber pole is not just for show. I know a guy who once came to Korea to visit a friend. In need of a haircut, he wandered the neighborhood looking for a barber shop. He saw a spinning pole and knew that he was in business, so he descended into the windowless basement shop, where he was greeted by an ajumma who informed him that a haircut would cost 80,000 won (about $80 US). He thought this was a bit steep, but went along with it. He was immediately stripped, showered, and then laid. But, in the end, he did get his haircut.

CHAPTER 7

HIGHER EDUCATION

BY August of 2005, I had survived one year on the peninsula. I had grooved into my 30 teaching hours a week by encouraging the kids to kill me; I had gotten tight with a new pack of friends, with whom I ate and drank several times a week; I had gone through two girlfriends and dated others, including a red-haired English woman who was doing her best to obliterate my desperate, needy heart; I had been to Vietnam and loved it, igniting a desire to travel that would blossom into a near-addiction. In short, I had spent almost a year of my life outside of America... and *thrived.* I had found my place, at least for the time being. For all my faults, I had worked in Korea; Korea, for all of its faults, had worked for me.

Not all English teachers who come to Korea work in the hagwons. These ubiquitous academies mainly house the short-timers (people who come for one or two years) and the newbies—those bright-eyed kids who stumble off the plane, having come from Manitoba or Missouri, armed with good intentions and liberal-arts diplomas so new that you can smell the dampness of the wood fibers. While teachers who arrive on the shores of the peninsula usually do start off slogging away in the hagwons—with their grueling teaching hours, short vacation time, cruel children, and sketchy directors—after a year or two or three, most move on to better gigs. Consider the hagwon to be the gateway drug of English teaching addiction. It certainly was for me.

After just one year at the Bayridge Language School, I was all geared up to ink my name for one more. After all, it had been a pretty good twelve months. Korea had been an adventure, an education, and above all, about five years' worth of normal people's fun compressed into one. I was not eager to return to the bleak prospects of working back home—the land of laws, rules, and credit checks.

That said, America wasn't so tough on everyone. Many of my high school classmates were doing very well. Many of them were employed by that smiling, khaki-wearing ogre of corporate hegemony, Microsoft. They were living happy, liberal Pacific Northwest lives, with beaming blond children, golden retrievers, and mortgages that could choke a dinosaur. They listened to NPR and drank café macchiatos while commuting in their forest-green Subaru Outbacks to Microsoft's "campus" in Redmond, Washington.

So most of my old classmates—at least the ones who, like me, had the wisdom to go to college—were doing well, sucking on that ever-so-generous tit of information technology, and living very proper American lives—the kind with fat 401Ks, diversified stock portfolios, and pre-paid college tuition for their gifted children. I, on the other hand, had taken an opposite route, one that led me through chaos and art, willful irresponsibility, dependency, and despondency, and had finally deposited me on the other side of the ocean, a bit older and battered, but still in one piece. And guess what? In my limited estimation, it was going smashingly. Sure, I couldn't vomit up a down payment on that three-bedroom house in an insular Seattle suburb, but for the first time in years, I wasn't broke. There was always some cash in the bank; in fact, at any time I could go take out hundreds of bucks and not even sweat it, despite the fact that I was shitting away much of my money like a tourist with a nasty case of dysentery. With the exception of the nagging daily stresses brought on by my parents' declining health, and the fact that I had fallen hard for a wispy English girl whose love for me evaporated every time I left the room, life was pretty good.

"As you know, Chris," my boss Jimmy said, "You are very popular teacher at Bayridge Language School. We would be so please you come back for another year."

"Sure," I agreed. "It's been a good year and I would be pleased to sign on for another."

In Korea, hagwons are at the bottom of the heap, but they're the easiest places to get hired. They're all over the country, in every city and every town, and most school kids attend at least one. I was lucky to have sleepwalked into a pretty good one. Sure, I had to work a lot of hours each week, but I was always paid on time, and both the heat and air conditioning worked. I had been to some of the ghetto academies where less-fortunate teachers worked (they always seemed to be Irish, Brits, Kiwis, or lowly South Africans), and I knew that I had a pretty good thing. But I was still at a hagwon, and even after only a year I was casting my gaze higher.

The Korean ESL food chain is essentially three-tiered. There are, of course, hagwons; above them are primary (elementary/middle) and secondary (high) schools, both public and private; at the top is that holy grail of English teaching jobs: universities.

University jobs are the most sought-after, and consequently the most difficult to get. The teaching hours are low (generally 9 to 12 per week, depending on the school), the money is usually decent, and the paid vacation time is massive—at least two months off per year, often three, four, or even five. Universities in Korea also have higher standards. They prefer candidates with master's degrees, though three years of in-country teaching experience can usually be substituted for this. Graduate degrees aren't unheard of among many of the ESL teachers on the peninsula, but they're still not common enough to make having one an ironclad requirement. With regard to qualifications, it's still a bit of a buyer's market, though this seems to diminish with each passing year.

Toward the end of my first year, I put in for a university job on a lark. I had become good friends with Angry Steve, who worked at one of the big universities in town. His undergraduate and master's degrees were both from respected American schools and were English-related. He had, in fact, been a *real* teacher in the States, specializing in English lit for some years at exclusive prep schools. Why he had defected to teaching half-dead college freshmen was anyone's guess (though it turned out that, like a lot of us, he really enjoyed the expat lifestyle and the new friendships that came along with it).

I had met Angry Steve at a weekend Korean class, where we had taken part in an all-foreigner staging of *Heungbu and Nolbu*, a famous Korean folktale about a two brothers. I played the poor, younger *Heungbu*, while Steve played the greedy, Scrooge-like *Nolbu*, who turns his back on his starving brother. I was happy to learn that he too had a background in drama, having directed plays on top of teaching back home. He was smart and funny and liked not just good books, but great music. He was dark and just a bit brooding and had little time for idiots or bullshit, though his good taste and piercing intellect could at times be mistaken for a kind of East Coast snobbery (the son of a prominent professor, he hailed from near Amherst, MA). The man simply did not suffer fools.

I gave Steve my resume, he passed it on with a recommendation, and before I knew it, I was wearing the one suit I owned and interviewing for the gig. Like many universities in Korea, this one was perched atop one of the city's many mountains and commanded a good view of much of Busan. Parts of the rock mass had been carved out to house department buildings and high-rise dormitories—this was steep terrain. Angry Steve accompanied me to the meeting, sitting on one side of the sofa while the secretary/translator sat on the other. I was sandwiched in the middle. A scowling middle-aged Korean man named Dr. Chun was seated before us. He sported a thickly-sprayed helmet of hair, and after twenty seconds or so of staring me down, he began lobbing questions my way, which, in contrast to his sour demeanor, were the biggest bunch of softballs I've ever had the privilege to field. My language skills were rudimentary, so I just listened intently and nodded, waiting for the stammering half-interpretations from the young female "translator."

Dr. Chun: *Ja… mungodmeoyengyeanimhageso… onjedulanhanminildaokinikka?*

Translator: Will… uh….will you… will you teach well?

Me: Yes. I will put forth my greatest effort and teach well.

Steve: Yes, Chris will do very well. He is a *good teacher*. (Thumbs up)

Dr. Chun: *Gurumnibabidayaminyikkahaesumal…alumnibum-nigom… kumshinuhalgsumnikka*?

Translator: Are you able to… to … can you not the late? Uh… keep the time? Will you… uh…will you please honor your promise?

Me: Of course. I'll make sure to show up on time and not miss any classes.

Steve: Do not worry. Chris is *very punctual*. He understands the importance of this issue.

The line of questioning was based on fears of things that I *might* do. "Will you not come to the class naked? Will you refrain from vomiting in the wastebasket? Will you avoid publicly masturbating near the school's front gate?"

Steve was one of the most respected foreign English instructors on the staff at the time. His words carried a palpable gravity with both Dr. Chun and the secretary, and despite my rather light resume, I felt that the gig was mine. How could I lose with such a cheerleader? And my suspicions were confirmed just two days later, when, at 8 a.m., the rooster crow I had picked as my incoming ringtone jarred me out of my beery sleep, and, through the hissing cotton in my head, I was formally offered a position at the university. I hung up, leapt out of bed, and danced a naked jig in front of the 10th-story window of my apartment. I had climbed up to a university after only one year in the country. This didn't happen too often. I was learning quickly that connections trump all in the Land of the Morning Calm.

****

That August I went back to America for three weeks, and when I returned to Busan, much refreshed, I started work as an English Instructor at Gaegum University, which had an enrollment of about sixteen thousand. I arrived at the foreign teachers' orientation woefully underdressed (I had yet to learn that on this campus, a shirt and tie were *de rigueur*), sweating through my white T-shirt in the maddening August humidity. Dr. Chun stood in front of the twenty or so foreign instructors, once again encouraging us to "teach well" and "keep the class time"—this time via a more-fluent translator. The suit-and-tie-clad foreigners mirrored his grave expression and nodded lightly, indicating their understanding and their hopes to speed his speech along and get to the buffet lunch that always accompanies such a meeting. And soon we were there. I stuffed myself with fresh sushi, crab, noodles, fried rice, and marinated beef. A little beer was also sipped (as it always is), and after the feed I was transported back up the mountain on which the school sat, shown the communal office, and given my own computer and cubicle (on whose carpeted walls I found an engraved plastic name plate: *Christopher John Tharp*). This gig looked and tasted real: I was a real pretend genuine fake *professor.*

The Korean frenzy to learn English is not just relegated to children. It's an all-age venture, and the universities are not immune. Most of us at Gaegum were not hired to work with students majoring in English. We weren't there to mentor students committed to mastering our native tongue in accordance with a path to their degree. We were instead hired to teach basic, conversational English at all incoming freshmen, representing every major in the school. These, for the most part, weren't students who wanted to study the language or those that even had even the faintest interest in learning it. English Conversation was a compulsory course for freshmen. The students took the class whether they wanted to or not. And it's safe to say that most would have opted out if given the option.

The Korean and Japanese education systems are remarkably similar, which isn't surprising: many modern Korean institutions are based on Japanese models, a result of both the colonial legacy and pragmatism on part of the architects of modern South Korea. Both systems emphasize high school, with endless hours of study, rote memorization, and an almost-militaristic obsession with mastering the annual college entrance exams.

These exams are taken each November in Korea, during which time the whole country is shut down to allow easy access to the test sites. After all, we wouldn't want young Min-ho's future dreams shattered because he was stuck in traffic. The makers of the exam are sequestered for months on end. For weeks beforehand, legions of mothers go to churches and Buddhist temples to pray for their children's success. On the day of the exam, students from the lower grades come to cheer their seniors on, singing songs, clapping, chanting—even removing their shirts and painting motivational slogans on their naked, freezing torsos. The entrance test is the pinnacle of years of education, and it is taken very seriously.

Once the test is taken, most of the students enter one of many universities. While the best are extremely selective, taking only the top one or two percent, the gate is open much wider as you go down the food chain. This is true of most any country, but the difference with Korea is that *almost everyone* goes to college. Four-year degrees are as common as kimchee refrigerators. But university, while important, is generally viewed as a time to relax after the hellish rigors of high school. Students are expected to commit to a modicum of study, but allowances are now made for drinking, cutting class, and getting laid. Approaching university without the monastic seriousness of high school is not only tolerated by both the students and the professors, it's expected. The result is an inconsistent, watered-down experience—a general shittiness in the level of education—especially for students in non-technical fields. This is especially true for students at lower-tiered schools. Korean universities are not widely esteemed outside the country's own borders; you'd be hard-pressed to find an American four-year institution that would transfer in even one credit.

I discovered this right away. Armed with a textbook and a CD player, I was thrown into huge classes filled with apathetic freshmen, the vast majority of whom wanted the best grade through the least amount of work possible. Classes were 30 to 50 students in size, and like anywhere, the most curious and diligent sat toward the front, while the back was inhabited by the larger group, who passed the time by shifting in their seats, talking, sending text messages, compulsively checking their make-up mirrors, and attempting sleep. This lack of interest I can understand: I'm sure that many American freshmen forced to endure a required course act similarly. After all, I knew the situation; I knew that I had been hired to instruct a paint-by-numbers conversation class.

What did surprise me at first was the lack of basic English proficiency. These kids had already been studying English since elementary and middle school, and many couldn't even get a grip on "How are you?" and "I'm fine, thank you." These kids had come up during the ESL boom. Apart from the mandatory study during their regular school time, many had spent long hours in English hagwons and had nothing to show for it. Sure, there were some students whose English was decent, and some whole groups of majors from the most competitive departments (i.e. Nursing, Oriental Medicine) could even claim excellence, but the vast majority were useless, as if they had learned the alphabet and quit right then and there.

How could this happen? How could so much time and energy be put into educating a generation of students in English and still fail so miserably? The answer is complicated. Ineffective teaching methods that overemphasize grammar, combined with large classes, rote memorization, little emphasis on speaking, stressed-out students, and second-rate materials all serve to create a perfect storm of non-education. It's also tough to really learn a language unless you take the initiative. Teachers can teach at you all they want. They can magically try to impart their knowledge into your empty head, but unless you try, unless you study, unless you throw yourself into the acid bath and speak the language on your own, nothing's going to stick.

Just like the hagwons, these freshmen English classes are a dog and pony show. I met with each group of students just one time each week for less than two hours. And despite the fact that I was teaching at a large, well-funded school, I was utterly untrained for the job. What methods did I have at my disposal to effectively instruct a class of forty students in English? Personal attention was out of the question. I could, and did, divide them into smaller groups where they'd work on the concepts I introduced—or instead, try for a nap. But the reality is that these classes were composed of too many people trying to learn a language in too little time. Actual acquisition was not the goal here. Woody Allen famously said that "80 percent of life is just showing up." This has apparently been translated into Korean.

I quickly found my feet during that first semester, though not through being an effective instructor. I did what had worked for me in the hagwon. I tried my best to be entertaining, to hold their attention, to be funny, to joke, to keep the energy up—in short, to put on a show. All my years training and working in the theater taught me how do that, and in the end I relied on it, which probably saved my ass that first year teaching university. Otherwise, I had no idea what I was doing.

Teaching at the Korean university isn't so different from teaching at the Korean hagwon. Whereas at the hagwon, your good graces are determined by the satisfaction of the kids' mothers, at the university it's the students themselves. Western academic careers live and die by the rule *Publish or perish*. In Korea, it's *Please or perish*. Student evaluations are carried out at the end of each semester. The strict teachers, the ones who bust balls and are there on a mission to elevate and instruct, are always first on the chopping block when annual contract re-signing time comes along. The teachers with the highest evaluations stick around, get raises, and can enjoy the relatively carefree life of the university instructor… but this is never accomplished by lowering the boom. This is pretty much the sole criterion that the administrators use when they decide who stays and who goes each year. Student satisfaction and high enrollment are paramount. Again, entertainment is the name of the game. Actual education comes in a distant, distant second. Unlike some of my colleagues over the years, this has never bothered me. Some may view this perspective as cynical, but it's simply the reality of the gig.

The actual disconnect between what I was trying to teach and the students' real understanding of English became shockingly clear one day in class. As I was teaching a large group of students, I noticed a girl sitting in the front row. She was wearing a sweatshirt bearing English words. This is not rare, as most of the clothing worn by younger people here is branded with some kind of English. Sometimes it's just cutesy, nonsensical phrases:

Horsey Time.

Fly to the Sky.

Beautiful Rainbow Story Forever.

Other times it's not English at all, but just an amalgamation of letters stuck together by a desperate clothing designer trying to jump onto the English trend, reading like an eye chart:

Howrk?

Doeglintgg if a Vlimttrw!

This girl's was more insidious, however. When I asked her to stand up, I saw

I FUCK ON THE FIRST DATE

screaming out from the front of her shirt in bright white letters. When I pressed her about the phrase, it became quite apparent that she—an innocent 19-year old girl studying English—had NO idea what it meant.

Only then, I realized how much work still has to be done.

CHAPTER 8

TRAIL UPSEOYO

HE was Sam's friend, not mine. In fact, I don't even think he even liked me. We both liked Sam and Sam liked us, so in the interest of not alienating our mutual connection, we did our best to be nice and not punch each other in the face. He wasn't in Korea to teach English. He wasn't in Korea to do anything, really. He was one of the handful of Westerners that I've met here that could actually qualify as a *tourist*, though Josh's idea of tourism was to rarely leave the confines of Sam's tiny one-room apartment, save a night or two a week to join us for a drink at the Crown.

"Dude, you gotta take him somewhere. Anywhere," Sam begged me over a quiet Sunday night pint. "He's my friend, but he's driving me fucking nuts."

"Where's Josh tonight?" asked Aussie Andrew, the black-haired bartender and proprietor.

"At my house. Where else?" Sam replied.

"How long is he gonna to stay for?" Andrew pressed.

"He's been here two weeks and has three more to go. I like the guy, I really do, but that's long fuckin' time."

"Getting on your tits, is he?" Andrew let loose a small smile.

"Yeah, you could say that." Sam took a drag off a Marlboro Light and glanced up at the TV screen in the corner, which showed a soccer game featuring Liverpool and Blackburn.

"Well, I do have this week off," I said. "I could take him with me… I guess."

"Please, dude. Get him out of my hair. I need some space."

****

Since starting at the university, I was shocked at how easy the schedule was. I only had to teach twelve hours of classes a week. It was the same lesson each time and very little prep was required. There was also the one month of paid vacation I would receive each semester. On top of that, I got even more time off for special school events such as the school's foundation day and festivals, as well as the whole midterm and finals week. It was school policy to have us administer our midterm and final exams one week earlier than the Korean professors. This was to spare the poor students the stress of worrying about their English tests at the same time they had to take exams in their Korean subjects. They got their English exams out of the way the week before, which granted all of the foreign instructors two more weeks of holiday a semester. I was not told this when I was hired and was, of course, stoked to learn about it. It was almost mid-October and time for my school's midterms. I had given my tests and now had a week in which I could go somewhere. So I agreed to take Josh off of Sam's hands, at least for a few days.

"You like hiking, Josh?"

"Sure."

"I want to go hiking for a couple days. Are you in?"

"Okay."

Josh was a big guy—a mule of a man. His nickname—Donk—was short for *donkey*. He looked like a combination professional wrestler, barbarian, and crab fisherman. He came from a family of Pacific Northwest backwoods eccentrics that was legendary for its exploits. Just before coming to Korea, he had evidently beaten up his own father in a drunken brawl. His brother had lived on the peninsula for a year—I had actually replaced him at the Bayridge Language School—and was now back in the US getting his Ph.D. Josh, for all his bearded, flannel-jacket burliness, also had the mind of a professor, though his eloquence only came out in isolated bursts. The rest of the time, he was content to respond with one-word answers, or grunts.

I had decided that we would go to Jirisan National Park, which is about five hours away from Busan by bus. Jirisan, at 1,915 meters (6,283 ft), is the second-largest mountain in South Korea. Like many of the peninsula's mountains, it is more of an extended ridge, with several peaks popping up along the top. The park itself is crisscrossed with hiking trails, the most famous of which follows the ridgeline and takes about three days to complete. Along this ridge trail are several communal shelters where you can spend the night. I planned on somehow hiking up to the main ridge and staying for at least a night in one of the shelters. I did a lot of backpacking in America and was anxious to try it out in Korea.

Josh and I left in the evening, silently boarding a Hyundai-built bus bound for the town of Jinju, which is about two hours from Busan. The bus crept down the car-packed highway toward the town, inching along in the river of brake lights. Josh sat next to me but said nothing, lost in the ridiculous fantasy paperback—*Berserker Prime*—he had stolen from the lonely bookshelf of the Crown. I tried to read too, but was distracted, periodically looking out the bus's window into the drizzly night. My mind was on Anna—the English girl I had fallen hopelessly for the year before. We had split up at the end of the summer, but my heart was still boiling, and on the weekend I saw her with a new guy; in my rice-wine-fueled rage I threatened to ram my fist down his throat. I now felt gut-shamed and sticky with regret that I had so publicly lost my cool, once and for all earning my new nickname of *Showbiz*, which some of my fellow expats had taken to calling me. Whatever the case, I had stepped over the line; I knew I had to get out of town to let myself cool down, and to try and shed the dead skin of my self-loathing.

Up to this point, I had done little Korean traveling outside of Busan, so this trip was a chance for me to take in some of the surrounding countryside. But what I saw from the bus was the bland uniformity one finds along any highway—blue signs announcing town names and kilometers; rest areas, gas stations, and toll booths. And though my eyes scanned the rainy night for any exotic sights or anything uniquely Korean, I was really looking inside for much of the ride.

Jinju means *pearl* in Korean, and like its namesake it is lovely, located on the Nam River, which winds down from the mountain range where Jirisan is located. It is famous for its fortress, which was sacked by the Japanese during the Imjin Wars in 1592 and 1593. The fortress has been rebuilt; overlooking the town and river, it is open to visitors both during the day and night. Inside the fortress is a shrine to the Korean martyr Nongae, who was a *gisaeng* (the Korean version of a geisha) during the Imjin Wars, when the Japanese leader Hideyoshi invaded Korea in an attempt to conquer Ming China and other parts of Asia. Nongae is revered throughout Korea for her legendary assassination of a drunken Japanese general, whom she grabbed before leaping from a cliff overlooking the river, killing both him and herself in the process.

Josh and I were lucky to roll into Jinju during its famous Namgang Lantern Festival, which takes place for ten days every October. As we crossed the bridge on our way to the bus station, we saw scores of colorful lanterns floating on the river below. They gave the whole place a magical and even psychedelic feel. We had known nothing about this festival and were fortunate to stumble right into it.

We got a cheap room at a *yeogwon*, a small, bare-bones hotel near the bus station. The place smelled of sex and cigarettes, and was located in a two-block district full of shitty love motels and small brothels. After checking in, we decided to explore the area, walking down the dark streets, lit up only by the red lights in the prostitutes' windows. As we approached each of the windows, the hopeful girls—in short shorts and micro minis—scurried to the front, presenting themselves for us to see, like fresh meat laid out in a case. However, once the light shone upon us enough to reveal the fact that we were foreigners, the girls turned away, obviously shocked, and disappeared from sight like terrified street cats. This bothered me. Neither of us was looking to score that night, but to be denied without even asking—solely because we were Westerners—felt like a slap. This righteous indignation quickly abated, though. To get upset about being denied sex with someone who you had no intention of soliciting is just silly, ethics be damned. And what sucks worse?

Being turned away by a prostitute or *being* a prostitute? Perspective, perspective…

Eventually, Josh and I made it out of the seedy bus station neighborhood and walked down to the river, where the festival was in full swing. We made our way to the tents on the shore. Inside, people sat at portable tables, eating steamed pigs' feet, *pajeon* (a kind of pancake with veggies and squid), *dubu kimchee* (warm tofu with kimchee), and the Korean blood sausage known as *sundae*. They washed it down with beige plastic bowls filled with the Korean rice wine known as *makeoli*, or with green bottles of soju. The din was massive, an assault of loud, drunk Koreans in rapt conversation. The place was thick with people, many smiling and waving to these two foreigners as we passed. Faces were red with drink and eyes followed us everywhere. At six feet, I'm reasonably tall, but Josh had me by a couple of inches. With a long, thick beard hanging from his chin, he looked exotic and scary, and people got out of his way as he lumbered along.

After the tents we approached a floating pedestrian bridge. After paying the gatekeeper our 1000 won, we made our way onto the bridge, walking single file with the stream of Koreans also making the crossing. The bridge offered us the best view of the lanterns—which were illuminated sculptures, really—many depicting animals such as river carp, frogs, horses, dogs, and large birds. Some were of men carrying swords or shooting bows, a nod to the great battle of Jinju Castle, which the festival memorializes. I, along with thousands of other people there, snapped photos on my digital camera in a ridiculous attempt to capture what could only be appreciated in person. The lanterns were beautiful and arresting, Asian in their essence. They managed to transport me for that short time. I forgot about Anna, about threatening her boyfriend, about acting like a fool. In the river were also thousands of little floating candles that had been cast adrift. I saw the spot upstream where people were putting the candles in and watched the slow-moving river take them. I imagined that these candles represented the wishes or dreams of the people who lit them. For a moment I wanted them all to come true.

After crossing the river we walked by more tents. It was getting later now and they were beginning to empty out. At one point we were waved over by an ajosshi seated at a table with three of his friends. From the overflowing ashtray, the look on their faces, and the six empty soju bottles in front of them, it was obvious that they were savagely drunk. The ajosshi greeted us in English:

"Hey! Come. Come. Come. You drink-ee?" He held out an empty white paper cup.

"Sounds good to me," Josh said.

"Twist my arm," I shrugged.

We sat down and accepted the shots of soju, politely if sloppily poured by the inviting ajosshi.

"Gonbae!"

"Gonbae!"

The drinks disappeared down our gullets.

"You… you… uh… [*mumbling in Korean*] whay… whay puh-rom?"

His slurring accent was thick as jam and it took a moment to register.

"We're from Busan."

"Busan? No no no no no no no. No Busan! [*more mumbly Korean*] Uhh… you… uh… coun-tuh-ry! Which-ee coun-tuh-ry?"

"Which country?"

"Yes! Coun-tuh-ry!"

"USA," Josh replied.

"Waaaaaa!" Thumbs up. "Okay buddy! Very good! Okay okay okay! USA very good! Very pow-uh!" Backs slapped. "Me. Mr. Son!" The English-speaking ajosshi dug his thumb into his chest.

"*Pangapsumnida*," I replied, Korean for *Nice to meet you*. Handshake. His was limp and sweaty.

"Oohhhhhhhhhhhh! Korea speaking very good!" More shots poured. "Gonbae!"

Toasts. "Gonbae!" Drinking.

"How much-ee… you… age-y… How… uh… how much-ee age-y?"

"Me? I'm thirty-four." Mr. Son looked alarmed. He translated my answer to his two friends, who looked on in disbelief.

"Whaaaaa… Sirty poh? Sirty poh? Whaaaaa…" Head shake. Hawk and spit. "Me? I pip-uh-ty pibe-uh! Pip-uh-ty pibe-uh! I big brother! *Hyung nim*." We shook hands. Again. More shots were poured.

His tone then became more serious: "You… you marry?"

"No, I'm not married."

Pause.

"Whaaaaaaaaaaaaaaaaa????" His eyes bulged from his sockets and spittle formed in the corners of his mouth. "No marry? Why? Why you… no marry?"

"I don't know. Just haven't met the right girl, I guess."

"But you *must*! You *must marry*!"

"One shot-uh!" says his friend. More soju downed, after which the lighting in the tent took on a crystalline quality.

"Okay okay okay okay. You… you have girl-puh-riend-uh?"

"Yes," I lied, not wanting to alarm him any more than necessary. To be thirty-four and single in Korea is known to cause aneurisms among concerned ajosshis.

He stared at me intently and licked his lips. "*Korean* girlfriend?"

"Uh, no. Actually she's English." Again a lie, but she was on my mind at the time.

"Okay okay very good very good very good! You Korean girl no! Korean girl NO!"

He made a large X sign with his arms, which is how a Korean tells you no when just saying "no" is not enough. We downed one more cup of soju, thanked them, got up, and slithered back to our smelly room, falling into a deep, boozy sleep.

****

The next day, after a lunch of *bibimbap* (mixed rice) and *gogi mandu* (meat dumplings), we boarded another bus that would take us all the way to the entrance of the park. The bus rolled out of town, following the slow-moving river and eventually entering countryside, winding through low hills and farming villages. This was rice country, and the landscape was dense with countless paddies, recently harvested.

One thing I noticed: everyone we passed seemed to be well over sixty, as if all the young people had disappeared, or migrated into the city. Korea's aging rural population is going to present huge challenges to the country in the years ahead. Most young people want nothing to do with farming, and a trip to a rural area will show any visitor just that. Truly elderly people work the fields and drive patched-together tractors. They perform the backbreaking labor that has become so unfashionable for the younger generation. There is a shortage of younger women in the countryside, forcing many of the men who do stay to take foreign brides from countries such as China, Vietnam, and the Philippines. Many of these women come for purely financial reasons and are sometimes trapped in miserable, even abusive relationships, with little or no legal recourse. But the age differential in the country is a real dilemma and forces the question: who will grow the food in twenty years' time? Perhaps the Koreans will be forced to import their farmers, with whole towns full of Indonesians or Vietnamese working the soil.

After the town of Hadong, the road joined up with a big, wide-banked river, with sandbars popping up throughout its lazily flowing water. At one point we passed a massive field containing an art installation comprising hundreds of scarecrows. The harvested fields reflected the sunlight in deep green and gold, and the leaves on the many trees were now the color of rust. Autumn was in full effect, though the sun shone confidently and traces of summer could still be tasted in the air. This was my first time out of the city since I had been home in the summer, and it felt *right.*

After turning off onto a two-lane road and rolling through some small green tea plantations, we came to Sangyesa, the famous temple and village that marked the beginning of Jirisan National Park. We donned our small packs and walked up toward the temple's main gate in hope of finding a room. We quickly located a *minbak,* which is a sort of country lodging very common outside of the cities in Korea. *Minbak* are meant for groups of people to stay in at once. You are provided with a very basic room, attached to which is an equally bare-bones bathroom. The room contains no furniture. Some blankets and thin sleeping pads are provided by the host, but otherwise the guests sleep right on the floor, which can be heated up in the cold months. Floor-heating is found everywhere throughout Korea and is a marvelous invention. It's a wonder that the rest of the world has yet to catch on.

Sangyesa means *Twin-Streams Monastery*, and is the head temple of the *Jogye* Order of Korean Buddhism. It was founded in the year 722 and has been an important center ever since. Like many others in the country, the temple was burned to the ground by the Japanese during the Imjin Wars of the late 16th Century. It was rebuilt after that and has since retained its form.

I have a confession to make: I'm not a big fan of temples. I don't really get *excited* about them. The truth is they often bore my nuts off. When I first arrived in Korea, I was curious about the temples and spent some time exploring them, marveling at the detail of their construction, and basking in their general glow of serenity. But after one year in the country I became kind of templed out, and to this day, whatever the Asian country I find myself in, I never run off to the first temple in the area; more than often I give it a skip. While I have been floored by some (Cambodia's Angkor temples live up to every word of the hype), I all too often lose concentration and start thinking about what I want eat for lunch or how good that first beer will taste.

Sangyesa is an exception to this rule. It is one of the coolest temples in all of Korea, if not Asia. While lacking the grandeur of other sites, it sits nestled at the base of a mountain, shrouded by both deciduous and pine trees. A small road approaches the temple, with vendors on the side, selling roots, bark, and herbal wood—all of which is used in traditional Korean medicine and cooking. The road follows a small, fast-moving stream which is spanned by a stone bridge. As you approach the main complex—composed of scores of buildings—you gently climb, rising from the valley, onto the foot of the stony mountain that protects the wooden temple. That day I poked around the site on my own, later following a trail that ascended up the mountain from the temple, leading to a famous 60-meter waterfall called *Buril pokpo.* As I climbed up from the valley I entered into a realm of silence, save for the wind through the trees and the sound of the river flowing far below. It was the most peace I'd experienced on the peninsula, up to that point. I had no idea that such silence was possible in this most cacophonous of nations.

Lost in the Valley of the Moon Bear!

I was a Boy Scout in those now-distant days of my youth. The Boy Scout Motto is simple: *Be Prepared.* These words have echoed around in my head through countless backpacking and camping expeditions. I grew up in the woods. I've spent years in, around, and on mountains, and I know how to prepare correctly before going outdoors. This was one of those rare times when I didn't follow my own rulebook, when I neglected to heed my own advice.

The following morning, when Josh and I strapped on our packs, they were pitifully light, which should give you an idea of just how under-prepared we were. We stopped at the village store and purchased the following items: three cans of tuna, four bottles of soju, and a park map, which was printed on a blue-and-white bandana that Josh tied around his head. At least we were now unlikely to lose the thing. What more would we need for survival, other than a bit of all-American gumption? Thus geared up, we trounced up the road and stuck out our thumbs, easily catching a ride up to the next temple, from where we planned starting our hike up to Mt. Jiri's main ridge.

On the do-rag/map, we saw that there was a trailhead next to this temple. This trail climbed up a ridge that eventually intersected with the main massif of Mt. Jiri. There was an established overnight shelter near this intersection, where I was sure we could sort out some blankets and perhaps a couple of bowls of noodles. Wherever Koreans gather in groups of ten or more, there is always food for sale. Knowing we were going to such a place, I wasn't too concerned that we lacked even the most basic necessities for such an endeavor. I didn't even bring a lighter, much less a coat.

Once we got to the temple, we couldn't locate the trailhead. We wandered around the parking lot where the trailhead was supposed to be, but it was nowhere to be found. So we made our way to the main complex, which was small by Korean temple standards. I saw a man—the temple's gardener, I presumed—hoeing away in the dirt. I greeted him in my very limited Korean and clumsily asked him about the trail. Josh had a Korea edition of *Lonely Planet*, which showed the trail we were looking for. I pointed it out to the man and listened to his response, which was delivered with machine-gun speed. He must have assumed that I was fluent, based on the fact that I was polite enough to address him in his own language, but the truth was that I spoke Korean with just slightly more fluency than, say, your average goat.

"Aiy…shiminchiludahsheebiruyagoimnikamina…upseoyo…tashimininminda!"

I had recognized just one word out of many that sprayed out of his mouth: *upseoyo.* It means: *it isn't there.* It's one of the language's more useful terms, and one that anybody who spends time in Korea will become familiar with right away, as it's often spat our way by shopkeepers or others who don't wish to bother dealing with a foreigner.

"Trail *upseoyo*?"

"*Nae!* Tuh-ray-ul *upseoyo.*" He shook his head and got on with his hoein'.

"What's he saying?"

"He says that there is no trail. I think."

"That's bullshit. It's on both our maps." Josh touched his book to his do-rag.

We trudged around the grounds of the temple a bit more, up past the main building, and into the trees behind it. It was there that we spied a small path heading deeper into the woods, and, more importantly, up.

"I bet this is it," I said. "It's heading in the right direction. I bet he just doesn't want foreigners to go on the good trail." It's amazing how you can convince yourself of the outlandish if you want to do something badly enough. I didn't trust the gardener. One thing I had learned after a year and some months in Korea is that you will often get ten different answers for one question, depending on who you ask.

So Josh and I headed up the trail, which indeed looked promising. For a while it climbed up and away from the temple's grounds and rambled along the hillside, high above a river valley. We could hear the sound of cascading water below. Thick forest covered the mountain-side, and the leaves were turning on the trees. The air was clean and it was sunny and cool—perfect fall weather. As we hiked on, I got the sense that we were heading into one of the wildest valleys that Korea had to offer. Korea is one of the most densely populated places on the globe, with little land left that isn't built-on or cultivated. The mountains are the only places that offer up any kind of solace or escape, and here we had found what seemed to be the biggest secret.

Suddenly we heard a massive rustling in the underbrush below. I stopped and peered into the dark bushes.

"You hear that?"

"Yeah."

Something thrashed and cracked as it moved along. I could see the branches and shrubs quiver and sway, but couldn't quite spy what was responsible. Whatever it was, it wasn't stealthy, and it was *big*.

"Maybe it's a bear," Josh posited.

"A bear? In Korea? Get the fuck out of here…"

Eventually, the trail snaked down to the river itself, and we began following a series of yellow ribbons that were tied to shrubs and tree branches. These marked the route. The "map" contained in the *Lonely Planet*—that most useless of tomes—was pathetic. So at one point we stopped and I asked for the do-rag map, which Josh now wore on his very sweaty head. He handed it to me. It was saturated in greasy man sweat. Despite this, I could see that the trail was supposed to be following the ridge, which was still high above us. We were deep in the hollow, but I was unconcerned. I had faith in my instincts: I figured the trail would eventually leave the valley and head up to the ridge.

We trundled on for a couple more hours, zigzagging across the river and ever so slightly climbing up the valley. After a while it became apparent that we would have to make better time. We had gotten a late start and now we were well into the afternoon. On top of this, Josh was the slowest hiker I'd ever trekked with. I'm a very fast hiker—I like to cruise down the trail and make good time—but Josh was the total opposite. He absolutely *moseyed*, meandering along the rocky trail at the pace of Jell-o, gently tapping his newfound hiking stick across the ground, and frequently sitting down for prolonged breaks. Perhaps he was taking it in, enjoying his surroundings. I'm sure my hell-bent rushing annoyed him to no end, but I wanted to get to the shelter before sunset, which would happen at around six-thirty in the evening—and even earlier in the dark of the valley. It was now almost four. We didn't have time to spare.

The terrain got steeper, which heartened me a bit, but as the sunlight began to diminish, I again became worried. And then we lost the trail. It just disappeared. The ribbons which marked the way stopped, and the river bottom now became a ravine—a stony obstacle course. The going got noticeably tougher. The hillside was now completely overgrown, and pretty much impassable without a machete. We lacked even a set of nail clippers. The temperature was dropping. And we had now had little more than one hour of daylight left.

I backtracked to the last ribbon, thinking I had somehow missed a deviation in the route; that the climb to the ridge that I had been expecting all afternoon would now magically appear. No dice. The flags just ended. The trail was indeed *upseoyo*.

Despite the wildness of the locale, the river was lined with miles of small plastic tubing. This tubing was used to siphon fresh water and take it to the villages and temples down the valley. It takes men to maintain such a line, and earlier in the hike we saw just that: they passed us as we hiked up the river. They carried huge packs laden with supplies. They were bearded with scruffy hair, and had faces like dark rawhide. These were true *mountain folks*, and probably worked the valley, keeping the waterlines flowing.

I stumbled back to Josh and told him that there was no missed trail;

that the thing just apparently petered out into the forbidden terrain. The end of the line. We were now facing the painfully real possibility of having to spend the night where we were. There, where we had stopped on the river, were two plastic tubs containing extra tubing and other waterline supplies. Next to one of the tubs was a stinking, half-wet blue tarp, underneath which was a moldy piece of thick blue material—a blanket of sorts.

"Well, if worse comes to worst, we could wrap up in the blanket and sleep under the tarp."

"We could," I replied.

I convinced Josh to try to continue up the river, one more time. "We'll just have to follow it all the way up. We know that the mountain shelter is near the water source."

After two minutes of scrambling and rock-hopping, we quickly gave up on that idea. We were bruised and scratched up from trying to force our way through the thick brush. We were out of options, and I sat down on a rock and put my head in my hands. It was then that Josh spied our salvation.

"I see something green over there. You see it?"

I looked to where he was pointing and saw something sticking out from the trees, a shade of bright green that stood out from the natural hues surrounding it.

"It looks manmade," he said.

We climbed up the hillside, away from the river a bit, and came upon a tiny house of sorts. A hut. And this was no rotten old hut. It wasn't a dilapidated, rickety, leaky hut, but a well-apportioned, *very lived-in hut.* It was made from plywood, and covered on top with a bright green tarpaulin—which is what had initially drawn Josh's gaze. Not only was it a fully-formed shelter, it also came complete with:

- sleeping bags, 2
- giant bag of rice, 1
- case of *ramyeon* instant noodle packets, 1
- toilet paper rolls, several

- candles, many
- cigarettes, 6 packs
- Nescafe, 1 box
- working gas camping stove, 1
- extra fuel, 3 tanks
- one complete set of pots, pans, cups, bowls, spoons, and chopsticks
- an *underground hearth* to heat the whole thing up
- a huge stack of firewood
- jug of gas for accelerating the lighting of such a fire, 1

It immediately occurred to us that the guys we saw several hours earlier--the two grizzled men heading out of the valley—must be the ones who lived in this little cabin, this lucky lean-to, this hut-of-plenty. Those men must have been maintenance workers on the waterline. Best of all, they were maintenance workers on the waterline who were taking the night off and going into town. I was sure that they weren't due back any time that night, so Josh and I were more than happy to play Goldilocks and hut-sit in their absence.

We immediately busted out the stove, cooked up a pot of rice and ate it with the tuna that we had bought down in the village. Josh started a big fire in the hearth underneath. We drank down some of the soju and listened to the strange Korean critters come alive in the night. I "borrowed" a pack of smokes and had my first in days. We drank more soju and actually talked to each other, finally breaking a glacier's worth of ice that had frozen over us for the previous two days. After the third bottle of soju, Josh threw up, his Western stomach being no match for Korea's gnarliest liquor. The image of Anna invaded my mind, along with thoughts of my recent, shameful encounter with her and her new man. The bundle of snakes which had poisoned me since our breakup in July suddenly released, and I could, for the first time, finally feel my bile ebb.

"*FUCK IT!*" I listened to my voice echo in the empty valley, perhaps the emptiest in all of South Korea.

After the last swallow of booze, I took one more breath of the mountain air, crawled into the warm hut, closed the door, slid into the soft bag, and went to sleep.

We arose at first light. We made some cups of instant coffee, washed the dishes in the river, and tidied up the place. We left a 10,000-won note for the rice, smokes, coffee, and "rent," and quickly skadoodled back toward the temple, slightly hung over, but happy in our bellies and well-slept.

This hut was well out of the way. It was totally—intentionally—hidden from view down at the river. It's a miracle that Josh even saw it in the first place. The man had the eyes of a raptor. His eyes are the only thing that saved us from spooning under a filthy tarp in the bushes, from pressing our warm manflesh against each other in a desperate bid not to freeze to death. May God rain praise upon Josh's eyes.

Once we managed to hike out of the valley, I discovered that Josh and I had never even made it to the trail denoted in his *Lonely Planet* and on the do-rag map. We had followed an unmapped route that, yes, did end at the top of the valley. We probably weren't far from the original shelter we had sought, but no doubt it was unreachable, thousands of meters above us up the mountain wall. We had, in fact, been in a closed area: a sign erected where the trail emptied out onto the main road informed us of this in bold, threatening Korean, as well as English. The part of the park where we had hiked had been designated a reintroduction area for the Asian moon bear, which was probably what we heard thrashing in the brush the day before. Visitors were strictly prohibited, subjected to all sorts of nasty fines. That's what the hoeing man at the second temple was trying to tell us, but sometimes not understanding the language can serve your particular interest at the time. Oops.

I knew little about Asian moon bears, other than they weren't particularly dangerous, and that they were severely endangered, due to loss of habitat and centuries of over-hunting. It seems that their bile does wonders to harden the dicks of the men of not just China, but those residing on the peninsula as well. Such a creature cannot be allowed to live, it seems. In this part of the world, erections take precedence over everything else.

We walked away from the trailhead, eventually making our way onto a small road that wound through farms carved out from the rock. We lumbered down the slope, searching for a car from which we could thumb a ride. The place smelled of damp soil and pine. Cows lolled in some of the fields, and at one point we passed an ancient man carrying an impossibly large pile of sticks on a backpack, which itself was made of wood. He didn't even glance our way as he struggled up the slope, a lifetime's worth of hard work pushing him on. I couldn't help but wonder where his children were.

CHAPTER 9

TAKING IT TO THE STREETS

AS an American growing up in the '80s, I had almost zero idea of what Korea was all about. As I mentioned earlier, my only impressions came from my military brat friends; the convenience store cashiers I encountered; the handful of shy, studious Korean kids at my school; and what I could glean from the nightly news:

"Anti-government protests continued in South Korea today, where militant students battled with riot police..."

This lead in-was a common one throughout the 1980s, and was always followed by footage of street mêlées featuring masses of bandana-wearing students, Molotov cocktails hurtling through the air, water cannon blasting through walls of people, plumes of tear gas, metal poles banging against police batons, riot gear and shields, and cascades of stones and bricks. Clashes of pure intensity; total chaos. I remember shaking my head while watching, not really knowing how to take in what I was seeing; I was both fascinated and horrified as I tried to digest clip after clip of these crazy students taking the cops and soldiers on. Though the reasons for these images escaped me at the time, I immediately knew one thing: these people were very committed and very pissed off.

What is wrong with Koreans? I thought. Why are they so angry?

Koreans have a rich history of street protests, dating (in modern times at least) back to the Japanese colonial period. In 1905, after defeating Russia in the Russo-Japanese War (to the shock of the Western world), the Japanese occupied the whole of the Korean Peninsula, officially annexing it as a colony in 1910. This happened with both the acquiescence of the U.K. and the United States, the latter of whom recognized Japan's "interests" in Korea in exchange for Japan turning a blind eye to the American colonization of the Philippines. President Theodore Roosevelt actually brokered this agreement, known at the Treaty of Portsmouth, for which he received the Nobel Peace Prize, an "honor" that still turns the stomach of many a Korean to this day.

The Koreans bristled and resisted the Japanese occupation from the beginning, but it is what's known as the March 1 Movement which really laid the foundation for modern street protest in Korea. In 1919, inspired by President Woodrow Wilson's doctrine of self-determination, thirty-three representatives of the Korean people drafted a Korean Declaration of Independence and presented it to the Japanese authorities, which resulted in their immediate arrest. Word got out, and students were the first to peaceably take to the streets, soon joined by farmers, shopkeepers, workers, and a variety of other citizens. These peaceful protests quickly spread all over the country and caught the Japanese occupiers entirely by surprise.

Unfortunately for the Koreans, Wilson's words did not translate into action, and the Japanese quickly and ruthlessly put down the demonstrations with military force. The Japanese shot protestors and set fire to schools, churches, and homes, which, according to historian Lee Ki-baik, resulted in 46,948 demonstrators arrested, 7509 killed, and 15,961 injured.

With their defeat in World War II, the Japanese were forced to withdraw from the Korean Peninsula, which then was split into two zones along the 38th Parallel, a dividing line chosen somewhat randomly by two US State Department functionaries in an office in 1945. Instead of granting full and immediate independence to the Koreans, the country was temporarily put under a trusteeship overseen by the Americans, Russians, and British. This resulted in massive, violent demonstrations throughout the country; after languishing under the thumb of the Japanese for forty years, the people had no stomach to trade in one colonial overlord for yet another.

Soon the Soviets set up a communist government in the North and withdrew their troops, with a minor anti-Japanese rebel fighter (and Soviet army vet) named Kim Il-sung handpicked to take the helm. By 1948, the Americans had set up a government in the South, with Dr. Syngman Rhee (the very Anglicized version of his name)—a US-educated anti-communist hardliner—elected to head this new, pro-Western republic. Both sides then squared off against each other for some five years (with minor skirmishes along the border), until the wee morning hours of June 25, 1950, when the Russian-supplied North Korean army poured across the weakly defended 38th Parallel. This ignited the Korean War, which drew out for over three gory years, "ending" in a stalemate in 1953. Technically, of course, the war never ended, but to this day exists in the suspended-combat state known as a "ceasefire."

We saw street protests and agitation all through this time—from the time the Japanese left, to the moment the terms of the ceasefire were announced. There were always segments of Korean society against what was going on, and they never hesitated to let it be known in the loudest and boldest manner possible. 1948 saw a bloody uprising on Jeju Island (which was met with severe repression, resulting in the death of tens of thousands of people); in 1960, after some fishy election results and the murder of a student, massive protests managed to bring down the great Dr. Syngman Rhee, who then fled to Hawaii to live in self-imposed exile. The next important leader of South Korea was Park Chung Hee, who came to power in 1961 in a bloodless coup. He ran the country as a *de facto* dictator, overseeing its modernization and economic development, all the while stifling dissent and doing constant battle with pro-democracy students. He was assassinated in 1979 by his own chief of national security (the head of the dreaded Korean Central Intelligence Agency), which ushered in the most politically volatile decade in the history of the Republic of South Korea: the 1980s.

Eruption

May 18, 1980 was a very significant day for me, growing up. On this day, Mt. St. Helens—one of the most beautiful peaks in the Cascade

Range—decided to blow its top, resulting in one of the most violent and dramatic eruptions ever witnessed in modern-day North America. I was 9 years old at the time and lived in Washington State. I remember sitting on the roof of our house and watching the massive plume in the distance, like a dark mushroom cloud. I remember listening to the initial news reports, my heart racing at the alarm so evident in the announcer's voice, and feeling a certain pride that we—the State of Washington—were on the world map for the first time in my life. We were famous. I remember playing in the volcanic ash that fell to the ground and having to wear a surgical mask to school—a novelty for us kids at the time. Like the Battle of Britain depicted from a child's perspective in the terrific film *Hope and Glory*, the eruption of Mt. St. Helens—a major natural cataclysm which had the potential for massive human death—was pretty much just fun and games for any kid who witnessed it. It was an excuse for not going to school, and for collecting grey, pulverized rock in Mason jars.

If the news reports mentioned South Korea or the city of Gwangju that day, I missed it, as did most Americans, I'm sure. The story of Gwangju was buried under Mt. St. Helens's ash, like everything else. It just couldn't compete with a big fat American volcano. And while St. Helens was a terrific story—nature at its purest; an intransigent old-timer named Harry Truman who in the face of death refused evacuation; the amazing time-lapse footage of an immense mountain literally blowing apart—less than sixty people were killed by the eruption. The city of Gwangju, which erupted on the exact same day as Mt. St. Helens, would prove to have a much higher body count.

President Park Chung-hee was immediately succeeded by Choi Kyu-hah, his prime minister, who acted as president in the wake of Park's assassination. The power vacuum left by Park's absence was just too tempting for an opportunistic major general named Chun Doo-hwan to resist: he took over in a coup d'état six days later. This move proved to be very unpopular among the population—with students in particular—who, after eighteen years of military rule, were desperate for the democratization of their country. Demonstrations once again broke out around the country, and on May 17, just over five months after he took over, Major Chun declared martial law.

Gwangju is located in South Jeolla Province, which sits in the southwest corner of the Korean Peninsula. South Jeolla people have long been considered among the prickliest and most rebellious in all of Korea. Residents of South Kyungsang Province, where Busan is located and I call home, generally don't care for their subversive neighbors to the west. This disdain is reciprocated, I'm told. So it's no surprise that the greatest resistance to martial law occurred amongst the most hard-headed folks on the peninsula. The protests in Gwangju started among students at Chonnam National University. Troops were called in to quell the demonstrations, and they were allegedly heavy-handed in their approach, cracking down not just on the militant students, but also on the other, more peaceful citizens of Gwangju, who at the time were just trying to go on with their daily lives. This proved too much for the locals to bear, and on May 18, the students were joined by many ordinary citizens in a general uprising against the military. Government armories were raided; weapons were seized. Some police officers were killed. The population of Gwangju began to arm itself against the troops called in against them. A general insurrection was on.

The people of Gwangju held their city for nine days, facing off a massive army force which had them surrounded. Chun Doo-hwan and the military command insisted that the demonstrators were communist provocateurs, North Korean agents who had infiltrated the country and were making an attempt at a communist uprising. Though there were surely leftist elements represented among the student protestors (as there always are), to write the Gwangju demonstrations off as the dirty work of commies was and is pure hogwash. It was a direct reaction to the institution of martial law.

On May 27, the government lost its patience and moved in, gunning down an unknown number of civilians in the process, both armed and unarmed alike. The death toll is hotly debated to this day: a later investigation by the civilian government put it at 200 dead and 850 injured, while others insist that up to 2000 people were killed. This question will never be fully resolved, to be sure, but what happened in Gwangju is still a sensitive subject among Koreans, and I have yet to talk to one who will fully open up to me about it. After all, many of them blame the United States.

Fucking USA!

On the surface, to blame Big Bad America for the massacre in Gwangju is a prime example of the knee-jerk anti-Americanism seen not just in Korea, but throughout much of the world. After all, it was Korean troops who actually pulled the triggers in Gwangju. Americans were not even on the ground. Those soldiers who did the slaughtering were also not under the Combined Forces Command, and therefore didn't have to answer to the American military. The Koreans were on their own in Gwangju, and US authorities insisted that they never signed off on any decision to go in with guns blazing. In fact, they claimed ignorance of the whole thing.

But we know that in law, ignorance is no excuse, and to many Koreans, the Americans at best chose to look the other way while Chun Doo-hwan ordered the butchering of hundreds of his fellow countrymen; at worst, they gave him a secret Yankee green light. Gwangju occurred during the first year of the presidency of Ronald Reagan, who was always willing to overlook an ally's bloodstained human rights record as long as they were doing their part in the global fight against Communism. In this respect Chun fit the bill exactly, cracking down on those pesky Reds with such fervor that Reagan invited him to Washington in both 1981 and 1985.

Gwangju did little to inspire love for America among the Korean people, instead exacerbating an already-deepening mistrust. The fact that America's motives on the peninsula are often viewed with suspicion (and at times hostility) by a large segment of the populace causes consternation among many of my fellow Americans who come here: *How ungrateful! After all, didn't we save their asses during the Korean War, shed-*

ding plenty of our own blood in the process? Don't we continue to protect them? They'd be speaking NORTH Korean it wasn't for us.

Anti-Americanism is alive and well in South Korea. It always has been. It's a complicated and potent cocktail of history, nationalism, xenophobia, real grievances, and scapegoating. Rather than existing as some unbending, constant force, it tends to flare up in spasms, where centuries of frustration and anger get vented on the largest and most obvious target: Uncle Sam. Many Americans have this idea that we're a force of good in the world, that despite some excesses and mistakes, American foreign policy has been dedicated to the fight against tyranny, the promotion of democracy, and the betterment of peoples' lives. But this view is pure Pollyanna, for anyone who has carefully studied US foreign policy can clearly see that it has been finely tuned to do just one thing: benefit the economic and political interests of the United States. Sure, the language of idealism is used, but in the end it's *our* ends that are advanced.

Koreans understand this better than anyone. It was America who, in an 1871 attempt to open its ports, attacked Korea militarily. It was America who sold them out the Japanese in 1905 (thanks, Teddy!). It was America who drew that line across the 38th parallel, causing undue pain and hardship to this day (the inconvenient fact that the partition was carried out in accord with the Soviet Union often slips their minds). Yes, America intervened in the war to save the Southern republic, losing over 38,000 young men in the process, but Korean losses number in the *millions*. Moreover, many of those were felled by US-made bullets and bombs. But most importantly, where was America during the long struggle for real democracy? Instead of supporting the Korean people, America threw its weight behind years of military dictatorships, all in the name of fighting Communism. This especially sullies the image of the United States in the eyes of many Koreans and confirms what many of them already believe: America has never had Korea's interests at heart.

This distinctly anti-American view tends to be held by people under the age of 50, those who grew up during the pro-democracy struggles of the '70s and '80s, when the radical left re-emerged as a real force in

Korean politics. Members of the older generation—the one that actually remembers the war—more often view America much more positively. Many are grateful for America's sacrifice to keep the South free from Communism. I've had elderly Korean men approach me on the street just to shake my hand and say "Thank you, America." Pro-American army veterans often rally in support of the alliance and against Kim Jong-il and the North in Seoul, sometimes flying the Stars and Stripes alongside the South Korean flag—known as the *taegukgi*—while they burn the vertically-challenged dictator in effigy.

A prime example of this kind of Korean is my old acquaintance, Mr. Bae, a 70-year-old former customs officer who now runs a customs brokerage near the port. Mr. Bae is fastidious and spry, almost never seen without a jacket and tie. He speaks English well, peppering his speech with well-prepared idioms:

"Oh, I see you are just the man for the job!"

"As you know, the early bird always gets the worm."

Mr. Bae loves America and is fascinated by foreigners. He will often walk up to random Westerners he sees on the street and strike up a conversation. If they happen to be American, the handshake they receive will be that much more vigorous.

Mr. Bae is a staunch right-winger. His house is full of documents and books that he's procured from the US embassy over the years, including a puzzling amount of literature from the Nixon and Ford administrations (Kissinger figures in highly). He was a big supporter of the last President Bush and worships at the altar of Ronald Reagan, whom he considers a near demigod: "Ronald Reagan was your best president! He was a good friend to Korea!" He speaks of the late Korean strongman Park Chung-hee in reverential tones, and spits pure vile when the subject of North Korea comes up: "Let them starve, I say! Let them starve!" Mr. Bae once traveled to Washington, D.C. to participate in a joint training course with the US Customs Service, and proudly displays a medal he was awarded from them in his display case, right next to his retired Korean Customs hat and badge. He is a patriotic Korean who, as a boy, was forced to hide from North Korean patrols on the occupied southern island of Namhae during the war. He loves his country, but finds no contradiction in loving America and Americans too.

Despite my expectations before I arrived in Korea, I have yet to be the knowing object of overt anti-Americanism. Sure, I've met some Koreans who had plenty of nasty things to say about the USA, but I've never had anyone take it out on me personally. This may have something to do with geography, as Busan is a conservative city where the pro-US Grand National Party dominates the scene, unlike the much more left-leaning environs of Seoul. I've really never been hassled in any of my travels, actually—not even during the height of the world-hated Bush administration. I'm sure that many folks—both in Korea and elsewhere—hate America and Americans, but most of them have the common decency to hate us behind our backs.

This isn't always the case here. When anti-Americanism bubbles over in Korea, it can get ugly and absurd quite quickly. The most obvious example happened during the summer of 2002, when, during the World Cup, two middle school girls were accidently run down and crushed by a US Army vehicle out on a maneuver. The soldier driving the vehicle—along with his commander—was subsequently found *not guilty* of negligent homicide in a military court-martial, resulting in one of the largest explosions of anti-American rage ever witnessed in Korea. Internet rumor-mongers helped to stoke up the ire, causing many Koreans to believe that the girls had been killed *intentionally*. We can thank the pro-North Korea hard left for that. Friends of mine who were here at the time talk of being refused service, harassed, even spat on, just on the suspicion of being American: Koreans reportedly weren't checking a lot of passports before unleashing the abuse. Westerner = American. This was two years before I arrived in the country, but I remember watching footage of the demonstrations on American TV: in one, thousands of Koreans ripped apart a massive American flag; in another, a similar mass of people set fire to their individual Stars and Stripes. To see this sort of raw hatred directed at us made me want to have nothing to do with Koreans. Commentators and politicians openly debated pulling out our troops and cutting South Korea adrift. I can't say I that I disagreed with them at the time.

The latest flare-up happened in the spring of 2008, when President Lee Myung-bak made the decision to re-allow the import of US beef, banned since 2003, due to concerns over mad cow disease. Suddenly the country was again gripped by a spasm of anti-Americanism, though less venomous this time, and cloaked in the language of "health" and "public safety." Spurred on by organizers on the far left, tens of thousands of people took to the streets of the nation's cities, demanding an immediate reinstatement of the ban. Attendees of candlelight demonstrations—made popular during the upheaval of 2002—swelled to around one million in central Seoul on at least one occasion.

Though supposedly about food safety, it soon became apparent that these protests were more about villainous Uncle Sam than about eating questionable beef. The original marches in Seoul were organized by the same hard-left agitators who were behind the ruckus of 2002, and though later joined by frightened and misinformed high school students (told they would be receiving the most dangerous beef in their school cafeterias), anti-Americanism was the engine behind them.

I wandered through several demonstrations in the streets of Busan, and the imagery alone told me all I needed to know: pictures of menacing cattle heads with glowing red eyes, on which were imprinted the Stars and Stripes. These posters and flyers said one thing, and said it very clearly: *Big, evil America is going to once again overwhelm small, pure Korea. America demands that we do its bidding and we say no!*

Like the tragedy of the two middle school girls, Internet rumors, misinformation, innuendo, and straight-up lies had poisoned the well of public discourse. Claims were made that Alzheimer's disease could be transmitted from tainted beef, and that the US only exported its sub-par, at-risk, diseased beef. A notorious "investigative report" on Korea's MBC channel argued that Koreans were genetically more susceptible to mad cow disease, and made several other bogus claims (legal action was later brought upon the producers by the government). I remember arguing with Da-jin, my Korean girlfriend at the time, who was convinced that the US government was purposely trying to export tainted beef into Korea in order to poison the Korean race. Kim Min-seon, a well-known Korean actress, famously stated that she "would gulp poison rather than eat US beef." This is how ridiculous things got, but, like every geyser of anti-Americanism here, it too died down, and today you can find delicious American beef in many stores and restaurants, at a fraction of the price charged for the domestic stuff.

APEC *Bandae*!

November of 2005 saw a big event in Busan: the APEC conference. APEC, which stands for Asian Pacific Economic Cooperation, is an annual meeting of all the Pacific Rim countries. Delegates get together behind closed doors, eat the host country's cuisine, dress up in indigenous costumes, and do away with pesky "trade barriers" like union laws and environmental protections. And it's not just a meeting of delegates from the member countries: it also includes each nation's head of state. So, for a few days in late 2005, Busan was graced with the presence of Russia's Putin, Mexico's Fox, Canada's Martin, Australia's Howard, China's Hu Jintao, Japan's Kozuimi, and yes, the devil himself, George W. Bush. If the presence of Bush on the ground weren't enough to inspire a good ol' anti-American Korean street protest, I don't know what would.

Let's just say that I wasn't disappointed.

The gathering of leaders took place on a Saturday and Sunday. I correctly figured that the action would be greatest on the first day, since the anti-APEC activists had had over a year to prepare for battle and would be chomping at the bit. So I made my way down to Gwangali—one of Busan's most famous beach areas—where I saw a gathering of marchers. I wasn't sure where they would end up, but I figured if I joined and followed them, that they'd lead me to the riot.

Most of these marchers were farmers who had been brought into Busan on buses. Opening up Korea's rice market to China was on APEC's agenda, and these mostly elderly old farmers were concerned that their homegrown rice—which was protected by entrenched government policy—wouldn't be able to compete with a flood of cheap Chinese grain. Their livelihoods were at stake, and they weren't going to sit passively while some delegates sold them out in the name of globalization. Two weeks prior to the demonstration, two of their ranks had committed suicide by ingesting herbicide. These guys wanted the world to take them seriously, and I was happy to march by their side.

I procured a NO BUSH sticker from a man in the procession, who slapped it onto the back of my black jacket, nodding and cackling in enthusiastic approval. We walked away from the beach, toward the Oncheon River, across which was the BEXCO complex where the bigwigs were rubbing elbows. I joined them in their chant, which was simple, yet effective:

"APEC bandae! Bush-y bandae!"

("Against APEC! Against Bush-y"—the latter an example of the Korean tendency to add an "i" sound to foreign words ending in "sh.")

As we approached the river, the crowd thickened: this was apparently where the anti-APEC brigade was massing up. The farmers comprised just one of many streams feeding into the huge lake of protesters. As we trickled in, I was waved over by another group of farmers sitting around a cardboard box that acted as an improvised table. They had their chopsticks out and were feasting on *jjok pal* (steamed pigs' feet), washing it down with little paper cups of soju.

"Where are you from?" one of them asked. His face was dark and deeply lined, evidence of a long life working outdoors. A yellow band was tied around his head, on which was written a slogan in Korean.

"I am from America," I replied.

"Ohhhhh… America?"

I turned around and pointed to the NO BUSH sticker on my back. The small group of old men immediately burst into cheers. They insisted I sit with them, and thrust a cup of soju into my hands. I drank up, ate a few slices of the pigs' feet, shook hands all around, drank some more, and soaked up the moment of solidarity.

My belly and head now warmed by soju, I headed straight to the riverfront, where thousands of people had gathered. On the other side of the water I could see BEXCO—all shiny steel and glass. I pictured a *hanbok*-clad George W. Bush sipping a near-beer and trying to chum it up with Vincente Fox, mangling the Spanish language while chucking the mustachioed Mexican president on his shoulder. Bridges spanned the river at two opposite ends of the carnival; the authorities had blocked off all access, creating a barrier of shipping containers stacked on top of each other. On top of the containers were groups of riot police—young conscripts, most likely—crouching behind metal shields while manning water cannon to keep the agitators at bay.

I was soon joined by Sammy and Josh—my hiking partner in Jirisan Park, who was still visiting from America. Josh was anti-authoritarian to the core. Fighting the man was programmed into his DNA, and his excitement to be taking part in this demonstration shot out from his very pores. We walked through the throngs of people, taking in the various banners and signs. One summed up the attitude of the Korean left—perhaps the most nationalistic of all left-wing movements—perfectly. It portrayed an imperial Japanese sunrise flag on the left side, which melded into the Stars and Stripes on the right: *Meet the new boss: same as the old boss.*

The protestors had secured an insanely long rope to one of the shipping containers at the bottom. Hundreds of participants gripped the rope and heaved and ho'd, dragging the container toward them a fraction of an inch at a time. The protestors at the front were blasted by the water cannon, but braved the frigid temperature, soaked to the core. They pulled and pulled and pulled, finally dislodging the bottom container, causing the two on top of it to topple down—along with the hapless riot police standing on them. The young conscript cops plummeted to the ground, resulting in a victory roar from the crowd. It was shocking to behold; the poor cops—kids really—could have easily been crushed by the falling containers, and avoided being killed by a minor miracle. Their comrades came to their aid and they limped back behind their still firmly-held line.

As dark approached, the majority of the protestors made their way to the other bridge. A dark line of hundreds of riot police now hulked in front of the containers—they would allow no more ropes to be attached. A van with loudspeakers pulled into the middle of the crowd and blasted protest anthems, including the infamous "Fucking USA"—a vitriolic anti-American rock tune made famous during the disturbances of 2002. A river of young men wearing surgical masks then jogged into the area, each carrying a long green metal rod, which they dropped into a massive pile. The organization behind it was staggering to behold, and then, as if on cue, hundreds of these hardcore students lined up and grabbed a pole each, immediately rushing the battalion of armored riot police waiting for them in front of the bridge. It was like a scene out of the movie *Braveheart*, as these men in their mid-20s, likely students in the same university classes, did a sort of medieval combat with one another. The clang of rods hitting shields reverberated through the night air. Josh, caught up in the action, grabbed a pole of his own and rushed the line, eager to take out his life-long frustration on a symbol of authority. The wounded began streaming to the back, blood running down their faces, where they had been clobbered by police nightsticks. Some of them limped on their own, while others were dragged back to improvised medical stations. It was pure combat, total violence—the most carefully-orchestrated riot I'd ever beheld.

The cops, having had enough of the initial mêlée, let loose a volley of tear gas, which cleared out the pole-wielding combatants in front of them. They then took the opportunity to move forward. When they stopped, they banged their clubs on their shields and let forth a huge yell, taunting their adversaries, who now held back, choking on the caustic smoke.

Calm now descended, like the mist of gas hanging over the improvised battlefield. The fighting was over. The protestors had faced off with the police and given them all they had. They had released their passion, their pent-up frustration, their very Korean angst. The whole thing had a ritualistic feel, as if both sides knew exactly how it would go down. The pressure valve was opened and the steam was allowed to escape. Some heads got busted and some blood was spilled, but at the end of it all, no one was severely injured. Just as quickly as it had begun, it ended, and the protestors sauntered away from the site, to swap war stories over late-night meals of grilled pork, soju, and beer.

INTERLUDE

FEBRUARY, 2006
SIEM REAP, CAMBODIA

I'M sitting in front of a computer screen in one of the town's tiny PC cafes. I'm coated in dust and sweat after a day of scrambling around the various temples that make up the Angkor complex. I sip a Coke from a long-neck bottle, amazed at the fact that they even have the Internet in Cambodia, as slow as it may be. This is a country that still reeks of tragedy. You can see the trauma in the eyes of everyone around you: the genocide wasn't so long ago, and many of the people you meet are survivors, while some surely took part in the carnage, as well.

The children of Siem Reap are all on the make, hawking photocopied books and T-shirts and guide services. They've memorized not just world, but state and provincial capitals in an attempt to ingratiate themselves with the international tourists that migrate to Angkor like Muslims on the Hajj. They're also more than likely to know a few choice phrases in your own tongue. They'll be sure to greet you warmly; look at a book and don't buy, however, and they'll spit curses.

"Fucking asshole motherfucker!"

I've never heard such venom shot my way from an eight-year-old girl.

I'm here with Kathleen, a dark-eyed ex-flame of mine from Seattle who agreed to meet me in Bangkok and come along to Cambodia. Our merry trio is rounded out by English Phil, an old friend from London who has not only quit drinking and drugging, but smoking as well. He huffs from a bizarre-looking plastic contraption that doses him regularly with nicotine, as well as satisfies his oral fixation developed through years of puffing cigarettes. It resembles an asthma inhaler, but acts as more of a pacifier.

Kathleen and I head down to Phnom Penh in the morning, then on to the beach town of Sihanoukville, where we'll meet several friends of mine from Busan for some chill time. Phil's heading overland back to Bangkok, where he's attending an AA convention. Bangkok is a cruel place to send people who are fighting their demons, but if you can stay sober there I suppose you've really got it beat.

I read an email from my brother Glen.

Our dad's been diagnosed with leukemia.

My tongue suddenly tastes like chalk, and I feel more perspiration bead up on my forehead. This is yet another malady thrown upon the sick pile, though from the tone of Glen's email, there's no pressing need for me to hightail it back to Bangkok and catch the first flight home. Dad has more time, but now we know this time to be quite finite, so right then and there I resolve to spend my next vacation back in the States.

CHAPTER 10

TIME TO EAT

AT the end of my first school year at Gaegum University—a couple of months before the Cambodia trip, before I got the news about my father—I joined the other foreign teachers, along with our boss and a few of the Korean staff, for a day trip to neighboring South Jeolla Province. We boarded a bus and headed off into the early summer mist, stopping off at a famous green tea plantation, a bamboo forest, and a mock-up of a traditional Korean village. The point of the trip was to celebrate the end of the semester, bond a bit as a group, and experience a bit of "real" Korean culture.

For lunch we went to a traditional *Han jeong shik* restaurant located next to the folk village. We all sat on the wooden floor around an impossibly long table and ate rice, soup, and about thirty different side dishes, known as *banchan*. These dishes ran the gamut from various pickled vegetables, fish, beef, quail eggs, assorted kelp and seaweeds, and even a few steamed chickens, called *baek suk*. We sat and ate and drank from bowls filled with rice wine, digging into the dizzying spread of banchan thrown out before us. Most of it was at least partially recognizable and almost everything was utterly delicious. A real *Han jeong shik* meal is an experience that's hard to erase from memory; it's an exercise is pure gastronomical variety. The amount of different banchan is staggering. I pity the dishwasher at such a place.

As I sat talking and munching away, a new dish was brought out. It looked like a kind of raw fish, sliced up and put onto a plate. I eyed it quizzically.

"You must try this one," a Korean colleague sitting next to me said. "This is *hong-eo*, which is the specialty of South Jeolla Province."

"What is it? Fish?"

"Yes, it's a kind of fish… it is fermented… fermented… How do you say?"

"It's fermented skate," one of the foreign teachers joined in. "You know, kind of like a stingray. Go ahead and try it. It's great." He smiled and stared.

I grabbed a piece of *hong-eo* with my metal chopsticks, wrapped it up in some lettuce and put a bit of red pepper sauce on top. My Korean colleague eyed me expectantly. I popped it into my mouth and chewed.

It was tough, like a kind of crunchy rubber. It was, in fact, the most unchewable piece of seafood that I'd ever put into my mouth. It was all cartilage and sandpaper skin. *Was there any meat in the meat?* I had little time to dwell on the texture however, for a split-second later I was hit with the smell. It was like a gas bomb went off, releasing a blast of pure ammonia, which singed my sinuses and throat. This piece of *hong-eo* tasted like it had been soaked in acetone and bile. It was rancid and toxic, the complete opposite of palatable. I felt like a cat had just peed in my mouth. It was the worst thing I've ever attempted to choke down, and soon I was gagging, spitting the half-chewed atrocity into my napkin, and frantically searching for some water with which to douche my panicking mouth and throat. My face went red and I gasped for breath, attracting all eyes at the table. The Koreans especially were tickled by the spectacle, breaking into deep laughter while I did my best not to puke all over the small dishes laid out in front of me.

The residents of South Jeolla province are considered the most prickly and rebellious in all of Korea. The fact that *hong-eo* is their signature dish does a lot to explain this perception. To this day I am astounded, not only because people eat the stuff, but also because it's a sought-after delicacy for many.

****

Koreans love their food. Eating is central to their way of life. Life in Korea revolves around dining: three meals are observed daily. Everything stops and everyone sits and everyone eats. And Koreans eat heartily. They dig into the food in front of them and go at it with gusto, munching and chomping and slurping without a hint of self-consciousness. There is a simple joy that is evident in many Koreans when they gather with family or friends with the intention of taking down some food. In this regard they are no different than anyone else in this world. After all, who doesn't like to eat?

Food is so central to the Korean experience that one of their standard greetings is *Bap meogoesseoyo?*, which literally means, *Have you eaten?* This has its roots in a leaner time, when the possibility of having not eaten was a painful concern, but the fact that it remains in common usage tells you something about the importance that these folks place on food. Food brings out the kindest, most generous side of Korean people: like many Asians, most everything is placed in the center of the table and eaten communally. Sharing is the name of the game: to eat alone and not offer some to those around you is viewed as some kind of cardinal sin of greed. I've often had complete strangers wave me over and invite me to eat with them. You see this sense of generosity in children, as well. I often taught kids' classes, and during break times they love to bust out their snacks—chips, cookies, dried ramen, chocolate squid balls (really). Unlike American kids, who tend to either horde or barter (a reflection of our hyper-capitalist selves), Korean kids almost always dole out their snacks equally, sharing with everyone in the vicinity, including the lowest kid in the pecking order—not to mention the teacher, who is usually offered the food first. Everyone eats. I regularly turn down fistfuls of snacks that the kids—grubby hands and all—feel compelled to thrust my way each time I walk into the classroom. For them it's a no-brainer. When you eat, you share. It's just what's *done.*

"Oh! You Can Use the Chopsticks Very Well!"

Sit down to eat for the first time with most any local in Korea, and these will be among the first words out of their mouth. It doesn't matter if they know that you've been in the country for years; it doesn't matter if you can even speak the language passably; it doesn't matter if you tell them that your home country is full of Asian restaurants with chopsticks piled on every table. Koreans somehow feel compelled to compliment us foreigners on our chopstick use, as if we've mastered the art of juggling or just played an intricate composition on the violin. Perhaps it's because they view us as big clumsy brutes, and effective chopstick use runs counter to this widely held belief. Or maybe it has something more to do with their cuisine: if we can wield chopsticks with dexterity, then perhaps we can begin to peel away the layers of their ancient and mysterious culinary ways. I don't think that anyone can really understand a culture without delving deeply into its food, and suspect that many Koreans also hold this view.

I love Korean food—I really do. My time on the peninsula has given me a great deal of respect for the local cuisine: it's delicious and healthy and extraordinarily varied. The idea of mining an almost completely unknown cuisine was one of the things that excited me most about coming here. Upon arrival I dove into straight in, plunging headfirst into another world of eating, wholeheartedly embracing a cooking culture that employs fermented bean and red pepper pastes, bizarre and be-tentacled sea creatures, salt water weeds, grilled meats, fish of all stripes, and an array of vegetable side dishes that could confuse even the most hardened vegan. However, I soon discovered that not all foreigners can eat like Koreans. Many Westerners can never get over the otherness of the cuisine. I've seen countless teachers arrive in Korea only to be intimidated by the seemingly strange food choices. Sometimes it's just the prevalence of seafood that puts them off (there are a lot of folks who have a bizarre, overriding hatred of all fish); for others, it's the pungent, spicy pastes and hot peppers that Koreans love to liberally apply to many of their best-known dishes. As a result, many of these foreign folks eschew the cheap and fresh food available to them anywhere in the country in favor of a diet of pasta, pizza, and various pub and fast foods, which, in modern, capitalist Korea, can be found everywhere. This reliance on comfortable, stodgy, known-quantities results in one thing only: fat, and lots of it. I've seen Western English teachers come to the country for just a year and seriously *hef out*, which is the opposite of what really should be going on. Look at the locals: most of them are thin. Have you ever stopped to think as to why that may be? Comedian Brian Aylward puts it like this:

"I like watching other expats at the food markets in Asia. They seem confused as to what kind of foods they are looking at. One of these days, I am just going to lean in toward them and say, *They're called vegetables, you fat fuck.*"

While Korean food's profile has risen in recent years, it still occupies a pretty obscure place compared with the popularity of other Asian cuisine, such as Japanese, Chinese, Vietnamese, and Thai. Most foreigners, when pressed, probably could not even name two Korean dishes. Sure, many people do know of kimchee, but after that the drop-off is massive. Someone may utter something about Korean barbecue, but what exactly does that even mean, other than that some meat gets roasted over coals?

Kimchee, of course, is king. It is the central component to all Korean meals. It is eaten at most every sitting, and it binds Korean people together more than any other food. Korean people are proud of kimchee, and in some ways it perfectly represents the Korean character: spicy, sour, strong, unique, and difficult for outsiders to really fathom. It's the one thing from their cuisine that they can claim to be *really theirs*. While other cultures of the world have sundry variations on pickled veggies and cabbage, no one has quite pushed it up to the levels of the Koreans, who have taken a traditional staple of their diet and elevated it to the level of national identity. To eat kimchee is to be Korean. To go without is to deprive yourself of a deep, cultural birthright. We see this when Koreans travel. More often than not, they pack kimchee to take along with them, as if leaving it at home would weaken them somehow. After all, *kimchee is power*. You see it and smell it everywhere in Korea—from the street markets and restaurants to the breath of the ajosshis on the late-night trains.

I tried kimchee my first night in the country and was hooked right away, relishing its sour, spicy taste. I took to it immediately, which seems to be how it goes. One either likes it from the outset or hates it forever. This split, among foreigners, is about fifty-fifty. Scouser Stu, an English friend who lived in Busan, hates kimchee so much that he expressed his dislike through his adopted Korean name, which, when spelled out in Hangul, reads *Kim Chi—no*.

Aside from being a physical embodiment of Korean-ness, kimchee is touted as a kind of health panacea by many of the Great Han People. Koreans claim that kimchee aids in digestion (which I am inclined to believe, based on my own experience—my once-chronic heartburn all but disappeared after moving here). Many even go so far as to put forth that it guards against serious sickness. During the SARS scare of 2003, not one case of the disease popped up on the peninsula. Koreans were quick to point out that regular and mighty consumption of their beloved fermented cabbage kept them safe. While many of us foreigners roll our eyes at such claims, I don't think it's unreasonable to credit kimchee as being an overall healthy food.

"Can You Eat the Spicy Food?"

Before complimenting you on your chopstick proficiency, most any Korean will likely ask you this when you sit down at the table. Koreans are convinced that their food is among the spiciest in the world—ignited rocket fuel, to the Western palate—which really isn't true at all. This isn't to say their food is bland. Koreans love garlic, onions, and peppers of all kinds. They also smother many of their dishes with an omnipresent red pepper paste known as *gochujang*. So yes, many dishes pack some heat, but not to the atomic extent that the majority of Koreans seem to be convinced. The hottest of Korean dishes could never compete with those from Thailand or India or even the provinces of central and southern China, such as Hunan and Sichuan. Yet Koreans often are incredulous as to any Westerner's ability to handle the spice of their food. Often, when dining with Korean friends, I'll order a dish, only to have the Korean server turn to my friend, and with raised eyebrows, ask them if they're sure I can take it. I've heard stories of foreigners being straight-up refused some dishes out of fear that it will be too hot for them to tolerate, despite repeated attempts to order. Sometimes this may be true, and Koreans are only looking out for their guest's comfort when they kick up such fusses, but, in the end, Korean food is nowhere near the top tier in terms of spiciness. The fact that most Korean people are totally ignorant of other Asian cuisines helps explain this gap in knowledge. Koreans eat and know their own food. Ask them to describe their favorite dishes from other Asian countries, and the list will be quite short. Many will just draw a blank and shake their heads.

That said, one of Korea's spiciest dishes did kick (and later burn) my ass when I first arrived. On my second night in the country, alone, I took a wander through the little market across the street from my new apartment, hoping to stumble upon something good and local and be surprised. In this I succeeded, walking a up to a second-story restaurant that had a picture of a cute little octopus on its sign, letting even those of us illiterate in Korean know what was on the menu. Business owners are fond of cartoonish representations of the meat served: if a restaurant specializes in steamed pork, more often than not the sign will feature a happy little fat pig that appears to be dancing or giving a thumbs-up sign; a spicy chicken joint may feature a flamboyant-looking rooster. I ascended the stairs, entered the octopus place, sat down on the floor and waited. I was soon approached by an apron-clad ajumma, who I presumed asked me what I wanted to eat, as my Korean then was as about as good as my Esperanto is now. I proceeded to randomly point at the first selection on the wall menu and signaled for a beer, as well. It was early August and I was overheated from the walk up the stairs. Soon I was presented with a pan full of baby octopus, onions, and glass noodles, all of which were covered with glistening red gochujang, and cooked over a gas flame at my table. Along with this was a collection of side dishes containing kimchee, radish, black beans, green cabbage, peanuts, and quail eggs. Once the spicy octopus was ready I dug in, ladling the bubbling goodness over a bowl of white rice and stuffing spoonfuls into my mouth, which, when looking around at the other patrons in the room, seemed to be the right way to go about it: Koreans eat rice with spoons, and never raise the bowl off of the table, unlike their troublesome neighbors, those uncouth and hated Japanese.

As I greedily ate in the thick summer heat, the pepper paste hit my system and I began to sweat like a fat guy in a sauna. My face was deep red and the front of my button-up shirt became drenched with sweat, which also beaded up on my forehead and dripped from my chin into my rice bowl. I was in serious meltdown mode, and the only thing to mitigate it was swigs from the small glass of cold Hite beer.

When I looked up, I discovered that all eyes in the restaurant were on me. The other patrons—a couple of families and groups of men eating and drinking together—stared my way with huge smiles, waving their hands to their lips as if to say, "Spicy, ain't it?" As I turned, I saw that the kitchen had emptied out and the women working there were now all looking my way as well. When I caught their eyes, they erupted in full laughter, deeply tickled to see this big white guy turning blistering crimson and secreting every bit of sweat in his system. They laughed and laughed and laughed, convinced of the spicy power of their food, satisfied that they had done their job. I shrugged, wiped my face, drank from the cool beer and laughed along, knowing that I looked ridiculous, but despite this, felt great. This meal was a true novelty, unlike anything I'd eaten before. It was waking me up, and to this day, spicy octopus—or *nakji bokkum*—continues to be one of my favorite Korean dishes.

Other than kimchee, the one Korean cuisine that is well-known beyond the shores of the peninsula is their barbecue. In big cities throughout North America, Korean grilled meat joints have popped up, adding to the variety of other Asian foods readily available in these urban centers. Korean barbecue is delicious: there's meat, coals, and a grill. You can't really go wrong. It's also a lot of fun—a communal and interactive way to share a meal. After all, the food cooks right there at the table. Everyone helps themselves, and the group is bonded by the literal flame in the center. It's a terrific way to eat and it's really no mystery why it's the one Korean cuisine that has caught on.

Of course barbecue—or *suk bul*—is even more popular at home than abroad. Meat restaurants are everywhere in Korea, and when walking at night you are often hit with the smoky aroma of grilling pork or beef. In warm weather, tables are set up out in the open air, and customers will sit for hours, picking at the small pieces of fired meat, eating from the numerous side dishes, and of course, drinking.

This barbecued food, while closely identified with Korea internationally, really isn't traditional cuisine by any stretch of the imagination. Up until the mid-'60s, Korea was one of the poorest countries in the world, on par with such places as Sudan and Bangladesh. Meat is a treasured commodity in any impoverished country, and Korea was no exception. Eating grilled meat as a main dish was considered an extreme luxury, reserved for the rich or for very special occasions. It wasn't until the last thirty years that Koreans have had the disposable income to blow on pure meat dinners. So to think of *suk bul* as "real" Korean food is to give it a bit too much credit.

Korean food encompasses a lot of things, but if you were to choose one thing other than kimchee that binds it all together, without a doubt it would be soup. Korean food is all about soup—especially kimchee and *dwoenjang* (bean paste*) jjigae*. It makes sense that soup is the centerpiece of almost all Korean meals. Up until recently Korea was dirt-poor, and poor people eat soup: you just take whatever ingredients are available, boil them in water, and serve with rice, if you have any. Soup is efficient: it's a way to feed everyone and waste nothing. It's also a good way to keep warm in the frigid, windy winters of the Korean Peninsula.

"Do You Like the Korean Rice Cake?"

Deok is the Korean word for rice cake, which is the nation's most treasured traditional snack. What is a rice cake? Well, it's not really cake at all, since no baking is involved. Deok is just sticky rice that is pounded with a wooden mallet into a thick, gooey mass. It is then stuffed with sweet beans or covered with various sweeteners to make it more cakey, I suppose. Koreans love deok. To them it is a treasured thing that reminds them of their past. When they eat deok, they think about their grandmother and the delicious deok that she used to make. Like kimchee, Koreans are proud of their deok. They are so proud that they thrust it on unsuspecting foreigners with alarming frequency. If you come to Korea, prepare to be regularly ambushed with deok.

Koreans often fail to comprehend that many foreigners don't like deok. We don't hate it, either. In fact, it's hard to have any strong feelings either way, when it comes to deok. It's like eating concentrated apathy. And it's always served up at official settings: in your boss's office, or at the home of a particularly lucrative private tutoring lesson. There it is, splayed out in huge slices, looking and tasting like a Nerf football carved up into eighths. But you have to eat at least one piece, choking it down and chewing on it for eternity, all the while faking a smile and nodding to your boss or the parents of the child whom you teach for heaps of money. They smile back and you keep up with the charade. Such is life here.

Deok is so traditional and festive that to hate on it is almost culturally disrespectful. Koreans have a great love for their rice cakes and you don't want to hurt their feelings, but sometimes the line must be drawn, sometimes you have to put a stop to it. I was recently teaching a class of housewives at my college. Several of the students had taken to regularly bringing me large slabs of deok, which I politely accepted for a couple of months. But the deok just kept coming and coming, and finally, in the gentlest manner I could muster, I confessed to not much liking it. These lovely women were shocked and horrified, as if a neutron bomb had just sucked all the air out of the room… or one of them had discovered my secret trove of barnyard porn.

In the end I've made my peace with deok. I smile and take it down; I pretend to savor it. This isn't hard to do, really, and is my burden as a guest in this country. Appreciation of deok is appreciated in turn. There are certainly worse foods foisted upon unsuspecting foreigners on the peninsula, and sometimes, just sometimes, I actually like the stuff.

Sunday Morning at Gupo

It was Sam's idea, and it sounded like a good one, at least four beers into a Saturday night down at the Crown. Thoughts of my father were gnawing on my insides and, despite the fact that I'd be home soon, I attempted to soothe them with lager.

"Dude, let's go to the dog market tomorrow."

"Really?"

"Yeah. Let's do it. Let's descend into the belly of the beast. Haven't you always been curious about it?"

"Sure. But part of me is afraid."

"That's exactly why you should go."

Koreans, like people in many other Asian countries, do, from time to time, eat dogs. You don't have to look to hard to find little family run restaurants serving up *boshintang*, the spicy dog meat soup renowned for its health properties… one of which is its purported effect on what's known as *stamina*. It is for this latter reason that boshintang is almost exclusively eaten by middle-aged and older men. Increasingly, young Koreans balk at the idea of dog-eating, and the government—in periodic attempts to avoid the condemnation of more canine-sympathetic foreigners—has even tried to curb the practice. But it is out there. It is part of the culture, and I, for one, am not about to wave my scolding finger at either the patrons or the purveyors.

So the next morning Sam and I boarded the subway and rode it to the other side of town. Our heads were hissing from the vat's worth of cheap beer we had downed the night before. We sipped from big paper cups of Starbucks coffee and said nothing, preparing ourselves for the upcoming encounter. We had both been in the country for two years at this point and had yet to visit the dog market. The time had come.

By the time we got out of the subway, I was officially starving. The coffee I had for breakfast was boring a hole in my stomach lining. Sam was in similar shape, so we decided that before we headed into the catacombs of the market, we'd grab a bite to fuel us for what was to come. The Gupo Market is not just a dog market. It is massive and comprehensive, selling fruit and vegetables, fish, pork, chicken, meat, household necessities, spices, rice, clothing, and hardware items. But Sam and I had no time to duck into one of the market's restaurants. We had come for dog, and we found it straightaway. The first thing that clued me in was the bark and yelp of a dog, echoing up the side street on which we found ourselves.

In a stall to our right, chickens and ducks were crammed into cages, lorded over by stern old women and their husbands. The place was badly lit and dirty; we sensed that we were in the rougher part of town, the fringe of the city of Busan. Next to the fowl was the first dog cage. Ten or so yellow dogs were crammed in. They looked out at us with warm, dark eyes, though you could taste their sense of resignation. They knew what was up. When Koreans talk about dog meat, they usually tell us how the yellow dogs—the meat dogs—are bred for that purpose only. This is true, I'm sure, but the dogs we gazed upon looked like sweet, friendly pets. These were individuals—social, healthy-looking pups. They had no look of livestock.

For the next two blocks we passed cage after cage of dogs—most of which contained these cute yellow guys, but with some other breeds thrown in for good measure... perhaps a canine butcher's affirmative action program? Next to the cages were the open-air meat cases, containing the skinned carcasses. The cavities were hollowed out, with only the liver and a few other tasty bits remaining. Legs stabbed into the air like those of inverted tables, with the naked tails poking and coiling, wormlike.

As we descended into this market, we tried to maintain our cool, our distance. We were foreigners, and while the sellers were eyeing us with obvious suspicion, no one was shooing us away. The people who worked the stalls were leather-tough in that way that only old Koreans can be—all spit and scowls—sometimes addressing each other in blunt Busan *saturi*, with its hisses, moans, and almost Arabic-sounding gutturals. At one point we approached a case to closely inspect a fresh-looking carcass, glistening blood-red and brown. The hard-as-rebar old woman tending the front tried to block us from taking a peek, but we ignored her, despite her lethal gaze.

"Looks delicious," I said to her in Korean. She turned away, unmoved.

We made it out of the side street and paused to take a breath. I had seen countless markets in Korea—with their raw organs, pig heads, and Lovecraftian sea creatures splayed out in full glory—but what I had just taken in stabbed me in a deep place. The sour reek of dog shit also hung in the air, and this combination of sight and smell not only caused me to gag, but succeeded in erasing my ravenous appetite; lunch would be delayed indefinitely.

After this break to gather our wits and avoid retching, we decided to take another pass down dog alley and snap some photos, which would be no easy feat, as the folks who man the stalls in dog markets are notorious in their aggressive resistance to photos being taken, especially by nosy, tsk-tsk'ing foreigners. As Sam surreptitiously attempted to click a few shots, he realized the battery on his camera had died: so much for the damning evidence, the main reason we had come to this pitiful place to begin with. The scene before us would have to be recorded by memory alone.

Though we got no photos, we did see more sights, some unexpected, including cages containing black goats, and one stuffed full of mewing cats. This had me scratching my head. Dogs, I knew, but cats? I later learned that sometimes the elderly in Korea eat a soup made from cats in an attempt to combat rheumatism and arthritis. The belief is that a cat's innate flexibility can be passed on to the joints through the broth. By this line of reasoning, California condor flesh should endow us with the power of flight, manatee meat should help us to become wise and gentle swimmers, and unicorn steak should give us the ability to crap rainbows.

Sometimes we just have to surrender to the notion of cultural relativity.

We ended up finding a new wing of the dog area. As we approached one stall, the old woman warmly greeted us and invited us to check out the wares. She held up a meaty leg cut and shook it vigorously.

"The leg is the most delicious part," she said, showing us her gold teeth through a grin. She gestured to the scale and nodded, ready to wrap it up for us.

We smiled and politely declined the offer, walking away from the cages and the keepers. As we passed one, I saw a man open the top of the cage and slip a snare around one of the unfortunate occupants, who let out a high-pitched whine.

"Life's tough, guys." Sam said.

The man lifted the struggling dog out.

As Sam and I turned down a side alley, and we heard its futile yelps and cries reverberate behind us. We kept on walking into the more welcoming section of the market, where perhaps our lunchtime appetites would return.

Just another day's work at Gupo.

INTERLUDE

JULY 9, 2006
LOS ANGELES, CALIFORNIA

I'VE just finished watching the last game of the World Cup. Italy beat France in penalty shootouts. The French side folded after Zidane head-butted that guy and was sent off. Craziness. To think that it's his last game, and that's how he'll be remembered…

I woke up in the wrong house. Pauly stirred me and handed me the phone. Evidently Irish Ray and I got into it at his place after eight hours of straight whiskey drinking. There are flashes of clarity: slamming into the cupboards in his kitchen. Being ripped from him on his front lawn. Threats of police being called. Me screaming something about my father.

As Pauly insisted, I call Ray, but he isn't having my apology. He has a black eye and is threatening to break my camera, which is sitting on his couch. He's ranting in his Galway brogue about me costing him $15,000 in a commission that he'll never collect. He's a stockbroker and lives on image: a black eye just won't do. The big meeting on Monday is evidently off.

So much for my happy trip back home.

I leave for Arizona in two days, first to Bisbee, to see my friend Ariel and his family, and then on to Glen's place outside of Phoenix, for a quick reunion of the Brothers Tharp. As Bruce Springsteen sings, "Nothing feels better than blood on blood."

My hatred for L.A. aches in my bones. I now remember why I left, and why I never want to return.

CHAPTER 11

DON'T BITE THE HAND THAT ISSUES THE VISA

AFTER living in Korea for a while, it's easy to forget the fact that you are a guest in a foreign land. It's easy to settle into the rhythms of your life and live much the same way you did back home, oblivious to the fact that there is a whole different set of rules—both codified and cultural—by which you are required to abide. It's tempting to lose your head and forget where you are, glowing in the false sense of freedom that can be so palpable here. After all, you can drink until seven in the morning, walk down the street with a beer, and ride your motorbike on the sidewalk; the cops pretty much leave foreigners alone.

When I go back to the States, I am constantly looking over my shoulder, in full knowledge that the police are just looking for *any excuse*—a gnawing paranoia that is refreshingly absent here. It's also easy to get sucked into the incestuous, self-feeding morass of expat life, and pass time exclusively with your Western, English-speaking comrades, carrying on as if you were in Chicago, Toronto, Christchurch, or Leeds. Any sense of cultural sensitivity is numbed with each successive night of drinking. You feel safe and ignored, counting on the language barrier as some kind of DMZ that gives you carte blanche to act as you wish. You drop your guard and loosen your tongue, and this is when things get dangerous. This is when you are most likely to step out of line; this is when you are most likely to do or say something that pisses the locals off.

As I've mentioned, I used to be an actor. I did theater as a kid and all throughout high school. I trained at an actors' conservatory during college and spent nearly ten years afterwards making plays and performing sketch comedy, improvisation, and even some standup. I lived for the thrill of getting up in front of people, especially when the goal was to make them laugh. I have been compelled to do it since childhood and, through practice and training, I have managed to get pretty good.

This instinct to perform didn't evaporate once I packed my bags and hit the rocky shores of Asia. My need to be the center of attention was quickly recognized, and earned me the nickname Showbiz by my drinking buddies down at the Crown, the shitty little pub where the most cantankerous of the ESL crowd would gather and hurl abuse at each other. The nickname was both a mild insult and a term of endearment, but it stuck hard because it was so damn true.

During my first year, I performed with Angry Steve in *Heungbu and Nolbu*. This was a silly little fifteen-minute affair for our Korean class, conducted mainly by non-actors who could barely spit out the most basic greeting in the language, let alone nail a convincing theatrical line. I couldn't even read Hangul at the time, but rather learned my lines phonetically, writing out the sounds in English. It was ridiculous and truly awful to watch, but in the end we did do a play: we memorized lines, put on traditional Korean costumes, and acted on a stage. That same year, I also participated a few times at Poetry Plus, a bi-monthly open mike of sorts, where I tested out my new Korea-centric comedy routine:

"Korea. That's a strange name for a country. Kind of sounds like a disease, doesn't it? Hey doc, I think have *Korea*."

"Sounds serious. What are the symptoms?"

"Well, I find myself spitting in elevators, shitting fire, and irrationally hating the Japanese."

Some of the jokes did garner decent laughs, but, needless to say, I kept my day job.

Not only was Steve an angry poker player, but he was quite serious about producing some English-language theater in Busan. After all, we were both passionate about drama and making it would help keep us out of the bar, which can be a sort of quicksand for the hobby-less English teacher. So in the fall of 2005, Steve put on a short one-act play, Eugène Ionesco's *The Leader*, in which I appeared. We staged it at Poetry Plus and people loved it. The response was massive and it became apparent to us that there was a hungry audience for this sort of thing, both among the expat community and some Koreans themselves.

In fact, a Korean producer took note of the show and soon contacted Steve about staging a full-length play. Steve ended up choosing Dario Fo's political farce, *Accidental Death of an Anarchist*, in which I played the main role of the Maniac. This was a fully-produced piece—rehearsed over several months, staged with set, costumes, lighting, and sound design, and run at an actual theater on the campus of Busan's Kyungsung University. The turnout was good, and while it was hard work (all theater is), it was a hell of a lot of fun. Everyone involved left the production stoked and eager to bite off something new. We had a basic ensemble of competent performers. We had an audience. We had a director. So the question was: what next?

Steve and I were chatting over cold beers at the Crown. It was a muggy night in late August and I had just returned from three-week jaunt back to the Land of the Free. I was supposed to grab some plays while I was home, so we could read them over and pick one to produce. But during my last few days home, I had a revelation.

"Screw doing another play," I said, gripping the glass mug of Cass lager. "Let's write our own thing. Let's do a sketch comedy show about living in Korea."

Steve's furrowed forehead slackened. "That's not a bad idea."

"We'll produce the whole thing ourselves. Do it in a small theater. We'll sell booze right there—do it late-night style." This is how a lot of the theater I had been involved before with was done: late at night in small venues with plenty of alcohol to lube the crowd. It was a recipe for success.

"And the material?" Steve's tone was serious. "We have to tread lightly here. We can't turn this into a Korea-bashing fest."

"Of course not. We'll make fun of both foreigners AND Koreans. It will be an equal opportunity affair."

And so *Babopalooza* was born.

Babopalooza was the first English-language sketch-comedy show ever produced in Busan, and perhaps the whole of Korea. The idea was to create a silly, rowdy night of comedy—a sort of expatriate *Feast of Fools*—where we playfully skewered each other as well as our Korean hosts. The cast consisted of most of the people involved with *Anarchist*, along with a couple of new folks—nine in total—as well as Cuttlefish, a foreigner rock band we recruited to play between scenes. Four cast members also served as writers, generating an hour and twenty minutes' worth of sketches. We took on a variety of subjects, including the prevalence of ignorant expats who do nothing but complain, things overheard from kids at the hagwon, a send-up of *Green Eggs and Ham* about eating dog soup, a parody of a popular character from a kids' English book series, and a controversial sketch which skewered the Korea Immigration Service.

After a couple of months of rehearsal, we rented a tiny theater and performed the show twice. Both nights sold out, with people literally straining to poke their heads through the door to get a glimpse. And the crowd was quite mixed: though the majority were foreign English teachers, a sizable Korean contingent was represented.

We charged 7,000 won for tickets and sold cheap Korean beer from a cooler. All the proceeds would be used to recoup the production's expenses. Even with full-capacity houses, we were doomed to lose money, which really didn't faze us, since we were doing the thing for fun. Actually, profiting from the show was never an intention. In fact, we intentionally chose to keep the tickets cheap, in the tradition of late-night theater.

The show was a small hit. The audience laughed generously at even the weaker jokes, and a couple of the sketches knocked it out of the park. Even the Korean spectators seemed to enjoy our sketches that made fun of them. Koreans are notoriously thin-skinned and, at times, can take the slightest criticism from a foreigner as a grave insult. Their own comedy also lacks a satirical element: there are several popular comedy shows on the television, but they veer toward extreme silliness and slapstick. Most of them consist of groups of men performing ridiculous challenges that involve lots of running, shouting, hitting each other in the nuts, and falling down. It can be quite funny (even to one with limited Korean skills), but I've yet to see one program that takes on positions of authority, which is essential for satire.

Most of the sketches were well received by all, with the exception of the Immigration sketch. This was not surprising, since we had known all along of the potential for this one to offend. In fact, Steve was so concerned with its over-the-line content and racist style that at one point during the rehearsal process he insisted that it be cut. I initially went along with him, but when we sat down with the writer—an essential and very funny member of the cast—he vehemently defended the piece and threatened to walk if we axed it. This guy had lived in Korea for many years and spoke the language nearly fluently. His impassioned defense of his piece appealed to my "free speech at any cost" instincts, and in the end I sided with him, overruling Steve, who served as co-director on the project.

I have always believed that the best comedy is that which isn't afraid to offend. This has been a mantra of sorts for much of my life. Fuck 'em if they can't take a joke, right? Isn't that what any artist worth a damn would say? Normally I'd say yes, but this mindset can be construed as a kind of artistic hubris. Back in America this no-holds-barred attitude may be absolutely salient, but in my blind defense of provocative comedy, I had forgotten one important fact: I wasn't in America. I was in a country that until very recently had jailed and tortured people for free speech violations. I was in a country still repairing its national self-esteem after being stepped on and humiliated by foreign powers for a good part of its 5000-year history.

Steve had been right: the sketch *should* have been cut. It did offend and did so mightily. The piece took place in an airport, where a just off-the-plane young English teacher is interrogated by a three-person panel of Korean Immigration officials. He is asked about various aspects of Korean culture. Foreign actors portrayed the officials in stilted, accented English. I wore a black wig and huge glasses—a kind of Asian blackface, really. There were jokes about dog-eating, suicide, Dokdo (the disputed islets between Korea and Japan), and the sanctity of Korean women. So yes, the sketch was totally racist, and above that, it committed a cardinal sin in this oh-so-Confucian of societies: it ridiculed people in positions of authority... over *us*. This is how our asses were later bitten.

Just over a week after the two performances of *Babopalooza*, two detectives showed up at the university where Steve and I both worked. They pulled us into an office and asked a few questions. Were we indeed involved with the show? Did we make fun of Korean culture? Above all, did we charge money? They also informed us that two undercover cops had come and videotaped the whole thing.

The visas of most English teachers in Korea are quite narrow in scope: you are allowed to work *only* at the school or institution sponsoring the visa. Any sort of outside income is strictly prohibited. *Babopalooza* was entirely organized and produced by English teachers. We charged for tickets and sold some beer. This was considered an outside commercial exercise, in direct violation of our work visas. No matter what other defenses we came up with, the law on this was clear. They had us by the balls.

The entire cast and many of the musicians were summoned to Busan's central police headquarters and questioned about our involvement in the affair. As the obvious ringleaders, Steve and I were brought in first. We were separated and subjected to three hours of interrogation, through a hired interpreter. I insisted on ringing the US Embassy to let them know what was going on, and the woman at the other end of the line curtly informed me that they were in no power to intervene, that I was subject to Korean law, but to keep them abreast of the situation. This didn't surprise me, but I thought I'd let them know what was up. Plus, I wanted the police to know that I was taking this seriously.

The police were courteous, yet extremely thorough in their questioning. At first they wanted to know general information about the show, along with who was involved. This was an exercise in redundancy on their part, since they possessed several programs with most of the participants' names listed clearly in black ink. There was no need for me to name names, so I just referred them to the pamphlet. Later they pressed me on the technicalities: was I aware that charging money for tickets violated my visa? How much did we pocket? The final phase of questioning was the most pointed: why did we do a sketch about boshintang (dog soup)? Did we hate Korean Immigration? Why did we ridicule Korean culture? Was I not thankful to live and work in Korea?

It became quickly apparent to me that the visa violation—while technically real—served as a pretext: the actual reason they had hauled us in was for lampooning Korean culture. These cops were quite concerned and even hurt that we had sent up certain aspects of their society. When I tried to explain to the questioning officer that, in the West, we have a free-speech tradition of satire, I was cut off and lectured on how "Korea is a modern democracy with guarantees of free speech."

The last question of the interview had nothing to do with the content of the show. One of the officers alluded to "allegations of drug use" during those two nights. With the exception of alcohol—an Amazonian volume of which flows throughout the peninsula—drugs are almost nowhere to be found. In fact, illegal drug use is often blamed on "foreign elements" within Korean society. Foreigners are watched and targeted. Just two years before my arrival in Busan, a number of foreign English teachers had been arrested and deported for possession and use of marijuana. It was a big story, splashed all over the national media, cementing suspicions that many foreigners are indeed drug addicts, despite the fact that the nation's militant attitude against simple marijuana use is rarely if ever questioned by any segment in society. Most Koreans believe that marijuana is a drug and all drugs are bad, so marijuana *must* be bad. Pot? Heroin? *Same same. NOT different.*

So I wasn't surprised by the request for a drug test. If the police could nail us for using drugs at the show, they'd have a slam dunk. One must also realize that, in Korea, a positive drug test is tantamount to possession. There really is no difference. Drugs in your bloodstream are drugs on your person. You can travel to a country where pot is decriminalized or even legal, but if it's still in your pee while you're in Korea, you're holding. It's enough to get you jail time, deported, or both.

At first I feigned outrage over the drug test. I loudly protested that drugs had nothing to do with this event (as I knew they did not). I knew that these cops were heading down a dead end, and I wanted to make sure they knew it. I also resented the fact that they requested a test in the first place, a further indignity to be suffered. I refused. The police tried the age-old "if you're not guilty, then you have nothing to hide" argument, which, despite the fact that it made my stomach lining crawl, convinced me in the end. After all, if we peed negative, it would be just one more thing that they couldn't go after us on. It would be the first step to exoneration—or at least, a dropping of charges and getting on with more important matters.

There was, however, another reason for my initial refusal. Just days earlier, over the weekend, I had been in Japan, where I had tagged along for a couple days on a tour with Skerik's Synchopated Taint Septet, some American anarcho-jazz musician friends of mine who were there playing some dates. I was hanging out in the dressing room with the band, along with a couple of the Japanese promoters. At one point a pipe was loaded and passed around. I was feeling a bit sick that night and opted out when it came my way, which makes it probably the best bowl of weed I *didn't* smoke in my entire life. But I surely had inhaled a few residual vapors, which was enough to have me worried. As it turned out, my fears were unfounded: Steve and I pissed clean. The hounds abandoned that tree, but the winds of the shitstorm were just starting to whip up.

* * * *

I came to Korea as an English teacher and was woefully uninformed about many aspects of the country before stepping onto the plane. One such thing was the Korean news media. *Prima facie*, it looked modern and healthy. There were many television stations with shiny, well-produced daily news programs; dour presenters delivered uninterrupted feeds from around Korea and the world. Glossy magazines and a variety of newspapers were widely available. The democracy itself—while somewhat young—was raucous and noisy and covered widely as such. One had only to witness one of the many brawls on the floor of the Korean National Assembly shown time and time again on domestic TV. This all seemed good and spirited and fitting with my idea of a free and responsible press.

But I'm no expert in *any* media, let alone that of Korea. Before actually seeing how they reported on the *Babopalooza* fiasco, I had just heard stories from other foreigners. Many expats complained that the Korean press was sensationalistic and quick to jump on the nationalist bandwagon. This was seen in 2002, during the massive anti-American protests over the deaths of the two middle school girls who were run down by a US Army vehicle. It is said that the papers and TV stations beat the emotional drum, repeatedly displaying inflammatory photos of the bodies, playing to base emotions in order to sell papers and garner ratings. On the Internet it was worse, with pure rumor-mongering, which we saw again during the anti-American beef uproar of 2008.

Of course the careless offenses of *Babopalooza* could not come close to the scope of the previous examples, but what this all points to is a general ethical laziness on the part of the Korean media, or at least a willingness to throw ethics to the wind when it suits them. We saw this straight away with a story that came out on *Babopalooza* in the *Kyunghang Shinmoon*, a newspaper out of Seoul. According to the article, our group's name was Right Down, and the title of our show was *Oriental Story*. What depths of his own ass the author drew these claims out of remains a mystery to this day, but what is painfully clear is that he had no real information at all, so rather than track it down, he instead chose to *make it up*. Much of the article goes on to make completely bogus claims, including:

- The seven band members were ordered to leave the country (they were not);
- That we called the practice of dog eating "strange" (we did not);
- That we said Koreans "even shit three times" (we did not);
- That we performed four times, rather than twice;
- That we performed for a total of 600 people, instead of 150.

Another, shorter piece was published on Daum.net, a popular Korean portal and news site. This piece went on to list the names of everyone who had gone to the police station. When a Korean friend of mine showed me the article, I could not recognize one name on this list. Once again, it was clear that the details had been fabricated. This may have been done for privacy's sake (Korea has stringent privacy and anti-defamation laws), but I nonetheless found it shocking.

We were braced for this thing to blow up in the Korean media, and for us to become the whipping boys and girls of Korea's notorious netizens—those anonymous nationalists who swarm and push Internet stories in attempts to light the flame to anti-Western and anti-American sentiment. Luckily, this time, the match failed to ignite the tinder. While *Babopalooza* proved to be a very popular topic of debate in the peninsula's English-language blogosphere, burning long threads on popular sites such as The Marmot's Hole, Scribblings of the Metropolitician, Dave's ESL Café, and Pusanweb, interest quickly abated among the Korean press… with the exception of the English-language dailies *The Korea Herald* and *The Korea Times*, which both ran fairly sympathetic (and much more accurate) takes on what had really gone down. The media coverage wasn't limited to Korea, either. Angry Steve's hometown paper, *The Daily Hampshire Gazette,* ran a story, along with Seattle's popular alternative weekly *The Stranger*, which couldn't pass up a write-up of a local theater son in hot water abroad for "artistic crimes."

After the police interviewed everyone involved that they could find, they shipped the files over to the General Prosecutor's office, where they languished on deck for six long months. During that time, everyone named in the investigation lived in a sort of limbo. We all kept our current jobs, as the uproar wasn't quite enough to get anyone fired on the spot and, for the moment, employers seemed to be willing to renew any contracts that came up. A couple of folks involved went back to their respective countries, flying the coop before any sanction could come down. The only people who got into trouble were the three people who changed jobs. Changing jobs required getting a brand new visa, and guess who still hadn't forgotten about a certain sketch? That's right: Immigration.

The three members of the Busan 9 (as we were known, despite the fact that about 15 were actually in hot water) who tried to change jobs were promptly denied new visas and told to leave the country, at least until the investigation had run its course. The first was my friend Sam, who got the news while vacationing in Thailand. The university that just hired him sent him a "We regret to inform you…" e-mail. This stung worse for him, since he had only appeared in one sketch, the only one that never even *mentioned* the word *Korea*. The two others managed to stick around: one by working illegally until everything blew over; the other by getting a new job under a second passport he just happened to own. Dual citizenship does have its privileges.

As for the rest of us, we stuck it out with the sword above our necks. I wanted to stay in Korea. After all, it had been good nearly three years, and the thought of going to another country and starting over—or worse yet, going home—didn't sit well. But none of us could predict what this prosecutor would do. It was up to him to move the case along or not. We had consulted with a Korean-American lawyer, but, without all of the information, he was unwilling to call an outcome, and to hire him to take the case was prohibitively expensive. My sense was, with the passage of time and general feeling of normalcy that had managed to return to our lives, that the prosecutor would wag his finger our way and let us off with a warning.

And that's pretty much what happened.

Angry Steve and I were finally summoned to the Stalinist-looking building which contained the office. We were led upstairs with our translator and seated in front the man himself, Mr. Yang. Mr. Yang smiled and tried to make us feel at home. He was definitely playing "good cop" to the more offended police who had originally questioned us. He produced a copy of the tape, which he said had been made by the detectives who came to the show. He fingered it and smiled, saying that he actually had *enjoyed* it, that he wasn't offended at all. It was as if he was playing his inferiors off as yokels and philistines for hauling us in to begin with, that he understood it was satire and good fun. But he did remind us that "this was Korea" and it would behoove us to be "more sensitive" in the future, and that there was no question we had broken the terms of our visas—something he was willing to forgive, providing we each wrote a brief letter "promising to not do it again," which we gladly did on the spot. In the end we shook hands and bowed, with Mr. Yang suggesting that we meet for a drink sometime, an offer that I have yet to take him up on.

But it wasn't over yet. The cops and courts may have been done with us, but not everyone was so willing to forgive. The first was my university, where I had worked for two years. Once the case was settled, they fired me. *Fired* isn't quite the right word, but in the summer of 2007, my request for a new contract was denied, via e-mail. No reason was given in their brief yet polite *fuck off* message. When I ran into the boss's secretary later that day and pressed her as to why, she informed me that it had something to do with "a performance" I had done. That was news enough, and I dropped it there. Six months later the same thing happened to Angry Steve, as well as to one of the musicians involved with the show.

I was quickly offered a new job at a two-year college in the middle of the city, and after a three-week stint in America I flew back to Busan and completed the necessary paperwork. *Babopalooza* was behind me, and despite the fact that I was canned over it, I had a new gig that in many ways was better than the previous one. I had just signed my contract and was waiting for my visa confirmation number when my new boss came knocking at my office door:

"Uhm. I am sorry. There is some… problem. The officer at

Immigration says that you did a bad thing. You must apologize before they give visa."

He led me into his office at once, where he sat me down at his computer, pointed to the open word processing program on the screen, and said "You must write a letter. Say *I'm sorry*."

"But I already wrote one for the prosecutor."

"Prosecutor? No. You must write for *Immigration*."

I nodded and began to type:

Dear Sirs and Madams,

Last year I was involved with a show that made fun of Immigration. This was a mistake which I wholly regret. I have nothing but the utmost respect for the men and women who don the uniform and risk their lives daily to enforce the most just laws of Korea. I apologize deeply and unreservedly, and promise to never ever ever ever do something so foolish again.

Sincerely,
Christopher John Tharp

Two days later I had my visa.

Though we all managed to make it through *Babopalooza* with just a stern talking-to, the effect of the ordeal was a complete chill for the performance scene in Busan. With the exception of a few musicians, most foreigners were afraid to step on a stage to do anything. We simply didn't know if we'd be hauled downtown for performing without permission. *Poetry Plus* wasn't performed for over a year, and when it did come back, there were just a handful of people performing to small, frightened crowd. It never found its feet again and since has been relegated to the past. Round Faced Productions—our nascent little theater company—was killed off before it could do any more. Everything went dormant for a while.

The expats up in Seoul were never scared off, as the cops up there have larger whales to poach, and over the last couple of years we have seen an explosion in theater, comedy, improv, and public readings done by expatriates. Emboldened by our brethren in the really big city, this is now happening in Busan. It finally seems safe to come out of the cave, and *Babopalooza* is just a memory for the old guard and a legend for the new. God willing, let's keep it that way.

INTERLUDE

AUGUST, 2007
OLYMPIA, WASHINGTON

IT'S good to be home, especially in August. Summer in the Pacific Northwest must be the best version of summer on Earth: warm days, cool nights, clear skies, cold water all around, and greens of every imaginable shade. The region's famous rains are nowhere to be seen.

I'm down at Batdorf and Bronson's, the town's signature coffee house. The place serves up coffees of the highest caliber and beans from around the world. The ceilings are high and light pours through the front window; it's airy and relaxing. Students mingle with state workers and hipsters and downtown business owners, making Batdorf's Olympia's true community coffee house. No elitist attitude here, folks. Just damn good coffee, mellow music, and newspapers all around. I just finished a Wednesday *New York Times* Crossword and feel very good about myself. We'll see if I can continue the streak into the week.

I love Olympia. I wonder if I could live here again?

I rode my bicycle down from Scott and Elizabeth's, which is where I always stay when I come into town. Elizabeth's at work at Intel and Scott's mixing music in his little home studio. Tonight I'll ride my bicycle into Lacey for dinner with the folks. I have dinner with them almost every night now. Afterwards, I stick around for a cup of coffee with Mom. We often watch a bit of TV—usually cop shows like *Law and Order* or *CSI: Miami.* Mom likes David Caruso's character; I think she identifies with his sadness, overcooked as it is. Dad does his best to stay up, but turns in very early. His energy is waning, that is for sure. The man is battling three life-threatening ailments and doesn't possess the spark he once did. That said, his appetite is still intact. Last night he downed enough spare ribs for three people.

Tomorrow we're heading to Offut Lake to catch some trout. Dad will stick to the dock, while I rent a little boat and take my nephews out on the water. We'll catch some fish and savor the day. That's all we can do, isn't it?

CHAPTER 12

COMMUNITY COLLEGE

AFTER the *Babopalooza* fiasco and my subsequent canning from Gaegum University, I experienced a spasm of second thoughts about staying in Korea. I had given the peninsula three intense years of my life and figured that this was a good time to make my exit. I didn't plan on moving back to America. I was determined to get into the ESL thing even deeper, to begin a teaching tour that would take me to more obscure, exotic, and dangerous locales. So I spent my afternoons scanning the international teaching job boards to see where my next adventure would take me: Mongolia? Kazakhstan? Ethiopia? I took in job ads from these places and more.

Suddenly Korea had become staid, old hat, no longer something that kindled the fire inside of me. Besides, I was single and had no serious commitments, other than a black-and-white cat I had adopted off of the street the year before. I had enough savings to easily cushion the shock of any move, and was actually buzzing at the prospect of something new. I was more than ready to go, but had yet to chisel the decision into granite. I was still open to staying in Korea, but only if things played out a certain way. So I told both my friends and myself this:

"I will only stay in Korea if a good job falls into my lap. I'm not going to go knocking on any doors. It has to come to me. If the phone rings and the offer is nice, I'll *consider* sticking around."

I had actually answered an ad and was now seriously considering a teaching gig in China. Not just anywhere in China, but in far Western China, on the edge of the Taklamakan Desert, in an oil boomtown named Korla. The pay was just a fraction of what I was making in Korea, but the cost of living was next to nothing and the location sounded interesting enough. Images of Bactrian camels, sand dunes, and feasts of roasted lamb flashed in front of my eyes. It was totally isolated, in a place with few foreigners. This would be a wildly different experience than this modern Korean life, where I was surrounded by hundreds of other expats and could access the net via the fastest connections on the planet. I felt the pull in my gut and had pretty much agreed to the job, when, one afternoon while I was sitting at home, the phone rang.

"Hey dude, it's Andrew." Andrew owned the Crown, as well as holding down a daytime teaching job. I lived just a ten-minute walk from the place and had passed uncountable hours sitting at the bar, talking and drinking beer. Andrew had grown to know me very well in the couple of years since he had taken the place over. The amount of trust that can be built between men through successive sessions of binge drinking can never be underestimated.

"Hey Andrew, what's up?"

"You want a job at my college? We need a couple of people."

"Uh… sure."

"Great. You got a job. Just bring me your resume, transcripts, and a photo sometime this week."

Click.

I felt my face flush as I hung up the phone. *Andrew just offered me a job at his cush little two-year college. This is exactly the phone call that I said would keep me here, and guess what? It came. So why don't I feel so stoked about it?*

Despite the fact that taking this job would squelch any plan I had to move on, that my dreams of brand-new, culturally disorienting environs would have to be put off indefinitely, I followed Andrew's directions and delivered the documents within a couple of days. I felt that I had no choice. I thought it totally unlikely that I would ever be offered a great gig *out of the fucking blue,* but here it was. I feel that sometimes, just sometimes, the universe sends us clear messages. This I could not ignore.

The next time we spoke, Andrew told me that he'd set up an interview very soon, but this didn't happen. I started to get concerned, because I was due to head home to the US for a few weeks, and as the departure date got closer, this crucial interview never materialized. The job in China was awaiting my decision as well, and here I was, in a limbo of sorts, entirely unsure of where I'd be in one and a half months' time. I talked to Andrew one more time the night before I was going to leave.

"Do I need to change my ticket? I still haven't met your boss and I'm scheduled to fly to Seattle tomorrow."

"Ahh… don't worry about it. I'm the head teacher there. I just tell 'em who to hire and they do it. Enjoy your trip, mate." Andrew flashed me his toothy Aussie smile. He had a cleft chin and blue-black hair, complete with a little forehead squiggle. He was covered in sweat and fryer grease from just having whipped up a few burgers in the war zone that was the kitchen of the Crown. This gave him the appearance of Superman, if the hero had traded his tights and cape for a t-shirt and sweat pants and had slathered himself in a light sheen of lard.

I ended up leaving the next day without having sat down to an interview. I had nominal faith in Andrew's promise, and just chose to surrender to my fate, leaving it in the hands of an Aussie barman, a Korean boss I'd never met, and, perhaps, God. But in the end, Andrew made good on his word. After only one week back home, I received an email from Suyeong College, officially inviting me to join their staff for the 2007-2008 school year. I now had a new job, with a contract that started exactly when my old one ended. The transition would be seamless. Andrew had come through, delivering me a full-time community college teaching job without so much as an interview. A year of drinking at the same bar can sometimes have its benefits. You gotta love Korea.

A Step Up or a Step Down?

Earlier, I made reference to the hierarchy that exists in the world of Korean ESL. At the top are the university jobs. At the bottom are the hagwons. And before, I had been at a large four-year *university*. It was by no means high or even mid-ranked—but it was a university. I was now at a two-year *junior college*. Within the ESL community, this is generally viewed as a demotion. After all, most anyone could enroll at our school. The place has almost no reputation: it's located in a nameless section of midtown Busan and to this day many of the people I meet here have no idea it exists. I had also taken a slight cut in my base pay (though this was easily made up for in the availability of extra classes—teaching adults and kids—that the college offered). So, when considered from a certain perspective, I had been knocked down a notch.

However, in other ways, I now had a much more prestigious gig. I was on a different visa: that of an actual, real, non-pretend professor, and this was reflected by my job title (as ridiculous as it may be). Instead of sharing a giant room with loads of the other foreign staff (there were only six at the new school), I was given an office, which I shared with only one colleague. We were given individual keys. The office was huge and had a good view of the city beneath, for Suyeong College was perched on a mountain even more precipitous than the one underneath my previous place of employment. Another perk of the new job was the class sizes. I taught small groups of students several times a week. Within a month I got to know their names. They all greeted me in the hall. The place was laid-back, lacking the institutional rigidity so pervasive at Gaegum University. I had a friendly boss who seemed to view me as something else than another foreigner who'd just come down the chute. Suyeong College just had a much more human feel, and after just a couple of months on board, I was happy for the move.

Two-year schools in Korea serve a few purposes, not so different from any community college back in the States. They're there to train people for specific careers, as well as to act as a stepping stone to a "real" four-year school. I was hired to teach in the Department of Hotel and Tourism English. The majority of my students were fresh-out-of-high school kids who had probably choked hard when it came time to take the college entrance exam. Some of them were pretty bright, a lot of them average, and a few about as inquisitive and mentally acute as driftwood. They were there ostensibly to improve their English, as well as to learn the nuts and bolts of the hotel and tourism business. About half planned on heading on to university, while the rest seemed content to enter the workforce after getting their two-year degrees. Not all of these students were 19-year-olds, however. In the mix were a good number of older students, in their late twenties and thirties. I never quite knew their story. I think some of them had flunked out of university when they were younger. A few never went at all. A handful of these students had actually lived abroad—in Australia, Canada, and the US—and spoke excellent English. To put them in a class where half the students couldn't even answer "What did you eat for lunch?" proved to be a challenge. The fact that the levels of ability varied so greatly proved to be a shortcoming at Suyeong College. It's hard to teach a class when the students are all over the map.

New Tricks for an Old Dog?

One student during my first year at Suyeong College stretched my patience to its snapping point. It had nothing to do with her behavior, per se, but more to do with her lack of ability to pick up even a whiff of English. She was an ajumma—probably in her mid-50s. For some reason she had decided to go back to school and study English. Why she chose English remains a mystery, given the fact that it was obvious she had no background in the language whatsoever. But this woman was a total sweetheart. She was incredibly nice and I very much liked her, personally. She attended every class and was never late. She'd sit with her book open and try to write down everything I said. She'd often bring a can of coffee or some juice, offering it up as a little gift before class started. But there was just one little problem: She couldn't say anything. I mean *nothing*. Even after several months of constant English bombardment, when I'd ask her, "Hello, how are you?" she was totally unable to reply with the requisite "I'm fine, thank you." A look of horror would invade her eyes, and she'd start babbling and stammering in an unintelligible garble of Korean and English, half-repeating the question over and over again in a frantic attempt to understand what it was that I asked her in the first place. She never improved: one full school year of five-days-a-week English study, and still no "I'm fine, thank you." Kindergartners learn this in *five minutes*. Not only was it astounding, it made me feel like a fraud, as well as a cynical jerkoff:

Why does she keep coming to school when clearly she's not improving at all? Should I sit down with her and gently tell her that it's hopeless, that she should give up, that she's clearly past the learning-a-new-language pull date and should spend her time gardening or learning pottery instead?

It was frustrating, because she bogged down the class. Once the speaking came around to her, the gears ground to an agonizing stop. I'd sometimes just skip her, but she was a tuition-paying student and deserved at least an inkling of effort on my behalf. I tried—I did try—but it was really like trying to get a Jell-o mold to speak. To put this into perspective, that same year I taught a mentally disabled man. He struggled and mainly just sat alone, in the back of the class, but by the end of two semesters, even he was able to hold a very basic conversation in English.

Is it just an age thing? Do we reach a point where our brain just says NO NEW *LANGUAGE!* I'm 40 now and still studying Korean, and while at times I wish for my more open teenage brain that picked up Spanish so quickly, I'm still doing okay, I am *improving*, slow as it may be. Or do I just think I am?

Yeah, we know that some people are better at learning languages than others. Like anything else, it's a knack that some folks possess to a greater degree. But is it possible to have a *total* language block, where no matter how much you study, you can never perform even the most basic task? I think maybe yes. I've seen it a handful of times with my students, as well with some expats here trying to get a handle on even the most elementary Korean. I think that sometimes the brain just refuses to go along...

Or maybe I'm just a really shitty teacher.

Beware of Thieves!

It was a really pleasant fall day during my first year at Suyeong College. It had been a great start to the semester and I was well settled into the rhythms of the job. The place was welcoming and really laid-back. I felt as if I had found a place where I could comfortably stay for quite some time without a problem or hassle. I had let my guard down.

It was three in the afternoon and I had finished my regular classes. I just had to head down the hill to teach an hour of kindergarten English and I was done. I only had ten minutes to get to the Social Education Building, where the class was held, so I went into my office and grabbed my bag and my keychain, which I had left sitting on my desk. I took the stairs down to the first floor and exited the building, taking the keys out of my pocket so I could hop onto my motorcycle and go. But the bike wasn't there.

Did I park it somewhere else? No. I never park it somewhere else.

I felt the blood leave my head, and my mouth suddenly dried up. When I looked at the keys in my hand, the truth slammed into me. My bike's ignition key, along with the one for the lock, was missing from the chain. Someone had come into my office, taken the keys from the ring, and stolen my bike.

Fuck fuck fuck fuck.

I sprinted up the stairs back toward the sixth floor. My boss needed to know that a major theft had just occurred. As I climbed the stairs, I ran into Tae-hyun, a student of mine. He saw that I was upset.

"Teacher, what is matter?"

"My motorcycle's been stolen. *Do-duk!,*" I said, throwing out the Korean word for *thief.*

"Oh, no. You are sure?"

"Yes, I'm sure! My keys are missing from my chain!" I held up the jingling mass.

"I will ask if anyone know about. I help you. Okay?"

When I erupted into my boss's office, he at once appealed for calm.

"This is very serious," he remarked, rising from behind his desk.

"I think it was one of my students."

"Oh, no… no… Maybe you should not say that. We must not… run to conclusion. Probably it is someone from outside the college. There are some bad people who come."

"But they stole the keys right out of my office. It has to be someone who knows not only that the bike is mine, but that I also sometimes leave the keys on my desk."

"You must always lock your door. Even when you use the restroom. Let us look some more. If we cannot find, I will call the police."

I walked down to the kiddy class in a Hitlerian mood, foul as a cold cup of black bile. The kids were oblivious to my situation, other than the fact that Gorilla Teacher was in no mood to play. I made a few copies of a coloring sheet featuring a giant clown, passed out some crayons, and sat in the front of the classroom, percolating in my own juicy hatred. Toward the end of class, my phone buzzed. It was Cowboy, a recent Suyeong graduate who now worked as the department's secretary and general assistant.

"Hello, this is Cowboy. You must come to front gate security building. We see thief on CCTV."

After class I met Cowboy at the security shed. He was on the phone when I approached, speaking lightning Korean in dark, threatening tones. He hung up and said to me: "Look." He led me inside the guard's kiosk and pointed to a screen. On it was a grainy shot of the back of my bike. A young man wearing a white jacket could be seen riding.

"Do you know who that is?"

Cowboy nodded his head in the affirmative, just as a security guard rolled up on his motor scooter.

"Go. Get on," Cowboy said.

I jumped on the back of the scooter and we were off, zipping up the hill and pulling into the gargantuan LG Apartment City development next to the school. The multiple towers rocketed over us like canyon walls, giving us the look of insects. We rode into one of the place's many parking areas and stopped in the front. Right there, sitting in a space between two cars, was my motorcycle—my black-and-orange Hyosung Troy 125.

Just moments later, Cowboy pulled up on the back of another security scooter.

"Here, Chris." He handed me my ignition key. "I am sorry."

"But Cowboy—who did this? Who did you see on the tape? This was one of my students, right?"

"I… I am sorry. I cannot say."

****

The next day I was summoned to Professor Kim's office. As I walked in, he stood up and invited me to take a seat. His expression was grim, as if we were heading to a funeral. I also sensed a tinge of embarrassment, recognition that my prediction had been right: one of my own students had indeed tried to steal my bike.

Professor Kim dialed his phone, uttering a few words before hanging up. One minute later there was a knock at the door. The door then opened, revealing Tae-hyun, the student that I had run into immediately after discovering the bike was missing.

The sneaky little fucker.

He hung his head as he shuffled in, placing his gaze firmly on the floor. He clutched a paper in his shaking fist.

Professor Kim barked a few terse phrases his way, to which Tae-hyun could only reply in Korean, *yes.* I tasted his shame. I felt a heat rise in my chest and fought the compelling urge to slap the kid's head.

"I had him write a note of apology." Professor Kim cued the student, who handed me the note, avoiding even a glimpse of my eyes. The note read as follows:

> *Yesterday, I went to your room to be given sam professor's lesson print. There were no professores, then I thought print is on the desk. I looked at deskes accidentally, I saw Bike' key. Ordinary time, I have thought Jone professor's Bike is great. As soon as, I saw the key, I though I'm very wish for riding the Jone' bike. I knew that casue big trouble. with no scared my, my hands went to the key. I stolen Jone's bike keys, as soon as out of room I went down riding the bike, but starting was difficult, I put the bike in an apartment parking space. not catch sight of the bike. Next I ran back to the college. I repented all along from when I stolen bike key and go out of the room. My big troubles scared me keeping up. then I knew mistakes. When I met Jone that stolen the bike, I couldn't tell you the fact. keeping*

> *up I was scared when lesson next lesson. I repented keeping up when lesson in the middle. then I got a calling from breaking I gave the key to breaking I know my fault. I beg forgiving to you. stealing professor's precious bike, that I told you the lie sincerly I beg pardon. I'm sorry you.*

After I finished the note, Tae-hyun bowed to me several times, apologizing both in Korean and English. He then left, leaving me alone with Professor Kim, who took the opportunity to press for leniency.

"It would be best not to involve the police in this matter. In Korea, a police record is very serious, and will stay with him for the rest of his life. He is young. Perhaps we should leave the punishment for his family."

"Well can't you at least expel him from the school? In the USA, he would be automatically expelled, *no questions asked*."

"That is a problem. If we expel him for committing a crime, then we *must* also press charges. So we cannot expel him without involving the police."

"Okay. Okay. But I don't want to see him in any of my classes again. Automatic F."

"Yes, I will tell him that. But please, please… please do not let any other professors or students know the name of the young man who did this. It is a very delicate matter. I hope you understand."

"Sure. It's just between you and me," I lied.

If this had been America, I may have acted differently, but I chose to shut up, to go along with my boss, to avoid making waves (as much as possible), since keeping your head down is what really translates into job security on the peninsula. To do so did chafe, however, since I knew for a fact that this student was no joy-rider, that his theft of my bike was as premeditated as it gets. Just a few days before, he had come into my office with a can of coffee from a vending machine. Very few students actually came into my office during that first year, so I already thought it strange. He gave me the can and told me he wished to hang out and practice English. I noticed that he was very jittery at the time, which I just chalked up to nerves from speaking English face-to-face with a foreigner. He lingered for less than two minutes—so much for the English lesson. Little did I know, he was actually casing my office that day. My keys were lying right there on the desk.

On the day he stole my bike, he parked it across the street, hiding it in a giant parking lot between two cars. He then came straight back into the school and made his next, afternoon class, erasing any suspicions among others that he was the thief. What the kid forgot to consider was that all three gates that lead into Suyeong College are monitored by CCTV. Any vehicle coming or going gets captured—including motorcycles, both legitimate and stolen. Tae-hyun had planned on finishing his school day and taking off with the bike later that night. It was obvious he was stashing it and trying to cover his tracks. The only reason he confessed was because he had been caught red-handed. I knew that, Cowboy knew that, and Professor Kim knew that, but in Korea, the truth often gives way to saving face.

CHAPTER 13

KIMCHEE FLOWERS

"Alcohol… it's a son of a bitch, y'all."

—The Butthole Surfers, "Alcohol"

LET'S get one thing clear: Korea is a drinking country. If you enjoy tipping the bottle, sipping the sauce, hitting the hooch, and getting straight-up *drunk*, this is the country for you. Alcohol is served everywhere, at all times. Drinking is not just what's done, it's *encouraged.* It's viewed as a way to bond with friends and co-workers, as well as a necessary pressure-release valve in this high-stress, work-around-the-clock culture. For a person who loves booze of all stripes, Korea is a kind of paradise. It's like Disneyland for alcoholics.

One of the most interesting thing about this country is how there is almost no stigma attached to over-drinking. It is, instead, often viewed as a badge of honor—especially among men—where nightly drinking rituals are seen as a test of manhood, a proving of your *cojones*. Shots are poured and backs are slapped and frosty glasses of beer are filled for all in the group to take down. To sit out a round can be viewed as an insult of sorts, or at least a way to show your true pansy colors. Real Korean men *drink*. It's just part of the gig. This goes all the way to the morning. You can show up at work in a wrinkled shirt, bleary-eyed with unkempt hair, and stinking of drink from the night before, and your boss will usually pull you aside and say:

"Yesterday, many drinking?"

You look him in the eye and slowly nod.

"Oh! Very good! Very good!" he gushes, vigorously shaking your clammy hand. In fact, you're that much more likely to get that big promotion. He knows he can trust you.

None of this is to say that women don't drink here as well. They do, especially these days, where the previous cultural prohibition against women knocking it back is pretty much a thing of the past. In Korea it is very common to see groups of women in their twenties or thirties sharing pitchers of beer, sipping soju at the ubiquitous barbecue joints, or getting into some cocktails at the club. Younger women feel free to drink, and no scolding or finger-wagging from elders is going to stop this trend, just one of many in the Westernization of a generation of Korean women. Smoking in public is still a different matter, though again we see this taboo broken with increasing frequency.

Drinking in Korea is different than drinking in the most Western countries, where we usually just drink recreationally with friends, or in an attempt to chase down desirable members of the opposite sex. Drinking for fun does, of course, exist in Korea, but consumption of alcohol takes on a whole other role: that of group bonding. Despite being the most visibly outgoing of all East Asians, Koreans can still be quite shy with strangers, so alcohol is used as a lubricant for Koreans who are unfamiliar with each other. At university this takes its form as what's known as the MT, which stands for *membership training*. This usually consists of an overnight retreat to a beach or mountain getaway with a meal, followed by some group trust and teambuilding games, all of which culminate in a monster drinking session, where even the shyest and most teetotaling of the group are plied with booze. Every spring I am forced to accompany my students on an MT. We wander from room to room, quaffing countless shots of soju, eating chicken and steamed pigs' feet, all the while watching while hapless students drink themselves messy.

After graduating from university and joining a company, this bonding-through-getting-smashed ritual takes the form of the *hweshik*, which is a dinner-and-drinking session with your boss and coworkers. This almost always consists of a meal of grilled meat and soju, followed by a visit to a beer house or *hof*, as they're commonly known (borrowed from the Germans via the Japanese—a holdover from the colonial era), climaxing in an hour or two at the *norae-bang* (karaoke room). These work excursions can be once every few months or several times a week, depending on the company, and while attendance isn't technically compulsory, to miss out is to put your good graces with your colleagues—not to mention your future with the company—in jeopardy.

I've been on many, many a hweshik and generally enjoy them, since I'm rarely one to turn down a good meal or a drink, and—being a performer by nature—am not shy to jump up on the mike and belt out a song… especially when lubed with booze. But others are not so game to eat and drink with everyone from work. Many of my Western friends chafe at being dragged out to a hweshik: some people hate drinking and others implode at the mere thought of singing in front of others. This goes for Koreans as well. Much of the drinking at a hweshik is nearly forced. When you finish your drink, another is immediately poured for you. Toasts are constantly made, and if you don't drink up with everyone else, you will often be scolded. This usually happens under the watchful of eye of your boss, as well, so more than often the alcohol will go down your gullet whether you like it or not.

This idea that you must drink because you *have to*, not because you *want to*, was recently challenged by a young woman working for an online game company. In 2007, unable to endure any more forced drinking sessions, she quit the company and sued. The Seoul High Court ruled in her favor, awarding her $32,000 in damages. Though this has led to some companies adopting rules to mitigate mandatory drinking during the hweshik, it has, in truth, done little to lessen the binge drinking that goes on nightly throughout the whole nation. You just have to walk the streets of Seoul, Daegu, or Busan around 11 p.m. on any given night, and you will see adult men in full suits passed out cold on park benches, in subway stations, and sometimes right on the street itself. Fresh puddles of vomit adorn the sidewalks: mixtures of half-digested rice, pork, and red gochujang. A common nickname for them is kimchee flowers.

****

So alcohol is indeed the Korean drug of choice. It's pretty much the only thing available and the only thing consumed. It's the one intoxicant allowed in this pressure cooker society. Other drugs—illicit drugs—which are rife though out much of the globe, are strangely absent in Korea. Though Korea is a peninsula, it is effectively an island, since the DMZ cuts off the only land route available. Contraband must come by air or sea.

However, this doesn't stop other island nations from procuring their fair share of illegal drugs. One need only look so far as the UK, New Zealand, or even Japan—all places where drugs of many stripes are widely available. But why not Korea? Why is Korea just a nation of boozers? Where are the stoners, the cokeheads, the tweekers, and the junkies?

I have neither read nor heard a lot of theories as to why, but one would have to chalk it up to demand. Koreans, for the most part, don't do illicit drugs. Few of them that I've talked to over the years—and there have been many—know the first thing about them. They know they exist, and that they're somehow *bad*, but that's usually the end of it. They certainly don't have enough information to compare them to each other: for many Koreans, marijuana and heroin are pretty much the same thing, never mind that one is vastly more harmful than the other. They both are against the law, and that's that. The prevailing point of view (I hesitate to call it wisdom) seems to be *Why would they be made illegal if they weren't nearly equally bad for you?*

In many ways, the Sixties really never arrived on this nation's rocky shores. That said, I have heard stories of some drug subcultures popping up, though these have been almost exclusively limited to the more worldly environs of Seoul. Meth made a bit of a splash some years back—it's a wonder it's not everywhere, considering the (temporary) boost it would give these work and study-obsessed people. Customs and the police do periodically bust people smuggling both opiates and ecstasy tablets—I've seen a few stories in the national news—with the contents lain out on table in front of a legion of cameras; this does indicate a demand. Although marijuana does make it onto these shores, and some is grown domestically in small-time operations in the hills and countryside, it is not and has never been used on anything approaching a large scale. So to say that South Korea is entirely free of illegal drugs would be a lie, though it must have one of the lowest usage rates in the world.

The Korean government also takes ALL illegal drug use very seriously, and vigorously prosecutes anyone caught using or having used drugs (positive piss test = possession). There is a zero-tolerance attitude toward drugs in the country, and this no doubt deters those kids who may be curious to at least try them once or twice. The government especially keeps its eyes on the foreign community—us English teachers in particular—for evidence of illegal drug use. It's no secret that many of us enjoy marijuana in our home countries—where, in some places, it's basically legal. Some ESL teachers do manage to smuggle or procure a bit while on the peninsula, and the police do not hesitate to aggressively go after anyone from the expat community found in possession. The authorities have been known to go through the phones of those caught, demanding drug tests from every foreigner listed in the phone book, in an attempt to net as many users as possible. Just *knowing* someone involved with drugs can get you in trouble with the police here.

This local naiveté about drugs is refreshing sometimes, given the jaded and violent drug culture that ravages communities in many of our home countries. For example, hip-hop music and culture are wildly popular among the youth of Korea, and, at least for a while, marijuana imagery was prevalent throughout the genre. I've seen countless pot leaves adorning the hats and shoelaces of young people, almost none of whom, I'm sure, have ever tried the stuff. One time, walking down the halls at Suyeong College, I spotted a student wearing an oversized t-shirt with a massive cannabis leaf printed on the front. I was curious whether he knew what it was, so I stopped him, pointed to his shirt, and asked. He looked down, shook his head, and sheepishly admitted that he had *no idea.*

* * * *

This country is awash in booze of many varieties, though drinking it may not be as simple as one may think. Koreans are very ritualistic in their drinking practices, with rigid customs and protocol which must be adhered to, lest you commit a faux pas that causes everyone in the group to cringe. While I'm certainly not an expert on Korean culture, I have learned a thing or two about downing *sul* (alcohol) while I've been here, and the following are some of my observations:

Some General Guidelines about Drinking with Koreans in Korea

- *Never pour your own drink.*
  This is the cardinal rule of Korean drinking etiquette. Pouring your own drink not only makes you look like a greedy bastard, but it deprives your drinking partners of doing you the courtesy of pouring your drink for you, which is the height of respect in this culture.

- *Always drink with food.*
  With the exception of severe street alcoholics, Koreans pretty much never drink without some sort of side dish to snack on. These sides are called *anju* and are often mandatory at Korean-style drinking establishments, where the beer and soju may be dirt-cheap, but the anju dishes run between ten and twenty bucks a pop. This mandate to buy food can be disconcerting for Westerners who just want to sit down for a few beers, but for Koreans the practice goes without question. Even a couple of beers consumed on a plastic table outside of a convenience store will be accompanied by a bag of crunchy snacks or some *juipo*—a dried and compressed fish jerky of sorts. This practice may seem a bit of overkill to Western drinkers, but this is how Koreans do it, and it does help to soak up the alcohol and slow down the pace.

- *Always share your bottle and drink from a glass, or in the case of rice wine, a drinking bowl.*
  In Western countries we usually drink liquor and wine from one bottle, which is shared by the group. In this respect we are no different from Koreans. When drinking beer, though, we often just drink out of our own bottles, even large ones. Most beer in Korea comes in big bottles and is meant to be poured into smaller glasses; to take a bottle for your own and drink straight from it is seen as the height of savagery. Sam, unaware that he was no longer in Idaho, was guilty of this practice when he first arrived, much to the horror of the local Busanites, who stared at him with mouths agape. *Not done.*

- *When pouring drinks, always pour the eldest's first. When drinking with co-workers, this will almost always be your boss or manager.*
  This is very important, and reflects the respect for and observance of hierarchy in this still-very-Confucian society. Moreover, it's just really polite. A foreign guest will often be the exception to this rule, however. In this case, the most senior of the group will pour the guest's drink in an attempt to honor and defer to the foreigner. If you find yourself in this situation, just smile and graciously accept the honor.

- *When pouring a drink—especially for someone older than you—do one of the following with your non-pouring hand: place it over your heart, touch it to the middle of your pouring arm, or pour the bottle with two hands.*
  Two hands is the rule here. To give or receive something with only one hand is seen as disrespectful. This goes for money as well, a custom that I believed to be universally Asian, until the first time I went to Japan and noticed the confused looks I garnered every time I touched my arm when receiving change at the store.

- *If you really want to show someone respect and affection, give him your glass and then fill it up.*
This is a custom that only applies to men drinking with men, and pretty much only when soju is involved. When you are finished with your glass (soju is usually sipped out of shot glasses), flick out whatever trace remains are in the bottom with a snap of your wrist, hand it to the man in question, and respectfully fill his glass. He will invariably reciprocate and probably be intensely impressed that you have learned the custom. Your Korean points will go up massively if you can execute this one well.

- *Always participate in the toasts.*
Koreans love nothing more than to clink glasses together with a rousing shout of "Gonbae!" every sixty seconds or so. Make sure to always join in and drink afterwards, even if it grows tedious, which it will.

- *When opening a new bottle of soju, give the base of the bottle a few good slaps.*
Whether or not this is a national custom or specific to the South Kyungsang Province area that I call home, I cannot say; I am told that one slaps the bottle in order to get rid of evil spirits, which is important in a nation where shamanistic rituals are regularly performed on the beach and fortune tellers can be found in most every shopping center. This, like the giving up of your glass, will surely impress most everyone who you are drinking with.

- *Know what "love shots" mean.*
If someone does a "love shot" with you, which involves intertwining arms and pouring drinks into each others' mouths, they are most likely *very* interested in you.

- *Never drink and drive.*
  While this is a no-brainer in any country, it is especially good to keep in mind in Korea, where drunk driving is just about the only traffic law that is regularly and vigorously enforced. All of the main cities have roving checkpoints working seven days a week, and even one or two beers in your system could see you facing a fine of around US$1000, or worse. Taxis are generally affordable, so don't hesitate to jump in one instead. Another option is to have a Korean friend call a designated driver. These are licensed drivers who will come to where you are and very soberly drive your car and you home, where they, in turn, will be picked up by their own driver. It costs only 10 or 20 dollars and is well worth it, when compared with the risk of doing it yourself.

****

A whole book could be dedicated to the history of alcoholic beverages in Korea and the variety available today. I will make no attempt to document the no-doubt countless ways to booze it up on the peninsula, but rather give a rundown of the most common ones presently out there.

Korean Concoctions Described

- *Soju*
  Soju is the national drink of Korea and has already been referenced and described *ad infinitum* in these here pages. It usually comes in little green bottles and tastes like a kind of vodka lite. This clear beverage is drunk with most Korean cuisine and on its own as well, though always with side dishes. Soju was originally made from sweet potatoes, but these days its origin is mysterious… though I've been told it is made from diluted industrial alcohol. It's wicked stuff that can wreak havoc on

your system. Even though it's (usually) only half the strength of proper vodka, it is deceptively potent, and often causes people to lose their phones, their keys, their wallets, their clothing, their better judgment, and many cases, their minds. And be warned: a soju hangover is only slightly better than a case of Ebola.

- *Baekseju*
  Baekseju is an herbal-based fermented rice wine, which is made from traditional methods and contains ginseng. It is viewed as a kind of health liquor; legend has drinking it will allow you to live to one hundred years old. This is reflected in the name of the drink, which contains the world *baek*, meaning *one hundred.* It's a little sweet and much easier on the system than soju. Though not so popular these days, it is widely available and is sometimes consumed as an alternative to the latter.

- *Makeoli* and *Dong Dong Ju*
  Makeoli and *dong dong ju* are essentially the same drink—a sweet and milky white brew made from rice and water. They are served up in big bowls and ladled into smaller ones. *Dong dong ju* is said to be less refined, with bits of rice floating throughout the drink, though most Koreans will probably be at a loss to really tell you the difference between the two. I've often asked and can never get a straight answer. These rice wines were originally consumed by farmers and are considered the most rustic of Korean alcoholic drinks. They are often sipped on the mountain, complimented by the popular Korean pancake known as *pajeon. Makeoli* has grown in popularity outside of Korea, especially in Japan, where there is said to be a *makeoli* craze these days. It is really fun to drink and will get you loopy as hell, though the high sugar content can make your head feel like a toxic waste dump the next day.

- *Beer*

  Korean beer is basically limited to three brands: Hite (Shite), Cass (Ass), and O.B. (Oh Pee!), though these days several sub-varieties are being introduced (the best of which is Max). These generally attempt to imitate American-style lagers and pilsners, resulting in a light, watery brew. As evidenced by the nicknames garnered, a lot of foreigners deride Korean beer for being awful—Hite especially. Most Korean brews are evidently made using corn (among many other ingredients), giving them a slightly sweet taste and causing any visiting Germans to turn up their noses and shake their heads in disbelief: there are no brewing purity laws in the Land of the Morning Calm. Sometimes the beer has a slight chemical taste, no doubt the result of preservatives. Rumor has it that formaldehyde is used, and though I've yet to have this confirmed. That said, the beer is light and crisp and goes well with grilled meat and is easy to drink during the sweaty Korean summers. I still drink it regularly and generally regard the haters to be whiners; while not great, Korean beer isn't *that bad.* Or could it just be that I've lost all perspective—that I've been in this country far too long?

CHAPTER 14

THE TALE OF AUSSIE MACK

DESPITE the statistics to the contrary, some of the expats here are indeed not angels. And while almost none even approach the downright sociopathic behavior described in Amit Gilboa's *Off the Rails in Phnom Penh*, which highlights a pack of champion scumbags slumming it in mid '90s Cambodia, Asian expat life always seems to attract a certain unsavory element, to put it in its mildest terms. I've met and known a fair share of raging boozeheads, compulsive brawlers, and serial fornicators. I remember a wall of a Canadian man who swung at everything that moved and once smashed in a taxi's windshield with his fists. I knew an Englishman who would get so drunk that he'd wander from bar to bar in his pajamas. I knew a Kiwi who bragged about smoking cigarettes in class (he taught kids), an Irish guy who spent every moment of his generous university vacations whoring in the Philippines, and a Texan whose racist utterances would make a KKK Grand Wizard blush. And then there was Aussie Mack.

As the name implies, Mack was from Australia, and when I met him he had been teaching in Korea for already a number of years. He was an obvious thug, though he was very friendly with Andrew, the proprietor of the Crown, where some of the most hard-drinking of the expat crowd used to pass the time. Mack was a mass of sinew, with dark, close-cropped hair, and angry-looking tattoos slithering around his arms. His expression was a perpetual scowl, and he spat out his words, as if each utterance stung his throat, palate, and tongue before being hissed at a hostile universe. Mack had known Andrew back in Oz and felt comfortable around him, so the Crown was pretty much the only place you would ever run into the guy. This was an unfortunate fact for many of the patrons, for Mack was a bully of the highest order, and after two or three white Russians, he was always looking for a fight. And as he was a bully, this was usually with the weakest-looking guy in the room.

Mack looked tough and was tough. Some bullies are all bluster and hot air—this guy was not. When he threatened you, he meant it, and was more than capable of backing up his words. He'd grown up in a mixed-race family of rugby players. A close relative of his had once started for the Wallabies, Australia's beloved national rugby squad. The man was no stranger to violence.

I first met him over an informal poker game. Texas Hold 'em poker had spread around much of the English-speaking world, and was just getting its start among the expats of South Korea. The Crown was the first bar to host a regular game, before it spread to almost every joint in town, only to disappear over the course of a year, like any fad is fated to do. Mack had never played the game before, and while I was certainly no expert, I understood the basic form of play, and began to get a bit impatient when old Mack could never figure out what was going on each time the bet came his way. Hold 'em tournaments are already interminable exercises—this is one of the reasons that I've pretty much quit playing the game—as I suspect it is with most everyone else. But I have a hard time masking my annoyance, and Mack, while slow to pick up the betting rules for that particular card game, was no idiot, and quickly got his hate on for me, glaring across the table and saying, slowly and deliberately:

"I don't like you. I don't like you at all."

Andrew, who was playing next to me, tried to assuage the growing anger of his Aussie acquaintance. "He's all right, mate. Just make your play."

Mack put down his cards and continued his death-glare. "No. I don't like his fucking attitude. I think he needs to apologize."

Seeing which way the table was tilting, I granted his request and apologized at once, which really didn't make things good, but allowed me to walk away that night with my limbs attached and my jaw intact.

Like most of us, Mack was in Korea teaching English, specializing, amazingly enough, in kindergartners. He made his living teaching the youngest of the young—tiny, tiny kids. I had never once seen the guy crack a smile; instead he'd always stare right through people. The chip on his shoulder was a towering, dreadful thing to behold. If he put the fear of God into the deep centers of adults, how must he be viewed by 6 and 7-year-old Koreans, who can cry for weeks on end at just the sight and sound of a foreigner? I think that we are often seen as huge, horrific monsters by these little guys. How must have they viewed Mack?

"He graduated from college? No way, man." One night, after Mack had staggered up the stairs of the Crown to an unfortunate taxi out front (his Korean was nonexistent), Sam confided his disbelief in Mack's credentials. "There is *no way* that guy has a college degree."

Mack wasn't just a bully in that he intimidated other people. He had beaten several guys up and loved to brag about it. One of his victims was the hapless Rob, another one of the poker crew. Rob was a short dumpy guy from Wyoming who had crossed words with Mack and paid the price: a complete beat down. Mack had reportedly kicked Rob in the head and ribs, resulting in a three-week hospital stay that Mack was forced to pay for over the course of a year.

"Yeah, I put him in the hospital and paid out six grand. He deserved it and you know what? I'd do it again. When he was there he whinged the whole time. He cried and called his mother. He called his *mother*. Can you believe it? How can he call himself a man?"

Mack eventually grew to like me, which may have been worse than having him hate me. I had picked up my guitar one night and gave a bit of a concert down at the Crown, singing some original tunes mixed in with some rock and roll covers. Mack was very impressed by this and decided that I was now cool. After this he always wanted to talk to me; he would sit beside me and clink a glass and tell me how good he thought my playing was. But I never could trust him. It was like being around a terribly aggressive dog that has grown used to you. Sure, it may wag its tail and lick your hand, but you still knew that at any moment the thing could snap, that it could chase you down and chew your face off. Any conversation with Mack was like this.

Even though he professed a new liking for me, Mack hated Sam and would usually try to goad him into a fight at the bar. He tried to fight everyone, unless they were obviously bigger than him. One night Sam and I had had enough: we plotted to ambush Mack, to follow him home while he was drunk and take him down with baseball bats, just to shut him up. This was just beer-fueled bravado, however. Despite our drunken oaths for justice, we swallowed our plan and never spoke of it again. That didn't stop others, though. We weren't the only ones dreaming of Mack's demise.

One night he was followed home by little Rob—whom he had gravely beaten a year before—along with Arthur, who was the most massive Texan on the peninsula. Mack had also run afoul of Arthur, and Arthur, with the aid of a revenge-seeking Rob, exacted just that, beating the hell out of the boozed-up Mack.

The next day I saw him at the Crown. He was just about to board a plane to Manila to visit his Filipina wife, and was medicating himself with booze. Both eyes were black and a front tooth was shattered, its jagged remnants jutting toward his swollen tongue. His left arm was in a sling. He looked as rough as it gets, but was nonplussed.

"It's not the end of the world, mate. It's just a fight. It's not the end of the world." He shrugged and gulped down his mixture of vodka, Kahlua, and milk.

I got the impression that this wasn't the first beating old Mack had taken, nor would it be his last.

Mack came back from the Philippines a month or so later, with his wife in tow. She was a lovely girl he had taken out of a Manila bar and married. Her English wasn't great, though I wouldn't know, since I made sure that my conversations with her were brief as possible. Mack would often bring her along to the bar, leave her at one end, and then go around and talk to or threaten whichever unfortunate patrons decided to brave his presence that night. It was always the same. He would—white Russian spilling in his hand—walk up to an unsuspecting customer and make small talk, eventually culminating in ominous words related to how he planned on negatively impacting their dentistry. This had a chilling effect. His poor wife would be consigned to sit alone and stare into space, no doubt bored beyond comprehension. She was pretty and friendly, but no one dare even cast a glance her way, for fear of stoking Mack's sizzling ire.

The last time I saw Mack was the only time I saw him get his fight. Again he was there, smoldering at the bar, gulping his milky fuel. He had tried to go after Sam, but Sam knew how to avoid trouble with Mack and pretty much ignored him—so he then turned his sights onto Wes. Wes was a slight American guy who greeted everyone with an "aw shucks" smile. He was sweet as honey, though bright as a five-watt bulb. He just liked to have a drink, listen to some rock and roll, laugh, and smile in that happy, relaxed, California beach style. He was the opposite of tough, and if not the sharpest guy in the room, he was a real heart. Mack had cornered him, and Wes, sensing tension, offered to pour Mack a drink out of his personal bottle of Jack Daniels whisky which stood on the bar.

"I don't want your fucking whisky, mate. You taking the piss? You trying have a go?"

"No, man. I'm cool. I just wanna have a good time."

"I'll show you a good time, you cunt. Let's go. Let's have a fight."

"I don't want to fight with you, man," Wes looked around for support. Eyes averted his gaze.

"I'm not asking you if you want to or not, Yank. We're going to fight."

"All right, Mack, all right. That's enough, mate." Andrew's tolerance for Mack had reached a limit. "You can't pick fights with everyone in the bar, mate. I think it's time for you to go."

Mack stood and squared up with Andrew, who had now stepped out from behind the bar, looking him in the eyes.

"Enough's enough. You've had enough to drink. You need to go home."

Mack held his ground for a moment, shrugged, then took down the rest of the white Russian in one swallow.

"Have it your way, mate. I'm fucking off."

He swayed and lost his footing, stumbling into the bar and knocking his glass to the floor in the process, where it fell and shattered. Andrew got under one of Mack's tattooed arms and walked him to the door. Mack's wife meekly followed. Andrew then opened the door of the pub and aided Mack on the long hike up the steep, treacherous stairs.

Sweating, Andrew returned through the door, and made his way around the bar.

"Sorry, lads. He's an old mate but a bit of a psychopath. I just can't have him acting like this anymore. It's just bad for business."

We all nodded and took a sip; the sentiment was shared by all. *Good riddance.*

With that, there was an enormous clamber outside of the door:

BUDAGA-BUDAGA-BUDAGA-BUDAGA-BUDAGA-BUDAGA-BUM!!

A figure lay at the bottom of the stairs. It was Mack. He was half-conscious and bleeding badly from two gashes on his head. He was a wreck. He had slipped at the top of the stairs and tumbled down to the bottom. He had done everything he could to provoke a fight; he had needled, cajoled, and threatened. He tried to fight with the bar all night and, in the end, he got his wish. But the bar won.

Mack was deported soon after that. He had told me that Immigration authorities had already questioned him several times about his chronic brawling, but that's not why they ended up giving him the boot. It seems that under close scrutiny, his bachelor's degree didn't pass muster. It was, in fact, a forgery, most likely procured down a Bangkok backstreet, where such things are readily offered up. Sam was right. There was no way that Mack had graduated from college. He was a fraud. And like Al Capone, he was done in on a technicality.

INTERLUDE

CHRISTMAS DAY, 2007 TE ANAU, NEW ZEALAND

I'M in the far south of the South Island, spending my first Christmas ever in the Southern Hemisphere, though you wouldn't know it from the slicing winds whipping off of the huge lake in front of the town. It's supposed to be summer, but warm weather has yet to arrive in Te Anau. The winters must be murder.

Sam and his brother are back at the hotel, eating from the Christmas buffet. At fifty bucks a head I found it a bit dear, electing instead to fill my belly at an outdoor burger truck—the only thing open in this comatose town. I gobbled down a double-patty grease bomb with a fried egg on top. Kiwis throw fried eggs on almost everything. No wonder Peter Jackson filmed *Lord of the Rings* down here. These people eat like hobbits.

Yesterday we came down from the mountain after a four-day trek up the Greenstone River. We spent the whole time stalking monster trout in the gale-beaten valley, battling wind, rain, and swarms of biting sand flies, which turned my ankles into raw meat. I landed several giant rainbows on black woolly buggers, though the fish are so big that they're actually snapping a lot of my leaders. I've already lost a lot of expensive flies, as well as my digital camera. This already-pricey trip costs more every day.

New Zealand is even more beautiful than expected, but it is a sleepy place, seemingly mired 20 years behind the rest of the Western world. Everything closes early and the streets are as empty as ghost towns.

Suyeong College regularly sends students to New Zealand on internship programs, and while these kids always return to Korea refreshed, they inevitably complain about how boring the place is, especially compared with the 24-hour charge that is life in Busan.

I called home yesterday, talking to my dad from the front desk phone at the hotel in Queenstown. Dad put his best voice forward, forcing a cheer that I knew was truly absent. He was interested in the fishing, of course, and I was proud to tell him of my success. I told him I loved him before hanging up. It was the last conversation we'd ever have.

CHAPTER 15

DAD

THE call came in the morning. The buzzing stirred me from my sleep, and I climbed over the still-dozing Da-jin—who had risked her mother's wrath by staying over—jumped out of my bed and stumbled over to the desk where my phone lay. The number on the display screen was long and unrecognizable, a sure sign of an international call. What time was it in America? After several years, the math still turned me around, especially at 8:30 a.m. on a Saturday, before I'd even had a whiff of coffee.

"Hey Chris, it's Mark..."

Despite the murkiness of my head, I recognized that Mark never called at this time of day; in fact, he rarely called at all. Most of my family phone time was spent with either my mother or my brother Glen. And once he spoke, I immediately heard that his voice carried the *tone*, the tone we all recognize and hope to never feel oozing out of the end of the receiver. Deep and concerned. Pressing. Grave.

"It's Dad..."

I held my breath and waited for the worst—waited for the words that almost always follow the tone—but I was spared, at least for the time being. He wasn't dead... at least, not yet. He was in the hospital and it was bad and yes, this may be it. The information was spotty and inconclusive. Mark didn't know for sure how things could or might turn out, but it just didn't look good.

Over many years there had been many scares. Dad had been seriously ill since 2004, but he had not been well for at least ten before that. He had been in and out of the hospital so many times that, despite the constant jitters set off by such news, the blow was deadened with each email or vibration of the phone. I had just become desensitized to the cycle of sickness—or dare I say, used to it? Whereas other friends would shift into the depths of panic at the mention of even a beloved aunt having surgery, the news of my father—or my mother, for that matter—spending time in the hospital became routine. It's not that such news stopped bothering me. Far from it. I just became used to being bothered. This thing, this sickness, this distant view of my parents' long, sad decline, was just my circumstance. I had to endure it and press on with my own affairs, my so-called Korean life, despite the growing hair-ball of anger, pity, guilt, and self-loathing that no amount of alcohol or casual distraction would allow me to cough up.

So I was not surprised, when, on that clear January morning, my brother finally summoned me home. I had been expecting that phone call since the first day I set foot on the peninsula. I had known that Dad was sick and would get sicker as each day passed. Every time a call came through from home I could feel my heart begin to sprint; I'd breathe in deeply and take hold of the nearest support, fully expecting to be slapped by the worst possible news. But the worst news never came. What I got instead was an infuriating succession of bad news. One chilling diagnosis piled upon another. Money woes exacerbated by an almost-criminal disregard for even the most basic attempts at financial solvency. Stonewalling. A lack of details. An unwillingness to change even a fraction of their lifestyles for the better, despite the fact that both of them—my mom and my dad—were killing themselves. Slow and total disintegration.

I received the first bad news about Dad just two weeks into my first contract in Korea. I was in the staffroom of the Bayridge Language School during one of my ten-minute between-class breaks. Usually I'd fire up the Internet and check my email (this was before the all-encompassing online hellmouth known as Facebook) and maybe sip on some green tea, which, along with nasty little packets of sugar-laden Nescafé, were provided gratis to all of the workers at the school. When I looked in my inbox I immediately noticed a message from Mark, with the word *Dad* in the subject line. My stomach dropped to the floor while I clicked on it and waited for the message to load, tapping my fingers on the desktop. Once again, Dad was in the hospital—this time, with serious trouble breathing, so bad that the paramedics had to pick him up from home. Mark said Dad was now stabilized and on oxygen, so this wasn't necessarily an *emergency*… but I should still call home as soon as possible.

Late that night I called my mom, who recounted the story. I could hear her light and suck down successive cigarettes as she described how scared and helpless she felt, how she'd never seen Dad so vulnerable. She'd thought she might lose him right then and there, and thank God they lived so close to the hospital. Help had arrived within a couple of minutes of dialing 911. It was my brother Glen who, after calling him the next day, informed me that Dad had been diagnosed with chronic emphysema and would never breathe without an oxygen tube again. He would be strapped to a tank for the remainder of his days. How long this remainder would be was anyone's guess, though Glen reckoned we were looking at a handful of years, at best. He had worked in hospitals for many years and knew firsthand how some diseases cripple and kill. I knew then that it was the beginning of the end.

Soon after that I met my workmate Scott for a one-on-one meal of *bul dalk*, Korean "fire chicken." We nibbled at the impossibly spicy bits of meat while downing glasses of Cass beer. I told Scott about my situation, how my father was now in what I understood to be the early stages of a steep and ugly slide toward death. Here we were, in a brightly lit restaurant with the aroma of grilled chicken clinging to the air, surrounded by tables of Koreans who were endlessly clinking glasses, eating, and laughing. The Lotte Giants baseball team played on the television and all I could do was look down into my glass. Though I was newly arrived and loving this new expat life, for the first of what would be many times to come, I deeply felt the distance between me and home. Scott just listened and nodded, refilling my glass as I emptied out my anxieties.

He looked me in the eyes and said, "Well, you're not alone in this. I lost my older brother when I was sixteen. He was in a car wreck. He barely survived the accident and hung on in a coma for six months before finally passing. The only thing I can say to you is make your peace while you have the time and hold on to the good memories, because they are the ones that will survive."

* * * *

Dad had a heart as big as a truck and a laugh that could move a house. This was a hearty, sonic boom of a laugh, drawn from a seemingly endless well of mirth. It was released most often around the dinner table (where Pops was the happiest), suddenly erupting and literally shaking the room. The man had an unstoppable joy, a playful, joking spirit that had a life of its own. He laughed, teased, prodded, and razzed, all the way until the end. My father was, among other things, a mighty jester. After all, he was born on April 1.

He's been gone for a few years now now, and while the material memory is beginning to fade, I'm left with these well-etched images:

- bushy hair and a thick moustache that laid bare his Italian roots;
- huge boa-constrictor arms, complete with tattoos: one a red heart declaring *Johnny loves Gloria* to the world; the other a busty brunette in a skimpy negligee (she used to be naked, but after the wedding, Mom demanded clothes);
- a web of crow's-feet around twinkling eyes, the result of a lifetime of laughing;
- a half-asleep man shuffling through the kitchen for a midnight snack, not-so-tighty-whities sagging off his butt, V-neck undershirt stretched over his boiler of a gut;

- a proud man spiffily dressed for family get-togethers, noble in stature and smelling of Old Spice;
- glasses, cup of coffee, and cigarette, as he busted out a crossword at 6:30 a.m.;
- nodding out and snoring in the chair as the Seattle Mariners played on the TV, this early bird unable to stay awake through the 9th inning;
- serene at Mass, hands held out in prayer, palms-up, basking in a deeply-felt faith that I at once envied and never understood.

Pops was a gentleman, in the most basic sense of the word: he was a gentle man. He was built like a bear but never once raised his hand in anger. The closest he would come was on one of those not-infrequent occasions when my sister and I were fighting and he was trying to rest.

"That's ENOUGH!" he'd roar, bursting from his chair and jerking his big leather belt from the loops that held it around his waist. This alone would turn our blood to ice and terrify us into instant submission. The threat was enough. Never once did he actually carry it out.

This isn't to say that Dad didn't have a temper. He did. It didn't arise so often, but when it did come, you and anyone else within a three-block radius knew it. I once saw him take a lifetime of aggression out on a push lawn mower that wouldn't start. Each fruitless pull on the cord cause a wave of ire to wash over his body. Like any time he was frustrated, he bit his tongue and furrowed his brow, until the stubbornness of the machine pushed him over the precipice. With the strength of an ogre, he picked up the mower and repeatedly slammed it on the ground, then chucked it the entire length of the driveway with one awesome push from his chest. This was one of the few times when I saw both the strength and the fury that my otherwise docile father was capable of.

Another time I was out with him fishing in our boat, near the town of Gig Harbor, Washington. I hooked into a massive Chinook salmon—to this day the largest fish I've ever had on a pole. It slammed the herring-baited hook and nearly bent the pole into the freezing dark waters of Puget Sound. I was just a kid at the time and this fish was out of my league, so Dad grabbed the pole and proceeded to fight this monster, which rolled on the surface, giving us a glimpse of its slab-like flank. The fish then proceeded to run straight out from the boat—the reel whizzing as the salmon pulled out yards of line. At this point it was about one hundred and fifty feet out. Just then we saw a giant sailboat—a yacht, really—heading our way. It was running parallel to us, right between my pole and the fish. We began to yell and wave in an effort to get the skipper's attention, but the yacht would not deviate from its course. It pressed straight ahead. As it got closer, our shouts and gestures became more desperate, until finally the behemoth of a boat sailed right over my line, the rudder acting as a knife. The line went slack and the fish went free.

My dad never cussed much, but the fountain of profanity that exploded out of his mouth that day was nothing like I had ever heard. He bellowed f-bombs and other violent oaths with an unfettered rage. He literally shook his fist to the sky, the closest I'd ever see him challenge a God that he not only believed in, but feared and loved. He was helpless to net his son's fish because of the arrogance of some rich asshole. This inflamed my dad's soul. He would have gladly gone to blows for me that day. This was my first lesson in class consciousness.

* * * *

As soon as I hung up the phone with Mark, I told Da-jin what was up, and she was right on the computer, searching Korean sites for any last-minute airline tickets available. Flights to America usually left Korea in the afternoon, so we'd have to act fast. The cheapest we could find was for nearly two and a half grand. Desperate for a seat, I punched in the card info right then and there (the airline later informed me that bereavement fares weren't available on international runs). I called a few of my friends and workmates to let them know I had to leave and to get my classes covered, and immediately began packing, grabbing my darkest suit first. All optimism would be staying in Korea. I learned that day that I can be out of my door in Busan and on the ground in Seattle in about sixteen hours, if I time it properly. That's not bad for crossing the whole Pacific Ocean.

The flight to Seattle was the first non-sold-out plane I'd been on in a while, affording me a bit of space to attempt relaxation, which never came. The on-demand films on the small screen in front of me were successions of color, movement, and sound; I was thinking of Dad the whole time, sure he'd be gone before I touched the ground. I readied myself as much as possible for the chance that I'd never see him alive again. This thought had always hovered in my mind, every time I had seen him since coming to Korea. I remember that last hug in Olympia during the previous summer visit, when my mother and he stepped out onto the street in front of their mobile home in the retirement park where they lived. I grabbed him for all it was worth and wrapped my not-small arms around his even bigger frame, holding him close—bear-hugging a bear—and smelling the remnants of his cologne. As my sister started her van and we pulled away, I watched the image of him standing in the passenger's mirror, until we turned the corner and he was gone. Was that it? Was that going to be my last memory of seeing him alive?

I arrived in back in Seattle with no hassle: Immigration and Customs were both courteous and quick. I stood with my bags in the SeaTac terminal and, with a huge cup of coffee and the *New York Times* crossword puzzle, killed the hour before my brother Mark's arrival from Texas. Again, my concentration was nowhere to be found. Finally, I saw my brother approach. He was smartly dressed in a dark jacket and jeans, and looked handsome with his close-cropped Air Force officer's hair. We managed a quick hug as I got out the question, "Any news?"

Some of my tension eased when he told me that Dad was still hanging on. I'd get to say my goodbyes.

We raced to the hospital in our rental and made it to the intensive care unit. Mark filled me in on the goings-on of the night before—what had transpired while I was in the air. My suspicions were correct: Dad had almost died. He had gone into cardiac arrest and stopped breathing. The medical team had revived him by sticking a breathing tube down his throat to keep him alive. This ran contrary to what I had believed would happen, since I knew both of my parents had signed *Do Not Resuscitate* agreements. No longer able to breathe, my father was now hooked up to a machine to do it for him. I knew this was something he would not want, but I was in no mood to be adamant: I just wanted to see him alive, one more time, even with the aid of some unwelcome technology.

My family was there when I arrived—my mother, my sister Molly, my brother Glen, my Aunt Anne Marie, and my two uncles, Bob and Dan. My aunt led me into the room where Dad now lay, squeezed my hand, gave me a nod, and left me alone with him.

Wearing only a white-and-blue gown, he lay amid a mass of equipment which monitored all of his vitals. His arms were bruised and bloody from the IVs that had been stuck into him over the last many months, as well as from the leukemia. His eyes were closed. A plastic tube—secured by a mass of tape and connected to a regulated air pump of sorts—sprouted from his mouth. I sat next to his bed, kissed his forehead, and grabbed his hand, hoping he could feel me, hoping he knew I was there.

"I'm here, Pops. I made it. I made it."

The following morning we—the immediate family, joined by my aunt—met with the doctor, a keen-eyed woman with short brown hair, who managed compassion without skirting the realities of the situation.

"We can remove the breathing tube, but only with your consent, Gloria." She looked to my mother, who nodded in understanding. "He will unlikely be able to breathe well without the tube. The body will begin to shut down, leading to an eventual failure of the organs. It will then not so much be a matter of if, but when. He could last minutes, hours, days, weeks, even months. We really can't know for sure, but my guess is that the eventuality will happen pretty quickly. He's a very, very sick man."

My mother's hesitation was brief. She shook her head and let out a deep sigh and said, "Do it. That's what he would want. It kills me to say, but he would not want to go on like this. Please remove the tube."

The doctor scheduled the removal for the following morning, giving us all a day to ready ourselves, though this was likely more for my mother than anyone else. My parents had been married almost forty-seven years, and in that time had become nearly one organism. The process of letting go of such a deep, ingrained partner must be almost impossible to come to terms with. To see my mom's anguish stabbed me even harder than taking in my dad's diminishing form on that hospital bed. Dad was nearly gone and nothing could change that. The real pain would exist among the living.

That night the family gathered at my Uncle Dan's house, were we had a huge meal of pasta, salad, and garlic bread, while swapping stories about Dad. We ate, drank some red wine, and laughed well, sitting side by side as family, never speaking of what we knew we would have to face the following morning. That needed no comment. It was the bitter water that pooled underneath. So we just lived as Dad lived best, through a hearty meal and joking words. This was the only way we really knew how to honor the man.

I was there the next morning when the doctor pulled the tube out; I was there as his breathing got lighter and lighter, until it was no more. It took less than ninety minutes. For one moment, after they pulled the tube, Dad came to. His eyes opened and he took us all in, and for the first time I saw him there. I saw inside. Whether he was actually conscious or not, I can't say; perhaps it was nothing more than a physical reaction to having to try and breathe with ravaged lungs once again: panic. I just hope that, if only for one second, he saw me. I hope that he knew that, even though I was on the other side of the world, I had made it; I had made it there to hold his hand when he died.

****

My dad died destitute, leaving behind a morass of debt that left our mouths agape. Things were much worse than we thought. My mother knew little of the details, or more likely had chosen to deny them, so it became my aunt's charge to sort out the mess—which ended up taking her the greater part of a year. We kids had to pay for the funeral and other expenses straight out of pocket. My sis, who lived three minutes away from my parents and had assisted them in every conceivable way while they ailed, was exempted; she had more than pulled her weight. That left it to my two older brothers and me to open our wallets and cough up at each onerous hidden charge hurled our way.

The funeral industry has perfected the art of quietly nodding and looking at you with caring, sympathetic eyes, all the while ramming a broomstick up your ass. It really is one of the greatest rackets running today. We were slapped with fees at every point. A funeral cannot be paid for in one go: it's a series of itemized measures that grows like a tumor. The cheapest funeral runs in the thousands of dollars, and though we loved our dad immensely, we opted to go budget. We had little other choice. The fact that no arrangements had ever been made stung hard, and we weren't about to go extravagant in spite of it. We couldn't afford to.

My father was a devout Catholic. He loved the Church and often said that he would have gone into the priesthood had it not been for that pesky little vow of celibacy. He just loved my mother—and women in general—too much. But he was at home in the Church and for many years volunteered, at one point even becoming a lay minister. He read about the Church extensively and used to educate us about the various orders of the priesthood, how they were founded and what their missions were. When Dad was at Mass he would relax and let the spirit enter his body. You could sense the grace that he felt, and whatever your feelings on God (mine run firmly on the agnostic side), to say that religion gave my father no peace would be folly.

Some years before, both of my parents had agreed to be cremated. Evidently the Vatican had reversed its views on the practice and no longer looked upon it as some kind of pagan abomination. Perhaps the Church was trying to catch up with the times, atoning for its unwillingness to budge on birth control by saying, "Okay, we realize that our policies are leading to overpopulation, so sure, go ahead and start burning bodies. Don't ever accuse us of not looking after the environment, *capiche?*" Not only is cremation an environmentally friendly way to dispose of the dead (choking smoke excepted), but, lucky for us at the time, it also happens to be the most economical.

We used a service called Memorial Choices to arrange the cremation and the nuts and bolts of the interment, as it's called, which consists of placing the urn containing the ashes in a wall. Memorial Choices claimed to be the cheaper way to go, and they were, but even they weren't above gouging us when the opportunity arose.

My brothers and I were in downtown Olympia at the time, sipping coffee at a local coffeehouse while attempting to compose a eulogy—which Glen would deliver—for our father. Mark's phone rang and he picked it up:

"Hello, Mark? This is Bill Halton from Funeral Alternatives."

"Hello, Bill."

"Hi, Mark. Um… listen… there's a small thing that's come up."

"Uh-huh?"

"Umm… yeah… listen, I'm not sure how to really put this, but… was your father a *large* man?"

"Uh, yes. Yes, he was… he was large." I took my eyes away from the screen of the laptop. Mark caught our gaze to indicate that trouble was afoot.

"Okay. Well, um, you see, unfortunately, for anyone over 250 pounds, there's an extra charge."

Mark rolled his eyes and sighed. "Hold on, Bill." He put his hand over the mike. "They want to charge extra to cremate Dad. They say he's too fat."

Glen slapped the table with one hand. "How much?"

Mark shrugged. "Hi Bill. How much is this gonna cost?"

"I'm afraid the fee is three hundred dollars. That's on top of the original eight."

"Three. Hundred. Dollars?"

Pause.

"Fine. Fuck it." Glen got up and headed to the bathroom.

"What?" I had had enough. "DO THEY REALLY HAVE TO

BUY THAT MUCH MORE GAS?" The other patrons shot stares my way.

Mark shook his head and licked saliva from his lips.

"Okay. Done," he said, snapping the phone shut.

****

Dad's funeral went off without incident several days later. The priest was a graying man from Ghana, who was serving in the local parish for one year, a result of the current priest shortage. Some of my family had a hard time adjusting to his thick accent, but other than that they appreciated his warmth and the sense of joy that he brought, even to a funeral. After the Mass I gave him a lift to the cemetery, and I impressed him with my knowledge that the former UN Secretary General Kofi Annan was also Ghanaian. He seemed shocked to meet an American who actually knew this. He was further astounded to discover that I could talk international soccer with him as well. It turns out that, aside from his national team, he was also an enthusiastic supporter of Chelsea. I liked him at once, and upon finding out that I lived in Korea, he peppered me with questions about the place:

"Is it true they eat kimchee with every meal? I have worked with Korean priests and I do not understand how they can stomach that stuff. Do you eat it? The smell!"

"Can they speak English well? I think maybe not so good."

He also reflected on living far away from home, for he too was an expat:

"I get here to America and everything is strange. People get into their car to drive everywhere. Me? I don't even have driver's license! To have so many cars—this is crazy!"

That night was the annual Knights of Columbus crab feed, which my father used to volunteer for—it was one of the highlights of his year. It took place in Anscar Hall, a gym-like pavilion next to the main building that makes up Sacred Heart Parish. My brothers and I decided to attend as sort of a tribute to the old man. I sat at a table with them, eating garlic bread and prime rib, sucking out the meat from the steamed claws of Dungeness crab, and downing watery beer from plastic cups. One nice thing about being Catholic is that drinking is never a problem. We aren't afraid to bust out kegs at church functions, unlike so many of those puritanical Protestant sects, some of whom are said to substitute grape juice for communion wine. (As if church weren't boring enough.)

Sam Pellegrino, one of my dad's closest friends and the main organizer behind the crab feed, came over to our table. He, of course, had been at the funeral just hours earlier, but had now traded in his dark suit for an apron, and carried two paper plates covered with tinfoil.

"Please give this to Gloria. I know how much she loves crab."

I made the rounds under the hall's fluorescent lights, greeting a few people that my dad knew. The African priest was there, all smiles and laughs, with a pile of empty red-and-white crab leg shells in front of him. I looked at the tables filled with good, hungry Catholics, eating and drinking and living, unaware that we had just buried Dad. Most of them didn't even know my dad, but even the ones who did went on with life as it was before. Sam Pellegrino loved my dad and sobbed when I broke the news of his death to him, but that night he worked the kitchen and cooked the crab, just as he had done for many years before. My brothers and I ate and tried to talk above the din of voices and cracking shells, but few words came out. We did our best, but our hearts weren't there. We really tried to enjoy the feed, but the beer was too weak and the food had no taste, and no matter how much we ate, it just didn't fill.

INTERLUDE

JANUARY 26, 2009 SHANGHAI, CHINA

THIS beast of a city is alive with the sounds of war. Machine guns. Artillery shells. The explosions reverberate down the narrow streets of the French Concession and the air is thick with gunpowder and sulfur smoke, obscuring the European architecture in a blue haze. Everywhere are booms and bangs and pops and whistles—an orgy of fireworks—the opening minutes of the Year of the Ox. People are on the sidewalk and in the middle of the road, lighting off huge box-loads of rockets, missiles, and firecrackers. The amount of pyrotechnics is as staggering as the city itself. The Chinese revel in it and make our 4th of July seem flaccid by comparison.

I sit with Da-jin, Scott, and our friend Caf at Yin-Yang, a small bar run by what appear to be well-connected Chinese hipsters. The tables are full and smoke lingers in the room, though unlike outside, this smoke has a much more Amsterdam-esque taste and smell. Trance music pulsates through the speakers, punctuated by the rumbles from the decibel party in the streets. We sip from tall glasses of Spaten beer and take in the décor of the place. Portraits of Mao figure prominently, along with red stars and hammers and sickles. This isn't commie kitsch; these guys are showing respect, and are likely left alone because of it.

The celebrations are exhilarating, but ill-timed. Dad has only been gone for two weeks now. I'm still reeling and feel like a heel for coming to the party, but I bought the tickets well before he left us. He also always wanted to visit China, so I'd like to think that I've brought at least a piece of his spirit with me. I'll keep him in mind as I wander the city, a place almost too immense to ponder, over the next three days.

My emotions are a river. They change from day to day, hour to hour. I know such ups and downs are the natural result of the grieving process, but it gets annoying. Just today I lost my cool in a taxi ride to the Bund—the riverside walk that is Shanghai's most famous attraction. Caf asked me if my father had left me any money or property. I responded with a venomous rant, almost cursing my dad's name: "No! He died as broke as it gets. We had to pay for his fucking mess and will probably have to pay for more. Isn't it supposed to be the other way around? Thanks, Dad." Twenty minutes later, my mood changed: I was laughing at a restaurant sign which read *SPICY PLATE OF RAPE.*

Da-jin is happy to be traveling with me but doesn't like the Chinese so much. "They are so rude and loud," she says. When a street-food seller seemingly overcharged us for some lamb-skewers this afternoon, Da-jin made up her mind. "Fucking cheating Chinese," she spat, shaking her head and settling into a very deep Korean scowl. The fact that she is constantly mistaken for a local doesn't help matters. She wants Shanghai to know that she's not Chinese, that she's different. She's Korean and always will be. They must respect this.

Tomorrow we will celebrate her Korean-ness by visiting the site of the Korean government-in-exile from the Japanese colonial period. We will solemnly take in the grainy photos of the independence martyrs, bow, and maybe even eat a bit of the kimchee that she's brought along to get through the holiday. China may be geographically close to the peninsula, but in other ways it's as far as it gets.

CHAPTER 16

HERE FOR THE HOLIDAYS

CHRISTMAS is most always an awful day for expats in Korea—it's a time when we feel truly alone—separated from our friends and loved ones, living strange and solitary lives an ocean away from home. This Christmas was more soul-wringing than usual. Being late December in Korea, it was windy and cold. I lay on the heated floor of my small apartment, barely able to stand due to a lower back that had decided to stage a painful insurrection against walking upright. This was also the first Christmas since my dad's death, and I felt his absence in the deepest reaches of my gut, despite the fact that I hadn't actually spent a Christmas with him in years.

Even more painful was the thought of my mom, whose condition had worsened in recent months. Because of chronic diabetes-related infections in her feet and legs, Mom's doctors had deemed it necessary to perform a double amputation. She was now confined to a nursing facility back home, with only my sister to drop in on her. I was beyond homesick, wracked with grief and guilt. Above all, I simmered with anger at my inability to either comfort my mother or do anything to alleviate her situation. My mood was pure black, and I would have more than welcomed the cancellation of Christmas—right then and there—but the day had arrived. I decided to at least try and make the best of it.

I decided to stick with my evening plans, in an attempt to crawl out of my physical and emotional funk. So Da-jin and I jumped into a taxi and joined our friends for a Christmas feast at the Novotel in Haeundae. A group of us had made a reservation to hit their Christmas buffet, which—despite the fifty-buck-a-head price tag—was well worth it. In addition to the shocking amount of food, the spread included a no-limit wine bar, consisting of small barrels filled with white and red, respectively. It took me no time to begin to numb my self-pity with glass after glass of wine. After all, I had to feel as if I was getting my money's worth.

After we had eaten ourselves pregnant, several of us, including Sam, Scott, Da-jin, and me, headed to a private party being held in one of the new beach condos directly next to the hotel. A party of young, new-to-Korea teachers had rented it for the night, and we joined in the festivities, bringing a bottle of Johnny Walker Black and several big beers to ease us into the yuletide cheer. I hung in the kitchen with Da-jin, Scott, and Sam, liberally filling paper cup after paper cup full of straight, neat whisky, feeling surly and mean and not really wanting to make "Where are you from?" small talk with the room of fresh-off-the-boat newbies. At one point we joined in a gift-swapping game, despite the fact that we had brought no gifts. There were a couple of extras, so we were allowed to join. When it was over, I found myself with a used copy of *A New History of Korea*, which, despite its textbook dryness, looked like a decent enough resource on the history of the peninsula.

At this point I was straight-up drunk. I was also surprised to learn that it was midnight. This is normally not so late for a Korean party hour, but Da-jin and I were to leave for a beach holiday in Thailand in two days and needed to buy some Thai baht the next afternoon, while the banks were open. She also had to work for a few hours in the morning, and very reasonably suggested that we get a taxi to our respective homes, which were just minutes from each other. Despite my already lit-up state, I wanted to stay out more, but acting the part of the good boyfriend, I acquiesced.

As we pulled up next to her family's house, Da-jin said, "You promise to go home and sleep?"

"I promise baby, don't worry. Merry Christmas."

"Merry Christmas." She pecked me on the lips and turned toward her front door.

Within seconds I was on the phone to Sam.

"Sammy, what's up?"

"You drop your girl off?"

"Yeah."

"Let's go get more drunk at the Crown."

"Good idea. See you down there."

When I arrived at the Crown some fifteen minutes later, Sam was already there, nursing a thick pour of Jamesons and chatting with Andrew, the towering Aussie co-proprietor. Andrew greeted me with a "Happy Christmas" while immediately going for the bottle of Irish whisky, filling the iced glass to the brim and shoving it in front of me as I nestled myself up to the bar.

"Have a good feed, did ya?"

"Not bad, not bad," I muttered as I made my way into the glass of steamy liquor. It soothed my stomach and turned up the heat inside, a heat which was already burning steadily due to the wine, Johnny Walker, and piercing anxiety which had taken a permanent hold of me during that year of my parents' decline.

We were the only three in the grungy little bar, and at one point Sam stood up and climbed the steep stairs that led to the dreadful little toilet above. After about fifteen minutes I noticed that he had never come back down. When I trounced up to take a look, I saw the side door which opens up to the alley outside was ajar: he had pulled a runner, something he was known to do when pathetically drunk. I came back down, shrugged, and finished another whisky.

After paying my bill, I walked out into the sharp winter air, taking in the world in shiny, gelatinous sparkles. Despite the cold, I was warm all over and feeling a sort of boozy invincibility. Nothing could stop me and sleeping was out of the question. I felt the fire grow inside and knew that I had to do something, that the night could not end, that I needed to let go, to purge, to make an adventure, and what better place to do that than in the casino?

There are two casinos in Busan. Both are attached to hotels and are open to foreigners only: no Koreans allowed (save those holding foreign passports). Gambling is technically illegal in South Korea (with some exceptions), though like prostitution and traffic laws, these laws are inconsistently enforced. But the fact that Koreans are barred from entering these casinos is probably a good thing, since the compulsion to gamble is so great among many locals that to allow it to go on wholesale would invite devastation. But the powers that be are more than willing to separate foreigners from our hard-earned won, and many of us are more than willing to give it up in an attempt to cash in. While not like many people I knew who were casino fiends, I'd pop in and do some serious gambling from time to time, which is what I did that ominous morning.

I sat down at the Caribbean Stud Poker table and immediately ordered a beer, gulping it down while playing cards, throwing a modest amount of chips back and forth, quickly winning about one hundred dollars in the course of a couple of lucky hands. Just then I saw Scott walking my way, along with a friend of his from the buffet earlier. He was on his way to the roulette table and stopped by to say hello and wish me luck.

"What happened to the girl? You manage to slip away?"

"You could say that, I guess…"

For the next couple of hours I played and gradually increased my stack. At one point three men joined me. They were Russians. They chain-smoked and drank straight vodka.

"Where you from?" one of them asked.

"USA."

"Ah… *Americanski*…" He looked to his partners and rattled off something in Russian. They laughed among themselves.

I continued to tread water with my winnings, keeping my stack around the three-hundred-dollar mark. The Russians stayed at the table with me, though they fared less well, losing several times and buying more and more chips. I sensed some resentment that I too wasn't being cleaned out by the house. I just sipped and played minimum bets, ordering beer after beer. I must have been visibly destroyed at this point, but the casino—perhaps in an attempt to win back their small amount of cash—kept delivering the drinks. It was around six a.m. that Scott sat down with us and played a few hands. He lost quickly and stood up from the table.

"Hey man. I'm heading out. You probably should come with me."

"Nahhhh… I'm okay… I just wanna win a little more."

"You sure?"

"Yeah, I'm all right… really…"

"Okay man…" He leaned in close to my ear. "Watch out for these Russian guys. I don't like the look of them." Scott was an ex-hockey player who could smell a fight brewing hours before a punch was thrown.

"Oh, no man… they're cool… they're cool."

Scott walked off at that point, leaving a near-empty casino, save the three Russians and me. At this point I began slipping in and out of lucidity. This happened for a couple more hours. I was drinking and playing the minimum, losing and winning, never making a real change in my stack. The Russians were smoking and talking and at one point, the one of them who spoke some English addressed me:

"You."

"Wha…?" I came to, snapping my head up from a nod off at the table.

"You like Booosh? George-y Boosh?" He glared my way.

"No no. Fuck Bush. I hate Bush. Fuck him." I took a swig to punctuate my disdain.

"Yes… fuck Booosh. We too hate."

"Good. Bush is an asshole. Many Americans—we hate."

More Russian speaking, shaking of heads. "You know Putin?"

"Yeah, I know Putin."

"What about Putin? You like Putin?"

"No, I don't like Putin. Fuck Bush. Fuck Putin."

"You no like Putin?"

"No way. He's an asshole too."

This is where the mirror cracked. I can remember insults spat my way. I heard garbled words about America and Americans—disparaging my people, disparaging my parents, disparaging me. I felt the weight of the Cold War on my body and I needed to fling it off until it crushed the ugly trio in front of me. My Yankee gander was stoked and I was burning.

"Fuck you Russian assholes. Guess what? We won the Cold War! And if we had to do it all over again we would! And you know what? We'd win it every fucking time, you dirty pieces of shit!" I shouted, now standing at the table. Immediately I was surrounded by a phalanx of black-suited security guys, who gently attempted to push me toward the main door. As my senses returned, I realized that I stepped over a line: I had caused a big commotion in the casino, a real no-no in face-conscious East Asia.

"You have too much drink. You must go home now," one of the black suits told me in English.

"Okay okay." I held up my hands. "I am sorry. But I need my chips."

"Chips?"

"Yes, my chips." I still had three hundred dollars worth of chips on the table. "I want to cash them in before I go."

He translated to his colleague, who went to the table to collect. I saw the man ask the dealer a few questions before he returned, empty handed.

"He say you gamble your chips."

I thought for a moment.

"No, no. I had a pile of chips. I am certain of it."

"I sorry. You gamble. You must go home."

They tried to force me out of the door one more time. But, despite drinking for over thirteen hours straight, I was clear on one thing: I had not gambled away my chips.

"Listen. I really must insist. I DID NOT gamble away my chips. Yes, I have been drinking, but I'd know if I lost all of my money. Do you understand?"

"Yes. Understand, but…"

"Do you have video? Surely you must have video. I demand to see the video."

"No. You go now!"

The guards once more tried to force me out, but I was now empowered with righteousness. Even if I deserved to be ejected I knew for a fact that they were wrong about the chips. I grabbed my phone and switched from English to the best Korean I could muster:

"Stop! I'm calling the police!"

With that, they took their hands off me, stood, and watched me make good on my threat.

Ten minutes later I was in a back office with a casino manager, along with several security people and two uniformed police officers—both of whom appeared to be annoyed to have to deal with this angry drunk foreigner. The manager put in the video. They all spoke rapidly to each other; I understood almost nothing. At one point the manager stopped the video, rewound it, and played it again. He gestured to the screen and pointed. Everyone else in the group nodded their heads.

"Look," he said to me. He rewound and replayed: blurry images of hands putting in some chips. "You put in your chips."

"What?"

"The video shows you bet all your chips."

"Play it again."

He did. I saw a set of hands—said to be mine—make a bet… but I had made many bets. I did *not* see anyone pushing in a large stack of chips.

"I don't see anything."

He turned off the monitor and waved to the security guards, who grabbed me and tried to strong-arm me from the office. I resisted with everything I had.

"YOU LYING FUCKERS! YOU'RE STEALING MY CHIPS! I NEVER GAMBLED THEM! NEVER! RACISTS! THIEVES!"

I managed to loosen a hand, make a fist, and swing at the first black suit in reach. I solidly connected on his chin. A couple more guys grabbed my legs, and I was finally carried out of the main entrance, down the escalator, and thrown into the back of a cop car.

* * * *

After a few hours in the Korean version of a drunk tank, I was led to a desk by a hulking cop with vicious acne scars gouged into his cheeks. He hauled me by the scruff of my neck and slammed me into the chair, playing the ogreish role of bad cop with dead-on precision. There I was fingerprinted and booked. I made a phone call to Angry Steve, and let him know what was going on.

"There's no way the casino stole your chips," he told me. "The house already has an overwhelming edge. They don't need to steal."

After hanging up with me, Steve immediately called Da-jin, who then rang me. I was now double-caught.

The police wanted me to give a statement, but I refused. I kept telling them that I was sorry for the outburst; that my beef was with the casino and not them. The officer in charge just shrugged and shook his head. He let me know that the casino was more than willing to forget the whole incident—that charges would not be filed—as long as I agreed to make a statement. I finally gave in, and, after about thirty minutes of questions and answers, I was released, met by a stone-faced Da-jin, who had come to pick me up

"You lied to me."

"I'm sorry."

"Come, we must eat tofu. This is a Korea tradition for those who are released from the jail."

* * * *

I quietly slurped from a bowl of *sundubu jjigae* while Da-jin shook her head and castigated me for my stupidity: "You are such a *babo.* You will be forty soon and you act like child. I can't believe how stupid you are."

With my head down, I nodded in agreement, watching the strands of white tofu float in the reddish broth. Eating tofu, known as *dubu*, is indeed a get-out-of-jail custom. I recall the scene in Park Chan-wook's *Sympathy for Lady Vengeance,* where the protagonist, Geum-ja, takes a bite from a huge hunk of tofu offered when walking out of the prison gate. My release is less auspicious, and I will have to settle for the loose bits boiled into the *jjigae*, along with the lecture from an exasperated girlfriend.

By the end of lunch, I realized I was not getting dumped. She was sticking with me, at least for the time being. After all, we were set to fly off to Bangkok the next night, a trip that I was financing on my own. There were errands to run, piles of currency to convert. The Korean won isn't sought-after; it's hard to get a good rate outside of the country. It's not something you want to be stuck with anywhere *but* Korea, so it's always a good idea to exchange it before you leave. Soon we were off to Korea Exchange Bank. It was early Friday afternoon and the sidewalks were abuzz with people taking care of business before the weekend.

On the way to the bank, I realized that my Alien Registration Card was missing. This is an important ID that all foreigners working in Korea must carry. While I'd have been able to get out of the country without it, I might not have been let back in.

"Shit. It must be back at the police station. Listen, Da-jin… you go to the bank and I'll go back for my card. I'll call you when I find it."

I did an about-face and headed pell-mell back to the cop shop. I was loath to show my face around there one more time, but I needed the card. After a sad inquiry back up to the floor that held me, I was informed that the card was nowhere to be found. The cop at the security door just shook his head and made an X with his arms. I sighed, sauntered back down to the sidewalk, put my hands in my pockets, and walked back to meet Da-jin at the bank. It was then that I felt something strange in the depths of my right pocket: not something, but somethings, several objects, hard and round, made of plastic. I drew them out and opened up my palm, both amazed and humiliated by the sight of three 100,000-won casino chips. They were there, on me, in my pocket, the whole time. As I picked up the phone to call Da-jin, a stinging blanket of shame enveloped my face and worked its way down until even my toes were burning. I had got what I wanted: I lashed out at the world, exorcised my pain, my anger, and my self-pity, and, in the end, became the punch line to my own joke.

****

Da-jin led me back into the casino later that afternoon, where I slunk behind her, like a dog forced to revisit to the spot where it had peed on the carpet. The manager was courteous and professional, cashing in my chips (despite my insistence that they be given to the employee I socked in the jaw), and letting me know, through Da-jin, that I was no longer welcome in the establishment. Ever. This I understood clearly, despite my shaky handle on the Korean language. Inflection and tone are often more effective communicators than actual words; memory of deeds works even better. I bowed several times, uttered "I'm sorry" in the most honorific Korean I could muster, and walked out of the Diamond World Casino forever.

****

Two months later I received a notice—posted on the door by the mailman—requiring me to pick up a certified letter at the Busan City Courthouse mailroom, which of course caused me some concern. These notices are not usually harbingers of good news: according to Da-jin, they most often indicate that you are in some kind of trouble. And despite it being reasonably late at night, I jumped on my motorbike and zipped down to the mailroom. I gave the minder (yet another uniformed, smoking ajosshi) my slip and he returned with the letter, which I opened at once. After poring over it a couple of times, I managed to get the gist: I was being sued. The man I punched during the casino catastrophe was pressing me for "blood money"—a common practice in Korea after any kind of physical altercation. He was wronged, so he petitioned the court that I pay up, to the grand sum of three hundred thousand won… exactly the amount I took home from the table that night.

I went down to the court cashier and settled up the next afternoon, no questions asked.

CHAPTER 17

MOM

MY first memory is of my mother. I was three and half years old, with my family at a motel in Longview, Washington. It was summertime and my dad was working an out-of-town job, so he brought us all along. It was hot and bright and the four of us kids played in and around the pool attached to the Motel 6—all rough concrete and cheap plastic sunbathing chairs. My dad was out paving roads and my mom was working at what she did best: being Mom. She was looking after us as we splashed and swam in the heavily chlorinated water. She wore shorts and a blouse and big plastic white-framed sunglasses. A cigarette dangled out of her right hand; she clutched a vodka and orange juice in her left.

My oldest brother, Mark, grabbed me and picked me up. Despite my squirming, he walked me to the edge of the pool. I couldn't swim and recognized that the water went well over my head. Well aware that the pool was a turquoise, little-boy-swallowing abyss, I made my horror known through high-pitched shrieks. This only encouraged Mark, who laughed and proceeded to swing me over the ledge, threatening to toss me into the deep end.

"One!" (swing) "Two!" (swing) "Three!" (swing)

After the count of three, I had expected to swing back to safety, but the unthinkable occurred: Mark's grip on me was looser than he had anticipated and I slipped from his arms, falling straight into the nine-foot pool of water below: SPLASH!

Once underwater, my fear abated. I remember slowly sinking in the warmth of the heated pool. I opened my eyes and took in the sheets of sunlight slicing through the surface. I loved the feeling of floating; that pesky force of gravity was now largely done away with. I was suspended in a place of near-silence. The amniotic feel of the water soothed me, reawakening the sensation of floating in the womb, which, at that point in my life, was a not too-distant experience.

My mom went into action, jumping straight into the water to come to my aid—clothes, sunglasses, cocktail, and cigarette be damned. Her split-second heroism—as well as the fact that she brought all she held into the pool with her—became family lore, repeated over big, boisterous dinners countless times through the years to come. Mom was a terrific swimmer—she loved the water and was at home in it—and within seconds she had me back up on the surface, where I took a deep breath of fresh air and proceeded to wail, realizing then that I had been in real danger, if only for a few seconds, and thankful that my mother was there to rescue me.

****

I had known that Mom was really sick for about a year before even coming to Korea. Mom hadn't been well for a very long time—like my dad, she had been in and out of the hospital—but I didn't know how bad it was until she told me. I was visiting my parents in Olympia. It was dawn, and I had stayed up all night at a friend's place, drinking. I made it back to their mobile home and slipped in through the sliding glass door, hoping not to alert her two terrier mixes that endlessly yapped every time I sneezed, let alone barged into the place smelling of a night on the piss. But my mother was already up, sitting at the table in her pink bathrobe. Her grey hair was disheveled and the purple streaks under her eyes spoke of a night without sleep. A milky coffee sat in front of her and she drew from her ever-present Benson and Hedges cigarette.

"Late night?"

"Yeah."

I sat down with her and joined her for a coffee. I felt ashamed that here I was, a grown man, slinking in at dawn after a night of partying with my friends. She seemed unconcerned, though. My mother was no prude and got more tolerant as the years went on. Besides, she had other things on her mind—namely, her own health. As I sipped the coffee and looked at my mother, who was in her early sixties but looked older, we talked. My mom and I talked easily and for long periods of time. Unlike the stilted and forced exchanges that passed for conversations with my dad, talking with Mom never required any effort. She was a terrific listener, only this morning it was my turn.

"I'm not well, Chris. This neuropathy is just getting worse. My feet and legs hurt all of the time. I'm tired. I can't sleep. I don't know what to do. It's as if my body has had enough. I've had four children, two miscarriages, and a hysterectomy that I don't think I've ever really recovered from. I'm sick half the time and now have to deal with this thing in my legs. I don't know, Chris. I just feel terrible all of the time. I'm in constant pain."

"You could quit smoking," I said, as she lit up another one. "Surely that would help."

My mother had been a smoker all her life. She started in the Catholic parochial high school she attended, in Tacoma, where she would sneak smokes in the bathroom with her friends. She often told stories of evading the nuns and priests who taught there, in order to get a puff in. Mom smoked all the time, wherever she could. She was a committed smoker, a smoker with an almost fanatical dedication to the vice. She disdained people who complained about cigarettes and waved off the health risks with the stock quip, "My grandmother chain smoked Winstons and lived to be 87 years old." This claim was indeed true, but as my mother's health began to deteriorate—most of it breathing-related—the old line about my chain-smoking great-grandma's legendary longevity ceased to impress.

When I was a kid, she had no qualms about sending me to the store to buy smokes for her. In those days you just needed to supply your child with a note requesting the sale, and the local clerk (who knew our family) would gladly ring me up. Later in life, when I began to periodically light up myself, she welcomed the company, as if I had become a co-conspirator. She would have been happy if the whole world smoked, because that way no one could judge her for it.

* * * *

Like she had been for all of my life, Mom was my lifeline once I got to Korea. While I certainly wasn't homesick for most of the first year I spent on the peninsula, talking to my mother was always a thrill. I'd call my parents every two weeks or so, eager to regale them with tales of their youngest son's adventures in the exotic East. And even if my surroundings weren't as exotic as I would have liked, I could certainly make them sound that way. Mom was always a willing audience for my ramblings. She had been one of the most supportive people in my decision to come over to Korea and was probably the most supportive listener. During these talks I'd usually have a brief chat with my dad, but despite my deep affection for him, like many American fathers and sons, we never spoke easily. Dad would usually affect mirth and respond to everything I said with a certain enthusiasm (*That's great*, or *Sounds like a winner!*), but there was always a distance between us. I suspect me being the youngest played a part, but my father was at the tail end of a generation of men who could never relate fully to their sons. The touchy-feely Sixties and Seventies helped to do away with such dynamics—or lack thereof—but my parents were really products of the Fifties, with a dash of Sixties tolerance thrown in for good measure.

Dad was also sick. He had gotten seriously ill just one month into my first year here, and much of the time he was a tired man donning his happy mask. After all, who wants to worry their kid? My father was a master of this, but we all knew how serious the situation was, and his declining health eclipsed the fact that my mom was really doing no better. Often, when I called, Dad was asleep, and during these occasions I could quiz my mom on how he was actually doing. She gave me much more realistic assessments than perpetually-optimistic Pops could muster, but it occurs to me now that I rarely asked Mom, "And how are you? Really?"

I already knew the answer to that question. By the time my second year had rolled around, she had been hospitalized once. Every winter, usually around January or February, she'd get sick. I suspect it was often a common cold run amuck, but this would mutate into a severe sinus infection or even pneumonia, which required a course of antibiotics strong enough to kill a whole city's worth of bacteria. And each time she got sick it took her longer to recover. My dad was on full-time oxygen, and now she required it too, on and off, as her worsening condition dictated. My brothers and sister watched in horror as both of them were slowly consumed.

My sister, Molly, lived just a couple minutes away, and became their caregiver. She made their relative happiness the focus of her life, despite the fact that she was raising three kids on a fixed income. My two brothers lived far away—Phoenix and San Antonio—and like me, they could only look on helplessly. While Molly was handling the situation on the ground with a kind of selflessness that I still can't comprehend, the brothers were sending money when appropriate (my folks were broke) and attempting to plan for the eventuality that we saw speeding toward us. It was all we could do, short of moving home, which none of us was willing to undertake.

In Confucian Korea, the idea of filial piety is perhaps the culture's most cherished value: to serve and honor one's parents is one's deepest duty. Through much of my father's and mother's slide into invalidity, Da-jin often castigated me: "What are you doing here? You are making money and traveling and being selfish. You should be home taking care of your parents. I do not understand you Americans." She couldn't process how I could possibly stay in Korea while my parents suffered.

* * * *

My father died on January 28, 2008. I went home and managed to see him before he passed. I spent two weeks in America, burying the man and doing my best to pitch in with both the costs and logistics of a funeral for which no real preparations had been made. I returned to

Korea that February, stinging from the loss, but also relieved: it had been a savage four years, and I could only hope that he was somehow now happier, in that "better place" where we hope our loved ones end up.

Dealing with loss has not increased my faith in any sort of God or afterlife. If anything, it's shown me that life is often cruel and ugly. Back in my expat bubble in Korea, I was aflame with anger: angry that he was gone, angry that he was so responsible for his own demise, angry at the mess he had left, and above all, angry at myself for running away from the whole tragedy. This anger quickly morphed into a new feeling of dread, however: one that made me sick in the deepest center of my gut. What was to become of Mom?

She had already lost a little toe to the ravages of neuropathy, but now had a sore on her foot. She mentioned that it was getting worse, but that the doctor had prescribed a regime of antibiotics to clear up the infection. She took the lot but they were ineffective: "It just won't heal," she said over the phone. "It won't heal."

The infection indeed spread and after two surgeries to clean it out, she lost the leg. I was at the Crown, numbing my nerves with Korean beer when the call came from my brother Glen. I stood in the stairwell and knocked my head against the wall. The sounds of his tears echoed my own.

Within a couple of months a new sore developed on her remaining foot. We all knew where this would lead. Her lower body was simply incapable of healing itself, and it was just a matter of time before she lost the second leg.

I was at the Crown again, when, at midnight, Glen called me with the news:

"They had to take the other leg. She'll be in long-term care for the foreseeable future. After that we'll have to find another place for her, as she won't be able to stay in the mobile."

That November—in the middle of the semester—I flew home for a week to help clean out the parents' place. I talked to my boss, Dr. Kim, and told him that I must help my family. Although Koreans value these things more than anything else, this doesn't always translate into empathy for the foreign help. I've known many people who have found themselves out of a job due to family emergencies. The afternoon before I left, Dr. Kim called me into his office. I feared an earful due to my last-minute trip home. Instead, he handed me a white envelope, which contained 150,000 won, about 120 dollars at the time:

"Your students took up a collection, and wanted you to have this."

****

I should have been home, but I wasn't. I should have been at her bedside—holding her hand and whispering in her ear. I should have been there to sit and cheer her up, to tell her stories and push her outside for some air, but after years of false alarms and perpetual crises, of midnight phone calls, of bad news followed by worse—the death of my dad—I chose to stay away. I was on a beach. It was just a few days after my Christmas casino meltdown. I was beaten up, wearing my shame like a thick sweater. I also was stricken with food poisoning—the result of some sketchy oysters eaten at the hotel buffet that we visited on Christmas night. I needed rest and recuperation, so Da-jin and I headed down to Thailand to spend a week in the embrace of the tropics. She only had the five days off. I planned on remaining longer, to eventually head north, meet Angry Steve—who also happened to be in the country—and cross into Laos. But the first week would be with my girl, in a beachside bungalow in Koh Chang, surrounded by what seemed to be the whole nation of Sweden. I wanted to enjoy the beginning of a new year with few distractions.

I achieved this for four days, until I got the email from my brother Mark:

Chris. Call home. It's mom. Urgent.

I sprinted from the PC shop on Koh Chang's main tourist strip back to our dark wood, beachfront bungalow. Da-jin was sipping tea and reading a book. Luckily her phone was rigged for international calls (mine was not), and after a few attempts, I got my middle brother, Glen, on the phone.

"I just got the email. What's up?"

She was still alive, which was more than I was expecting, given the tone of the email. I'd received scores of alarmist emails over the years of my parents' decline, most of which usually informed me about a new diagnosis or hospitalization—but the word "urgent" had yet to appear. It is a word of power and we all knew it. When we see something addressed as "urgent," we think one thing: someone is dead.

Mom had suffered a year in which God threw a Jobian mountain of misfortune her way. In this time, she would lose not one, but both of her legs, her dogs, her house, and worst of all, her dignity. In her last few months she was at the mercy of nurses and caregivers, lacking the necessary upper arm strength for even the most basic mobility. A very independent and stubborn woman became infantile in her dependency. This, to be certain, is what really killed her.

Logistically I was in a pickle. I was five hours from Bangkok, where I could book a flight back to the States, but all I had with me was a small backpack full of shorts and t-shirts. I would require my winter clothes back in Washington, where the damp cold was in full effect. These clothing considerations were not just limited to the weather. With the situation as dire as it was, it would make sense to bring my best suit. All of this was back in Korea, so I immediately went to one of the many travel agencies dotting the strip along Koh Chang's White Beach, and tried to book both a flight back to Korea and then another home. This took some wrangling. I was attempting to fly during the absolute height of holiday peak season. Seats were at a premium, and I wouldn't be able to make it home for over a week, barring purchasing a first class ticket, which was well out of my price range.

My happy trip to Thailand suddenly turned into a spiral of anxiety. Here I was, with the girl I loved, in a location of pure beauty—emerald jungle and brilliant sea—yet my mind echoed with the refrain G*o home. Go home.* But what could I do? I was stuck there for several more days, so I made a charade of enjoying my vacation. I rented a motorcycle and toured around the island with Da-jin. We hiked to a waterfall and swam in the cool waters. We went night fishing for barracuda and got skunked.

On New Year's Eve, our little resort put together an elaborate buffet meal, with fresh, grilled seafood. Da-jin and I were seated with a sad, childless couple from Japan. The four of us were the only non-Europeans in the place, so we were put together by default. A performance area was set up in front of the tables, where we were subjected to the staff of the resort belting out awful Thai karaoke numbers, as well as the requisite Siamese dancing. The entertainment started at seven and was stretched out over five hours. After a pile of food and two glasses of wine, Da-jin and I retired to the bungalow and took a nap, rising only ten minutes before midnight, just in time for the shower of fireworks blasting off down the beach.

We walked the beach hand in hand, color-drenched explosions blooming over our heads. The beach was full of revelers—both locals and tourists. Everywhere we heard the sing-song tones of Swedish being spoken. Reggae and techno music bumped from the many beach-side bars and restaurants. Shirtless fire twirlers swung their flames to an apathetic crowd (kind of a one-trick discipline). We eventually made it down to a big stage, with yet more reggae: a full band of dreadlocked Thais were giving it their best Peter Tosh. We took it in for a moment and turned back around, sauntering back toward the bungalow. I was in no mood for dancing. We ended up taking a nightcap on the beach, at a bar run by an overweight ladyboy in a hot pink dress that acted as a second skin. The margaritas weren't bad, but the whole affair just felt wrong.

I was back in Busan within three days; five days after that I stumbled off of the Northwest Airlines Tokyo-to-Seattle flight that I knew so well. Washington was as bleak as it always is in the winter—a canvas of grays, blues, and dark greens, with the sky perpetually three feet above your head—and soon enough I was in my white PT Cruiser rental (the only car left), Neil Young in the CD player, screaming down Interstate 5 toward the facility where my mom was housed.

The smell smacked me in the nose as I pulled into the Puyallup

River Valley where Tacoma—Seattle's white-trash little sister—sits splayed out in all of her muddy splendor. It's known as the "Tacoma aroma" in Washington State, the result of the pulp mill that still operates near the mouth of the river at Commencement Bay. On the hill that sits beside the sad downtown I saw St. Joseph's hospital, the place where, almost 37 years before, I was born. Both my parents were from Tacoma. They grew up and were married there. I had spent the first six months of my life in one the town's unglamorous suburbs, and luckily remember none of it. It's an ugly town—Rust Belt-like—with boarded-up businesses and a palpable lack of optimism. But, as is often the case with such places, a huge heart beats underneath. It's unpretentious and all about getting to work. As good a place as any to die, I suppose.

Following complicated directions copied from my Korean computer, I arrived at the nursing home where my mother was staying. She had been moved there two weeks earlier, when it became clear that her care needs far exceeded those of the adult group home that we had grudgingly chosen for her two months before. It was a place of antiseptic smells, fluorescent lights, and an underpaid, indifferent staff. I rushed through the corridors in a manic attempt to locate her room. When I found it, I sucked in a sour breath and entered. She was in the back, one of two occupied beds. My brother Glen sat next her, stroking her hand and whispering soothing words. He stood when he saw me and wrapped me in an embrace.

"How was the flight?"

"It gets shorter every time."

She lay there, asleep, looking grey and empty. Each pained breath was piercingly audible—a struggling wheeze. I leaned down and kissed her forehead. It was sticky and cool; I faintly tasted her sweat on my lips.

"Where's Mark?" I asked.

"His flight gets in just about now. Hopefully he'll get his car and be here within the hour."

We sat there for the next forty-five minutes, staring at this woman who, up until this year, had been an immovable force in our lives. She had anchored us all through our worst times. She had given us words of hope and most of all, listened deeply, beyond language. She was now weak, reduced in limbs and spirit, her body and will irreparably broken. I gripped my brother's hand and he mine. Mom's breaths became weaker and less frequent.

"She's going now. She's going."

My brother—having worked as a paramedic and surgical tech, as well as having lost several close friends—knew more of death than most people should.

We now stood over her, made the sign of the cross, and recited the Lord's Prayer:

Our Father, who art in heaven, hallowed be thy name…

Within five minutes of completing the prayer, she died. I had gotten there just in time.

My sister Molly had come to the nursing home shortly before the end, but chose to stay outside of the room, just as she did for my dad's death the year before. She had been both my parents' best friend and caregiver during those last years, and despite dealing with the awful day-to-day realities of caring for the sick, she had no stomach for death itself. My brother Mark was still absent. Unlike me, he hadn't beaten the clock, so I waited at the entrance for his arrival. He eventually pulled into the parking lot, and as he emerged from his car, I calmly approached him.

"How is she?"

"I'm so sorry, Mark…"

I buried my mother on my 38th birthday and returned to Korea two weeks later, where I went back to work, and got on with life, pretending that everything was normal. And in many ways, things were no different. I had been away from home for several years, and even before that had almost always lived in a different city than Mom and Dad. I was used to not seeing either of them for long periods of time. Now, though, they were really *gone.* This truth loved to slap me in the face at inconvenient times. Both parents dead in less than a year. Both of them sixty-six. It was and is a dizzying thing to contemplate. Often I'd forget and reach for the phone in attempt to call them, only to have my hand stop in mid-trajectory: *Oh yeah, that's right.*

How long does it take the heart to accept what the mind already knows? Months… years, sometimes. These realizations came in flashes, momentary flurries of panic and horror, the knowledge that I was truly alone. Da-jin and I eventually broke up, partly due to the geyser that I had become in the wake of what I went through with my parents. For all her mistakes—her jealousies, her bitterness and resentments—she did what she could to support me. She stood by me through the most trying two episodes of my life so far, but any slight unhappiness on her part was met with rage by me. We tried for three years and she was there for the worst of it, but even that couldn't save us.

A few days after we parted ways, I went hiking alone. My head was full of static and I needed it cleared. It was a warm, fall day, and I headed up to Geumjeongsan, Busan's biggest and most famous mountain. I walked from my small apartment in the center of the city, along the busy streets, past old women selling lettuce and orange persimmons; past men gathered in the parks, playing *go-stop* and *baduk*; past the packs of white and navy-blue clad middle-school girls, with their frumpy short haircuts and fat backpacks. Visor-wearing ajummas sold the pressed fish-paste skewers known as *odeng*, batter-fried cuttlefish, and spicy *ddokbokki* from food stands on the side of the streets. Warbling voices hawked vegetables and frozen mackerel from blue flatbed pickup trucks, tape loops blaring their deals through old, distorted speakers. Eventually, I reached the mountain, climbing up under the orange cable car line that ferries the lazier visitors up and down the slope. The trail got steep and I quickly left the din of the city, relaxing in the peaceful quiet of the low pines. Lone older men passed me on the trail, giving small waves, smiling and greeting me with "*Pangapsumnida*!" always happy to see a foreigner hiking on the mountain, that most Korean of pastimes.

Close to the summit, I stopped off on a large rock that offered a viewpoint of the city below. I saw how beautiful Busan was from the air, a long reach of white and beige buildings with green mountains in between. I could make out the span of Gwangan Bridge in the background, with the blue of the ocean behind it. A game was on in Sajik-dong: the baseball stadium was packed full of fans, whose cheers and songs floated along the wind and up the mountain. I looked down at these streets that I knew so well, that in just five years I had traveled extensively, by bus, taxi, motorcycle, and on foot. For that one moment I didn't feel like a foreigner. I felt like I belonged to this city, that I had earned a place in it. Yes, I was alone. My parents were gone, and though I still had friends and family in America, I didn't have a *home* there. My home had moved. I had taken it with me, and it now resided in a place called Yeonsan-dong, in a crazy city named Busan, on the southern tip of the Korean Peninsula. Who could have predicted such a thing?

I suppose that day I came to some sort of peace, that the anger which had possessed me so greedily had now relaxed its grip. It turned into sadness, which in time blows away, I'm told. But it still cuts me to think about what went on, how death can come earlier than any of us wish, and how ugly it can be. I have many friends here whose parents come to visit. It's a very natural thing, isn't it? Parents come to visit their son or daughter who works in Korea. It's a great excuse for a trip to Asia. I often meet these parents. I shake their hands and attempt my best happy face ("Do you like Korea? What food have you tried? Wow!"), but I really want to fold in on myself. I see my friends' parents—usually in their late fifties, sixties, or even seventies—and it reminds me of what I don't have. These parents who come to Korea are vibrant and healthy, traveling across the world to see their kids, who in turn will go back home to visit them. I know that I will never have this, and it busts me up inside.

CHAPTER 18

ALMOST KOREAN

A few years ago I discovered a lump in the middle of my back, about the size of a large gumball. It wasn't painful; nor was it particularly uncomfortable; but it was unsightly, and it was a lump, so I thought it wise to have it looked at. I visited one of the large hospitals here in Busan and was quickly seen a by an internal medicine specialist, who informed me that I had grown a benign fatty tissue known as a *lipoma.* He told me that this condition was quite common and non life-threatening, but that it would be best to have it removed.

I came in the next week for surgery, which took just thirty minutes; only a local anesthetic was applied. The wound, however, took a frustratingly long time to close up, due to the stitches being removed too early by a different doctor (they were subsequently put back in). The thing became a bit of mess, frustrating my main doctor with each successive trip to the hospital. Finally, after about two weeks' worth of visits, my doctor looked me in the eyes and said, in stilted yet competent English:

"As you may know, the white man heals much more slowly than the yellow man, because the white man has the weaker tissue."

Weaker tissue? There he was: the picture of clinical professionalism—white coat, stethoscope around his neck, standing in front of a desk, behind which were framed several very fancy-looking diplomas. This man was a medical doctor, yet was relying on some half-baked notion of eugenics to explain what was going on. Did he graduate from the Josef Mengele School of Medicine? Or was he just repeating to me what he had been taught all of his life: that the difference between Koreans and other races goes all the way to the molecular level?

A Visit to a Dead President's Home

In May of 2009, former South Korean president Noh Mu-hyun committed suicide by jumping off a mountain behind his house, near the town of Gimhae. At the time, Noh was under investigation for corruption. Many believed that this inquiry was a politically motivated witch-hunt overseen by the new right-wing president, Lee Myung-bak. Noh came from humble beginnings and built a reputation as a human rights lawyer. He ended up succeeding Kim Dae-jung as leader of South Korea and continuing his more liberal policies, including that of rapprochement with the North. It is said that Noh took his own life to spare his family the shame and indignities that come with a full investigation. It worked: soon after his death, the lead prosecutor in the investigation resigned and all further inquiries were called off. It seems that in Korea, the authorities can be paid off in blood, especially if it's your own.

I was shocked when I read the news of Noh's suicide. The thought of a former American president taking his own life was and is unfathomable, yet in Korea such a thing, while upsetting for many, didn't seem to come as a huge surprise. There is a long tradition of suicide in Korea, especially in an attempt to shield one's family from dishonor. Both the ex-mayor of Busan and the incumbent mayor of Yangsan, along with several other nationally prominent figures, have killed themselves as a result of corruption scandals, so Noh's death could hardly be viewed as anomaly. Still, it was big news, and it happened just an hour away from Busan.

Two days after Noh Mu-hyun's death, my friend Big Welsh Will and I met for breakfast. It was Sunday. We had planned a motorcycle day trip, but still had no destination. So over a cup of coffee, Will suggested what I was already thinking: "Why not go to Noh Mu-Hyun's village and check out where he killed himself? Should be an interesting scene."

Objective sorted.

We took the long way there, following a road that snakes alongside the Nakdong River, rising and falling from the valley floor. The hot day that I had predicted failed to materialize; instead, we had to contend with menacing clouds and periodic sprinkles. I had been so confident about good weather that I left my leather jacket at home and ended up wearing Will's raincoat to stave off the chill.

We crossed the river and rode into the hilly countryside. Strange industrial parks were built up all through the area, sometimes side by side with tiny cattle farms, whose occupants were penned up in drab, metal barns. These industrial complexes are staffed mainly by foreign workers, working in jobs locally described as *3-D*: difficult, dangerous, and dirty. This was evidenced by the many foreigners we saw along the side of the road—mainly darker-skinned men from Southeast Asia or the Indian subcontinent. Eventually, after leaving the main road for a narrow country lane, we came across some road signs guiding us to Bonghwa Mountain, the very place where the ex-President had ended his own life.

A tiny dirt road led up the mountain and ended at a temple on the top. We dismounted and walked to the summit, joining a small group of Koreans looking over to the rock face from which he had jumped. Straight below us was the President's village of Bongsa, packed with mourners.

"Noh Mu-hyun?" I asked.

They nodded their heads in confirmation.

Will and I walked along the path toward the cliff, and began to climb. Part of the way up, we came across an ajosshi in a suit haranguing a security guard—who had obviously been posted to keep people away from the jump-spot. From what I could glean, he was upset about being barred from the exact spot of the leap, and that it was his right as a citizen of the Republic of Korea to go there. After calling the guard a motherfucker in Korean, he turned around and walked back down the path. Upon seeing us, he smiled and addressed us in loud but broken English.

"There!" [*pointing to the top*] "Noh Mu-hyun dive!" [*mimes jumping*] "Goodbye! Sayonnara!"

Laughing to himself, he walked away. I'm guessing he was a member of the conservative Grand National Party.

After getting as close to the death-cliff as possible, Will and I walked back to our bikes and made our way down the mountain. Along the gravel track, a skinny man in glasses flagged me down. He wanted a lift back down the mountain, so I obliged him. Just as he hopped onto my bike, the sky opened up with a barrage of rain. The various clouds had gathered to form one big, nasty über-cloud, and we were caught in the middle of a late-spring squall.

The three of us took refuge under a roofed entranceway of one of the buildings at a roadside industrial center. We smoked cigarettes and conversed the best we could. Our bike guest spoke swiftly and with a very strong provincial accent, so I missed a lot of what he was saying, choosing the good ol' nod-and-smile most of the time. I did tell him that we wanted to get to Noh Mu-hyun's actual village, and he agreed to show us the way.

After about thirty minutes, the shower abated, and we were back on the road. We dropped the skinny guy off a couple of kilometers from the village, and he pointed us in the right direction, which was obvious from the sea of cars headed that way. The police had the main road into the village blocked off, and like most everyone else (save a few bigwigs) we had to walk, so we legged it the three kilometers to the President's village, joining thousands of mourners in what now felt like a pilgrimage. Many were dressed in black and held white carnations (a Korean symbol of mourning). A news helicopter buzzed the crowds and rice paddies that lay adjacent to the bucolic village. Bonghwa Mountain stood in the background, the sheer cliff face staring all of us down, a grim reminder of the reason for the gathering.

At one point a line of hundreds of Buddhist monks and nuns came walking from the mourning site. They wore matching robes and straw hats. The crowd of shuffling visitors split as the Buddhists made their way through.

As we came into the village, the crowd thickened to a jostling mass. A photo of the ex-President stood on an easel. Hundreds of people gathered in front of it, bowing and showing their respect. Another building contained more photos and a large book, where visitors could write notes of condolence. Others scribbled messages on yellow flags strung up around the village.

I was no fan of Noh. The man got elected in '02 by whipping up anti-American sentiment, by exploiting the accident in which the two Korean girls had been killed by the US tank. I wasn't here then, but foreigners who were tell of a lot of harassment by angry, xenophobic Koreans. He also coddled North Korea, giving into their demands and sending them aid, without receiving a single concession in return. But for many Koreans—especially those who had come of age during the tumult of the 1980s—Noh was a hero. He rose from truly humble beginnings to the highest office in the land and was proof that the democracy they fought so hard for could actually work. The country went into full mourning, and for a full week performances were cancelled and many bars were closed, a rarity in this alcohol-fueled society. His suicide was an historic event, so I felt compelled to ride out to Bongha to check it out for myself. It was a strange and interesting day, one that reminded me to the bone that I live very far from home, that Korea—no matter how used to it I get—is very much a foreign country. I'll always be an outsider peering in.

Dae Han Min Guk Pighting!

I've been in Korea for the last two World Cup Finals, though I wasn't here in 2002, when they co-hosted with Japan. That year, under the tutelage of Dutch coach Gus Van Hiddink, the Korean national team made a surprise run to the semi-finals, taking out powerhouses such as Italy and Spain. They eventually finished fourth, exceeding most everyone's expectations, including their own. The country went nuts—a kind of patriotic soccer mania that reached a fever pitch. I was living in Los Angeles at the time and took in many of the games on TV. I was astounded by the Korean fans—how they worked in perfect unison. Everything seemed meticulously rehearsed: the chanting, drumming, and singing; the brandishing of cards and massive flags. The pure fervor put forth by the Korean fans was in a league of its own—and this was as viewed through a television screen half a world away. To have been there in person must have been overwhelming. It was almost disturbing in its intensity and uniformity. What it immediately brought to mind were the synchronized routines of the North Korean crowds during their annual Mass Games. One could see straight away that the DMZ was only a political divide, that Southerners displayed their own nationalistic fervor in a nearly identical way to their Northern brethren. The power behind it was unmistakable, and with such a massive boost provided by its supporters, it's no wonder their scrappy team almost went all the way.

Fast forward to the 2010 World Cup Final, where South Korea met Greece in their first match. I met Angry Steve and Sam in Seomyeon, Busan's central downtown area. We managed to get a table at a small grilled meat restaurant, near where we had watched a Korean match at the World Cup four years earlier. The whole district—as well as the restaurant—was filled with locals sporting their red t-shirts. Many of the girls wore light-up devil horns—a nod to their team's nickname, the Red Devils. When striker Park Ji-seung hit the first goal, the place exploded. You could hear cheering and people *losing it* throughout the whole city. It was as if someone had applied a lit match to a gas leak. Such enthusiasm was infectious, and the three of us were immediately on our feet, high-fiving and even embracing the Koreans, who were lost in the momentary ecstasy of a World Cup goal. We kept our eyes attached to the screens (there were two) throughout whole match, looking away only to refill a glass or tend to the sizzling pork on the grill. When the second goal was scored, the place once again blew up, and when the final whistle was blown, the whole of Seomyeon emptied out into the streets for a spontaneous party. Throngs of Koreans were singing and clapping. Groups of young men banged on drums. They all sported bright red, and many of them had small versions of the *taegukgi*—their national flag—painted on their faces. As we walked through the mass of people—thick as grass—we were greeted by strangers. I kept shouting *Congratulations!* and clapping my hands as we pressed on, observing a pure joy and pride that's not always so evident in Korean people. Everyone we came across was kind and looked us in the eyes, as if to say *Welcome to Korea. We are capable of anything, even beating the best European teams at their own game.* There was none of the anger, overbearing attention, or uneasiness that, as foreigners, is sometimes thrown our way. These people were confident, and confidence breeds no ill will.

On that occasion, and others like it, I found myself envying Koreans, if for nothing else than their sense of belonging. That night, it became nakedly apparent that these were one people, and that they relate to each other in a way that I would never fully understand. They knew exactly who they were and were very proud of what that was. They were Korean and experiencing it together. There was such an overwhelming sense of being part of something, of identity, of deeply bonded togetherness, that I found myself wanting to know what that must feel like. I grew up in an immigrant country with a short history. The culture that formed me is the most individualistic on the planet. I carry an American passport and speak American English and am a product of that culture, but I almost never *feel* American. I don't have a great sense of Americanness. And now here I was in a country, that, though familiar, was still very foreign, and despite the fact that I had already been there for six years, I would always be an outsider. Just for once I wanted to know what it must be like to really *belong*, to feel the deep connection that was so evident among the Koreans chanting and singing in the street that night. I wanted to taste that thing that they had, but knew that however much I tried, I never could.

Some Things I Will Never Understand

Despite my feelings of otherness, after six years my comfort level with this place has grown immensely. Sure, I'm still stared at and giggled at least once every day, and I struggle to be understood in the language, but I do feel like I have a place in Korea, that after so much time living and working here I am owed a modicum of normal treatment. Often, when speaking with the locals in Korean—usually about what food I enjoy or which places I know—I'll be honored with the phrase reserved for foreigners who have really made an attempt to fit in:

"Oh! You are almost Korean."

I'm usually thrilled when Koreans say this to me. It validates my efforts to respect their ways, it makes me feel like I've made progress, and that, even if for just a moment, I am perceived as being less foreign than before.

But these attempts are superficial: I'll always be a foreigner, and despite my periodic smugness, despite my feeling that I understand Koreans and their culture better than many other expats, something will happen to remind me that I really know very little, that I am still the consummate outsider.

"You are *almost* Korean."

Almost.

About a month into the last semester, while teaching at the college, I noticed that one of my students was absent. He had come to every class before but had now suddenly stopped.

"Jae Yong?" I asked, scanning the room. Nothing. Another red slash in the attendance book.

This went on for a whole week. He had been a reliable student and was now nowhere to be seen. Despite this, I thought little of it. Students get sick; they suddenly go into the army; or, more often, just quit. On the following Monday morning I rolled into class and called out the names as I always do. Again, I got to his:

"Jae Yong?" Silence. "Where's Jae Yong? Is he sick or something?"

The handful of weary students in front of me shifted in their chairs and glanced at each other. Finally, a young man named Jung-woo spoke up:

"Uhm... teacher... Jae Yong is dead."

For a second I thought he was joking. I've had many students joke that their missing friends are dead. Young Koreans have a dark sense of humor in this regard. I reflexively attempted a grin, but from the mood of the others I could tell that Jung-woo was serious.

"Dead? Really? Oh man... that's... terrible. What happened?"

"Car accident."

"Wow. I... I don't know what to say..."

It seemed that the other students didn't either.

"Well... turn to page 32 in your books. Today we will be going over giving directions to hotel facilities...."

After class I returned to my office and went over Jae-Yong's student card, which contained his participation and homework grades up to that point. I saw that he was a good student, headed for an A. Everything on the card reflected a success, and while it was certainly sad that this young man was no longer with us, it also bothered me that my boss had never even informed me. In fact, none of the foreign staff were told. Here I was reading a *dead student's* name four classes in a row, thinking that he was home with a cold. What does it take to get notified? One would figure that the death of a student would be significant enough to warrant informing the teachers. I cannot conceive for a second why the boss would choose to withhold such information.

This is typical of working in Korea in that, as foreigners, we're totally out of the communication loop. We're really considered off the totem pole in this status-obsessed culture. It's not that we're too low or too high—we're not even there to begin with. This cannot be changed. A foreigner in Korea will always be just that. No amount of language acquisition, soju tolerance, or chopstick dexterity will make up for it. You are an outsider, an alien. You can marry into a Korean family, become a Buddhist, and participate in their annual ancestral rites, but you will never be one of them. They will always consider you to be *other*, and as a result, it may not even occur to them to inform you when someone you know, teach, or work with dies.

Later that day, I went to my boss and told him what I had heard from my students. He got a very serious look on his face and said:

"Yes... it... it is true that Jae Yong is... is..." he searched deeply for a polite way to put it, but came up short: "dead."

"What happened? A car accident?"

"Uhm... no. Not car accident. It is an issue for his family."

"What do you mean?"

"His family does not wish to say how he died."

"Okay," I said.

"They've already had the funeral. They didn't want to inform the students until after."

It became quickly apparent to me that this kid had killed himself, hence the family's reticence to discuss the cause. A sense of secrecy and shame permeated the whole discussion. It was almost like my boss was saying to me: "It is a sad thing, but better to forget and not mention it again," as if speaking of it would invite a curse or cause the family even more grief.

Is that why he didn't contact us? Out of deference for the family? Did he think we wouldn't find out anyway? Didn't we deserve to be told?

I love this country, but sometimes Koreans mystify me. I suppose they always will.

INTERLUDE

JUNE, 2010 TUMWATER, WASHINGTON

IT'S a peaceful cemetery—but that's what people always say, isn't it? Except for a couple of maintenance guys, there's no one here. Bunches of flowers give a break of color between the green of the grass and the grey of the headstones. It is quiet, and a slight breeze blows. So it is peaceful, save the hiss of the freeway, which filters in through the evergreen trees that ring the field of the dead.

I stumbled off the plane after sixteen hours of travel—not a deadly amount, but enough to make you loopy, especially when you don't sleep a wink during what should be a whole night's rest. This added up to two nights, if you count the one before the flight that I spent with my girlfriend Minhee, holding her and gazing into her eyes, wondering why I had to fall deeply for a girl just before a long trip to America. But I needed to come home, to see my family—both the living and departed. My sister is getting married and we are all going to gather for a happy occasion, a welcome excuse after being called home for sickness, bad news, and funerals.

To see both of your parents' names—one next to the other—gracing a headstone will take the air out of even the toughest among us. I am alone, armed only with a bundle of flowers that I picked up at the Fred Meyer store down the road. I approach the spot in the wall where their remains are interred and am shot in the gut: I'm home, but they're gone. It's never been so tangible. An ocean's distance does wonders to blur the realities of life. The last time I was home was for

Mom's funeral, but that was too soon, as they say: her name had yet to be etched into the cold marble. Now, there it is, spelled out for me to read in disbelief, over and over again.

Not knowing quite what to do, I bow before them, in the manner of a Korean ancestral rite known as *jae-sa*. This is not planned, but it seems appropriate. I am so seized with grief that the ground is the only place that makes sense, at least for the time.

After Mom and Dad, I make my way to the veterans' section, next to the big Howitzer that marks the area for those who served.

"Can I help you?" a maintenance guy asks.

"No, I'm just looking for my grandfather's grave."

"What's his name?"

"Glen Christ-"

I look down and there he is:

Glen Christiansen
US Army major
WWII

I kneel down and kiss the stone, rubbing the smooth surface with the palm of my hand.

"Here's a little something for you, Gramps."

I open the bottle of Chivas Regal that I picked up in Narita's duty free and give the grass in front of the headstone a generous pour. Gramps was never one to say no to a taste of Scotch, and I'm not about to deny the man, even in the afterlife. He was a second father to me.

Again I bow.

Next to Grandpa C. lie my great grandparents, Matt and Marie Reisenhauer, whom I had the pleasure of being very close to until I was 12 and 13. They left this world exactly one year apart. These graves are nearly 30 years old now, and the surrounding grass encroaches well onto the faded stone. I rip at it with my fingers and sweep the excess away with my hands. I give them both a belt of booze and again I bow.

CHAPTER 19

GOING UP THE COUNTRY

IT was the end of the hottest summer I'd endured in six years. The heat was persistent and draining, an unwelcome guest who refuses to leave the party. The slightest exertion caused my clothes to stick to my skin like wet toilet paper. The new semester was grinding away and *Chuseok*—Korea's Thanksgiving, harvest festival, and biggest holiday—was right around the corner.

With the coming three-day holiday falling squarely midweek, most schools in the country chose to take all five days off. This doesn't happen too much in work-obsessed Korea, so our little expat motorcycle gang—the Rain Dogs—planned an epic journey around much of the southern part of the peninsula. So, after meeting Sunday night in central Busan, we were off, crossing the Nakdong River and shooting down the small highway toward the neighboring burg of Changwon. Our bikes were running smoothly and the night's heat made it possible to ride in our t-shirts. With light traffic, we made good time on the open road. We had a full roster this time around, the whole gang on board:

- Essex, England's David Scraggs, also known as Her Majesty's Man in Korea;
- B.C. Jay, who hails from Vancouver, British Columbia—though the B.C. in his name actually stands for *Boring Canadian*;
- Idaho's Sam Hazelton, my officemate and partner in crime, whose neck and head are shockingly similar in width;
- Big Welsh Will, a mild-mannered Welshman with feet as big as Frankenstein's monster's;

- And this here author.

****

After a night in a Changwon love motel, we woke up headed through the port city of Masan, down the coast road that would take us to Namhae—an island that sticks out from the peninsula like a stumpy toe—separated from the mainland by the narrowest strip of water. The road passed through the town of Tongmyeong and followed the coast east, winding up into the hills, through villages surrounded by terraced rice paddies, golden with ripened grain ready for harvest.

As the road twisted down out of the hills to a settlement near the water, we noticed a sign: *Dinosaur Footprints*. The southern coast of the Korean Peninsula is famous for its fossilized dinosaur remains, along with actual footprints, which can be found along at spots along the shoreline, etched into the rock. The signs directed us through a near-empty parking lot next to a pier. Old buoys and fishing nets lay in piles, and seagulls sailed in the breeze. The place smelled of old fish, rubber, and salt, and the blue-green water gently licked the rocks of the shore. We dismounted our bikes and hiked out to the black volcanic rock that held the evidence of these great beasts' wanderings, our eyes fixed for any sign of a claw or paw prints.

"Over 'ere," David said, pointing down to some splotchy spots on the rocks. "You see 'em?"

I did not. Certainly there were some kind of imprints, but millions of years of waves and wind had cratered the rocks. With no smooth surface in sight, we couldn't tell whether these imprints were dinosaur footprints or just holes. We gave a collective sigh, jumped on the bikes, and headed out toward the main road.

At the intersection, we saw three grandfathers sitting on a raised platform—a common sight in Korea—especially during the warmer months. They drank from paper cups filled with soju and snacked on kimchee and fried fish. Upon seeing a group of five foreign riders, they waved us over and filled a cup for each of us, poured from a disturbingly large several-liter plastic bottle.

"Where are you coming from?" Their accents were thick and countrified and different from the *saturi* that I usually heard in Busan.

"Busan."

"Oh. Busan! You have traveled far! Did you see the dinosaur prints?"

"Oh, yes," David replied in very competent Korean, though with a cumbersome Southern English accent draped over it like a woolen blanket. "They were very interesting!" I think he was lying for the sake of diplomacy.

"Oh... very good... very good." The old boys nodded in agreement.

"What country do you come from?"

As David told them each of our nationalities, the grandfathers emitted sounds of great approval. They were very much impressed at our international membership and likely had never seen so many foreigners in their village since the war. They were so impressed, in fact, that they unscrewed the top of the bottle and offered us more soju. This act of hospitality was short-lived, however, interrupted by a woman's shrill voice. An old grandmother, probably one of their wives, strutted across the empty road and waved her hand in annoyance.

"No, you old fools! Can't you see they are riding motorcycles? No alcohol!"

The men quickly recapped the bottle, sheepishly obeying her command. We gave bows and smiles and headed out down the road, slightly warmed from the alcohol in our guts—and a little thankful for her intervention.

"Hast du Kimchee?"

The last thing you expect when motor biking through rural South Korea is a village made up entirely of wooden homes, complete with 45-degree red-tiled roofs. Garden gnomes pop up throughout the impeccably-landscaped yards, many of which contain *real* grass. Mercedes-Benz, Audi, and BMW automobiles are parked in the driveways, and elderly white men can be seen pruning the flowers and heard talking to one another in guttural Teutonic tones. It's as if you have just driven through the Black Forest, exited the Autobahn, and rolled straight into a real German village. In fact, it *is* a German village. That's its official name: the German Village. This German village contains many of the trappings and details you'd expect from such a place, and like any real idyllic European spot, it too is filled with mobs of gawking, photo-snapping Koreans.

In the 1960s and '70s, thousands of Koreans emigrated to West Germany for work. Some toiled in the mines, but most of these transplants were women who went to work as nurses in German hospitals. Many married German men and made lives for themselves there. Fast forward to modern Namhae, with an aging population of just 51,000—less than half of what it was in the Sixties. Namhae, despite being one of the most beautiful spots in the country, is losing people, so the Korean government has undertaken different strategies to get them to resettle. One such scheme is the German Village, built with the intention of drawing back some of these emigrants by offering the actual Germans a taste of home, while giving the Koreans a chance to return to their real home. *Ja vol.*

Of course we, the Rain Dogs, could not resist the pull of the German Village. We twisted the throttle and pushed our weak bikes up the precipitous hill, rolling into a hamlet that was painfully quaint, Disney-like in its accuracy and artifice. Upon seeing such detailed design, such Northern European purity, I felt the urge to sing and speak in German—to *be* German. I had learned a bit of German from an exchange-student friend in high school. So, from the safety of my slow-moving bike, I belted out the lines of the German national anthem, which he had taught me so many years ago:

Einigkeit und Recht und Freiheit
Für das deutsche Vaterland!
Danach lasst uns alle streben
Brüderlich mit Herz und Hand!

This clamor at once attracted the attention of the Korean tourists, who turned their many cameras away from the pretty houses and lawns and onto me, figuring they had at last found a real German in the not-so-real German Village. As they smiled and pointed, I greeted them with a hearty wave and in my best Bavarian lilt, repeated: "*Hallo Deutsche freunden! Hallo! Wie geht's dir? Gut? Ich bin sehr gut!*" I did this throughout the village, bellowing my hackneyed greeting for all to hear. At one point we reached a dead end in the road, which was punctuated by a small guard-house. A diminutive old Korean man stood sentry. He wore a sagging, oversized uniform that emphasized his emaciated frame, giving him the look of a grumpy and malnourished child. His hat appeared to eat his head. Alarmed by the sight of our gang, he got up and stepped out of the house, taking us in with sharp suspicion. He had heard me singing and did not like it one bit. Real Germans do not sing alone, especially when atop a motorcycle. He had been a guard at the German Village long enough to know this basic fact. I was far too festive a German, and therefore probably not a real German at all. This could not end well. He muttered into his radio—perhaps calling for backup? We took this as our cue to leave. After all, we still had soju on our breath from the pit stop near the dinosaur footprints. It was best to take no chances.

On our way down, we stopped off at a few houses, if just to take in the lovely design. They were quite nice, absolutely correct in their German assembly and craftsmanship—wood worked with expert care. You just don't see such houses in Korea, where view-blocking gates, blood-red brick, and metal-barred windows are the mainstay of any abode that isn't an apartment block. It was good to breathe in a scent of something different, a reminder of how nice houses can be. (*Houses!* Yes. People actually live in houses! Years on the peninsula can cause one to forget such a fact.) For a moment, I envied those lucky enough to live in the German Village, despite the fact that they would never know real privacy. What if I could live the reverse? What if I could marry a Korean woman and eventually move back to America, only to settle down in a government-built Korean Village nestled in a valley in rural Oregon? We could live in crowded brick houses or one-room apartments. We could make kimchee and bean paste in pots that we stored on the roof. Overweight American tourists could waddle down the narrow streets, marveling at the grandmothers crouching on the pavement, selling seaweed and octopus. "Look at that! Isn't it neat? Is that squid moving?" Real ajosshis could eat dog soup, gulp from bowls of rice wine, and piss on the sidewalk in broad daylight, while I'd sit on the heated floor of my home with my aging, permed, and visor-wearing wife, popping rice cakes and watching *trot* concerts on TV. Yes, the Korean Village.

I could think of worse fates.

Naked In Sangju

Right before dark we managed to get to our destination: Sangju Beach, puttering into town on our not-so-intimidating 125cc bikes, failing to frighten either small children or the very old. Before long, we located a minbak near the beach, where we chatted with a beaming ajumma who was more than happy to have some guests so close to the Chuseok holiday. She was especially thrilled to learn that it was David Scraggs' 40th birthday, a fact that was lost on most of us as well. He had kept it a secret, but now we were settled in, on one of the nicest beaches in the whole country, with practically no other tourists about. The weather was gorgeous, we were on vacation, and now we had David's 40th to celebrate.

After three-hour raw fish dinner we ended up on the beach, which was wonderfully empty. Sangju is a long sandy beach, popular with visitors in the summer. A bright moon peeked up over the mountainous ridge of the island, but the ocean itself was dark and loud with surf, the result of a typhoon surging in the Pacific some hundreds of miles south. David took one look at the black water and said, "All right lads. I'm going in." And with that, he stripped off his clothes and sprinted into the waves, *au naturale*.

"How's the water?" B.C. Jay shouted toward David's pale form bobbing in the foam.

"It's fucking great! Get in ya wanker!"

B.C. gingerly removed his shirt and jeans and drawers as well. Sam followed suit, and soon they were both in the sea.

"Dude! The water's perfect," Sam yelled our way.

Will lit a cigarette and considered the scene. Something caught his eye. "What's that up there?" He pointed to a thin object, jutting out of the sand.

"I dunno. Let's go see."

We walked up the beach and checked it out. It was a long windsurfing board, stuck vertically into the sand.

"Don't suppose anyone would mind if we took it out for a spin…"

"I don't believe they, would, Will."

With that we grabbed the board and hauled it toward the water. I stripped and ran into the surf, followed by an also-nude Big Welsh Will, board at his side.

The water was purifying and cathartic, still quite warm from months of summer heat, which lingered well into September. The waves were some of the largest I'd ever seen in Korea. We took turns paddling on the massive board, trying to ride the good swells, but the board was too large: it invariably kicked out from whoever was trying to command it, causing a wipe-out that was surely more fun than any real ride. I was drunk and giddy, like a sugar-whapped kid let loose at Chuck E. Cheese's. It was cosmic revelry: raw nature and friendship, with enough booze to quash any fear.

None of us should have been swimming. It was definitely a bad idea, a roadmap to catastrophe—something that would horrify any mothers, wives, or girlfriends—but there are times when reckless fun trumps good judgment. I was alive and electric; all my hairs were copper wires, receiving signals from the fat, waxing moon. I was *there*, in the womb of the ocean, with my friends, with my new family, in my new home. Everything was warm and good and just felt right: bodies and water and the camaraderie that is brotherhood.

Our return-to-the-wild moment was eventually interrupted by the arrival of a small group of young Koreans, who, unlike us, came into the water fully clothed. David and I stood chest-deep as they came to greet us—two guys and two girls. They spoke some English and asked us the usual questions as they splashed each other and laughed with each deluge of a wave. They had no idea that we lacked clothes, our nudity masked by the fact that only our torsos were visible. This illusion was soon shattered by Big Welsh Will, however, who paddled by on the surfboard, his yogurt-white buttocks lit up by the angry moon.

"Hallo boys! Lovely night indeed, I'd say."

A look of horror shot into the eyes of the young Koreans, who immediately turned around and headed to shore, creeping away into the safety of the night, where they'd hopefully see no more stark-naked, raving Welshmen. It is fortunate that Will was lying on the surfboard, belly-down, for he is a massive man, both in frame and endowment. The guy has size-14 feet and a dick of similar proportions. I'm sure it's unlike anything those hapless kids had ever seen before. They could have been scarred for life, so let us count our blessings as they come.

One by one we came out of the water and put our clothes back on. At one point, David returned from the town's little store, where he had restocked on beer. We sat in the sand and drank some more. Despite my damp hair and tingling skin, I felt relaxed and content, if not just a little sleepy. It was then that I noticed a sound coming from the far end of the beach.

"Do you guys hear that?"

"Sounds like drumming," Sam replied.

"Look, down there, there's a group of 'em." David pointed to a dark mass of what appeared to be people, crouching over drums.

Why was there a drum circle on Sangju Beach in Korea? At one a.m.? Had the place suddenly been invaded by hippies? I didn't smell any patchouli, but you never can be too sure.

We grabbed our beers and made our way down the beach until we came to the group in question. They definitely weren't hippies, despite the drums and somewhat colorful garb. These guys—and they were all men—were dark-skinned Asians and made a mean percussion section.

"Hello my friends!" One of their ranks stood and welcomed us into the group. He wore a red-and-white shirt with a black cap.

"Hello!"

"Welcome."

"This is awesome. What's the occasion?"

"We are playing music from our country."

"And which country is that?"

"Sri Lanka!"

"Ahhh…"

It turns out that, like us, they were also foreign workers. Unlike us, they worked in the factories, which is the toughest work in Korea, especially for immigrant laborers.

These Sri Lankans were not bemoaning their situation on Sangju Beach that night. Like us, they were relaxing, and like us, they were celebrating. They were enjoying one of their precious days off by sitting on the sand and drumming into the night, by conjuring a bit of a home that must have felt far, far away. In a sense, we were doing the same. Upon hearing that it was David's birthday, they broke into a loud cheer.

"Actually," Dave looked at his watch, "my birthday's ended now. But thanks anyways, chaps."

With that, they hit the skins again: a spirited, up tempo rhythm. This went on for another hour. We stayed through the end, soaking up the drumming and warmth of the group, until the Sri Lankans stood up together, whisked the sand from their colorful clothes, and walked away into the dark.

The five of us were left sitting alone on the beach, with a half of a pack of smokes and nearly empty bottles.

"Happy Birthday, Scraggsy."

"Cheers."

We made our way back, forming a chain, weaving over the sand and through the streets of Sangju, up the treacherous stairs of our minbak and back into our tiny, shared rooms, where we could sleep away the approaching morning on warm, hard floors.

Return To Jirisan

The next day we rode north through a disconcertingly pissy rain, away from the coast and into the knotted, mountainous interior. Summer's final blast had exhausted itself, and the relentless drizzle which now fell was positively chilly. Actual Chuseok was just one day away, and the slick road was relatively empty of traffic. We took it slowly. We only had a two- or three-hour journey ahead of us, so there was no need to risk a spill. We were in no hurry.

We arrived at our destination thoroughly soaked and chilled, but with bikes and limbs intact. We were meeting another group of Busanites near Sangyesa Temple on the edge of Jirisan National Park, the site of my adventure with Josh "Donk" Graham some years earlier. I had since been returning over every Chuseok holiday, each time with a larger number of friends. Our compatriots—mainly folks from Busan's expat music scene—were holed up in a large minbak just uphill from the small river that runs down the valley. When we arrived, they were all on the premises, sipping beers and jamming acoustically under the building's flat roof.

"We thought you'd never get here." Scott greeted me with an open can. My stomach turned at the prospect. "Come on, a little hair of the dog won't hurt you."

* * * *

The next day, after an epic breakfast of eggs, homemade Mexican beans, and bacon, Big Welsh Will and I decided to go up the valley and explore this corner of Jirisan. We jumped on our bikes at noon, when the rain had ceased and the sun was splitting the clouds, and followed the two-lane road that wound along the little river.

As we pulled out, I noticed moving dots on the mountainside opposite our lodging: people, walking up to visit the numerous tombs situated on the steep grade. One of the main directives on Chuseok Day is to visit your relatives' graves and perform *jae-sa,* the Korean ancestral rite. Such graves are most often located on mountains and hills, but these were the highest I had ever seen. A tiny access road shot up the mountain until it petered out. The rest was an arduous hike to a small graveyard of sorts. Hauling the bodies up must have been a feat.

Will and I followed the main road up the valley, which was lush from the recent rains. Mist moved off the peaks, giving the place an ethereal, even tropical look. We passed small brown houses, many with wood fires burning, no doubt cooking Chuseok feasts. The smell of smoke and grilled pork filled the air, igniting our appetites as well. At one point a rough-looking one-lane road spurred up to the right, heading precipitously up the mountainside.

"That looks interesting," Will remarked, and at once we were in first gear, pushing our bikes up the track, following a small stream. After about ten minutes, the road reached a dead end in the smallest Korean village I had ever seen. The place was a cluster of little wood and stone abodes, precariously balanced on the mountain, crammed together and movie-set idyllic. We killed the engines and took the place in. Outside of a nearby house, seated on pieces of laid-out cardboard, were five middle-aged men. They stared our way. Will lit a cigarette and stared back.

"What do you reckon they'll do."

"Invite us to drink with them, I'm sure."

And with that, one of their ranks stood and approached, waving us over at the same time.

"Hello! Hello!" He brought his hand to his mouth, making an eating motion, followed by the inevitable mimed cup to the lips.

We were soon sitting in the circle with full glasses of beer. In the middle were several plates: wild mushrooms, carrots, peppers, bean-paste, and one whole, steamed chicken, known as *baek suk*. They handed us chopsticks, and I immediately dug in, relishing this delicious, fresh, *real* mountain food.

They were the Kang family, back to visit their mother in their home village over Chuseok. These men, cousins and brothers, were now scattered in cities all over the country, only returning to the mountain for the most important family occasions. I spoke with Kyung-hoon, the youngest brother, who wore glasses and was the most outgoing of the group. When I told him I lived in Busan, his face came alive.

"Busan! Really? I live in Gimhae! We are neighbors! Do you like baseball? The Lotte Giants?"

"Yes, I love baseball," I replied.

"Great. Next time we must go to a game together! Here is my business card."

While my Korean skills are by no means great, they're good enough to move a conversation along, especially when the topics travel along well-trodden ground. Will, on the other hand, despite a respectable time in the country, had mastered taxi directions, restaurant ordering, and not much else. He was reduced to nodding and smiling and relying on my very half-assed translations of what was going on.

The women of the Kang family were all in the rustic little house, working in the kitchen and cooking over the open fire stove. From time to time one of the men would bark an order their way, and a frowning wife or sister would emerge with the bottle of soju, bowl of rice, or whatever else was required. None of the women greeted either Will or me, but rather eyed both of us with tangible contempt—not, I think, because we were foreigners, but because we were men. We were two more mouths to feed, objects of the brothers' attempts to impress, and we certainly wouldn't be helping with the washing-up.

One of the Kang men did seem to have a problem with foreigners, which grew with every glass of soju he downed. He took a particular interest in my presence, sitting next to me and grilling me in a slur of indecipherable Korean. While I could make out much of what his more effusive brother said, I understood none of the speech oozing out of this guy's mouth, save the odd bit of profanity. He obviously didn't like me, and probably didn't like foreigners to begin with. This displeasure deepened with each successive, incomprehensible syllable.

"Looks like matey isn't too pleased with our presence," observed Will. "Perhaps it's time to leg it."

"Good idea."

With that we took our cue, bowing, shaking hands, promising to call for later baseball dates, sliding onto our bikes and making our way back down the mountain.

Our trip wasn't quite done for the day. We still had a couple of hours of light, as well as gas in our tanks. So we chose to explore the base of the valley, following the rocky reaches of the river down to where things got flatter and wider, where we found bushy rows of green tea and fields of ready-to-harvest rice. The small valley road eventually joined the busier route we had taken the day before, so Will and I cruised down this flat road, opening up the bikes and breathing in the sweet air of the Indian summer. To our left was a crudely fashioned sign (*Parasailing Jump-off Point*), followed by a tempting arrow, so we turned off onto the primitive road heading up the mountain and once again climbed. This route was steeper and rougher than anything we had been on previously. It shot straight up, with the surface concrete of the road disintegrating into pure dirt and rock the closer we got to the top.

A small walking path led up to the true top, no doubt the spot from where the enthusiasts launch their parasails, though we saw none gliding that day. What we did see, however, was the whole Jirisan ridge, along with many lesser mountains. The dipping sun hit the heights from low angles, bringing out shadows and colors unseen under the bright midday sun. Low-lying clouds had scudded in under us, blanketing the landscape, covering everything in a grey-and-white mist, out of which rose these ancient peaks of Korea. The moment was complete in its majesty and—best of all—we had the whole mountaintop to ourselves.

Harvest Time

The next few days saw us heading north into the heart of the country—and then back east toward Busan. The riding was pure butter, sliding through the most scenic and empty country any of us had taken in on the Korean Peninsula. We climbed up and dropped down many valleys containing nothing but rock, small pines, and farming villages. I felt like we had found *it*—that lost corner of Korea—the place that you hear about but never see. For great stretches we saw no Family Mart convenience stores; no blue-roofed industrial complexes; no monstrous green golf driving ranges; no commercial centers, cement trucks, or shitty love motels. We saw none of that, just open nature and small settlements scratching a living out of what the land had to offer. This part of the country is a living time capsule of how life used to be, presented as is, not packaged and theme-parked-up for fleets of tour busses. This old Korea is being erased at a kinetic pace, and there was something deeply soothing about seeing it exist in full splendor.

After spending two days relaxing and hiking the peaks of Deokyusan National Park, we headed back toward Busan. As we rolled through more countryside, we noticed that the rice was now being harvested. In Korea, the first thing they do after harvesting rice is haul it out of the fields in big bags and pour it over blankets set by the side of the road, where the kernels dry out in the sun. It was our last day of the trip and we'd stopped for a rest and pee break. I noticed two locals who were stooped over, spreading out the rice. Both of these farmers were old women, working without complaint. Their faces were etches of lives of toil. I approached the woman working nearest to us and addressed her in the most honorific Korean I could muster:

"Grandmother, that looks like hard work."

"Yes, it is. It gets harder every year," she replied in a rough country brogue.

"Where are all the young people?"

"They all left. In our village nearly all the young people have moved to the city. They prefer city life."

"Do you think they'll come back?"

"I hope so."

I nodded, smiled, and almost turned back, when another question urged me on.

"By the way… why doesn't your husband help you?"

"Ah… my husband died a few months ago."

"Oh, I'm so sorry."

"That's okay," the old woman said laughing. "I never liked him anyway."

She bent down and resumed her work. I walked back to my bike and joined the rest of the Rain Dogs as we rode east, back toward Busan.

CHAPTER 20

TENSION

THE snow seemed appropriate. It smothered the fields and dusted the tops of the otherwise brown hills, stripped of color by the winter extremes. Outside of Busan, the whole country was bathed in white. It thickened the farther north we went, following the KTX tracks across the spine of the peninsula and up into Seoul itself. Once I disembarked, I found that the sidewalks were impacted with hard snow, that even the mass of the city couldn't escape the icy deluge. It was piled up on the sides of the wide roads, while still covering the side streets. The scene was frigid and stark—perfect weather for visiting the last outcrop of the Cold War.

I signed in at the USO office at Yongsan, the US Army's sprawling base in Seoul. After killing some time outside, I boarded a bus filled with other Westerners, and soon we were off, snaking through Seoul's interminable traffic and heading north, out of the city, through the countryside, straight to the border with North Korea. This was a tour, pure and simple, with a chipper guide and backpack-toting tourists. There was an itinerary and a meal stop. It was as if we were visiting a temple, folk village, or famous waterfall. But this tour was different. We weren't going to a happy place. We had all paid about a hundred bucks apiece to step into what is technically a war zone, what some people describe as "the most dangerous place on Earth."

As we made our way north, the suburbs of Seoul gave way to snowy rice fields, low hills, and patches of pine forest. Traffic became suspiciously light, and the murmur inside the bus settled into silence. Before long, we passed through a checkpoint manned by automatic rifle-wielding South Korean troops, and soon we were at the site known as the 3rd Tunnel.

The 3rd Tunnel is just that: a tunnel, one of four found over the years by the South. It is assumed that the North has burrowed many more, yet undiscovered, and that 30,000 men, plus light artillery, could pass through the tunnel in just one hour, acting as a deadly portal less than 60 kilometers from Seoul. Today it's like an exhibit at Disneyland, with an interpretive center and a short film filling us in on the basics of the Korean War, for those who slept through high school history. The tunnel itself is deeper than I had expected, but in the end, it was just a long hole bored into rock. Still, to think about the tenacity it took to build the thing gives you an insight not just into the Northern—but the *Korean*—character in general.

After the tunnel, we attempted to enter the observatory on top of Dora Mountain, but were barred due to recent tensions. This small mountain holds a viewing platform, from which one can spy into North Korea via those coin-operated telescopes that adorn every tourist attraction with a view. The South Korean army maintains its own presence there… with much better telescopes, to be sure.

After a brief stop at Dorasan Station, the last before the Northern border (the rail lines are linked up, just not in operation), we headed into the JSA, the Joint Security area, in which lies the "truce village" of Panmunjom, a cluster of buildings where North and South Korea face off. As we pulled into Camp Bonifas—named for one of the two American soldiers killed in the infamous Axe Murder Incident by North Korean troops—things became noticeably more militarized. We were now actually in the DMZ. Fences and razor wire ringed the camp. As the bus rumbled into the parking lot, I pressed my face against the numbing cold of the window and eyed a gang of South Korean soldiers who horsed around in the field next to the lot. They wore full camouflage uniforms and were no doubt blowing off some of the steam that must build up from the boredom of working as guards. The buildings that made up the central cluster of the camp were beige and functional, reflecting the practicality of all military architecture. A line of flags drooped in the windless afternoon, representing each country in the U.N. force that fought alongside the South. After a brief wait, a young Latino US soldier wearing an MP armband boarded the bus. He walked down the aisle, checking everyone's identification, snapping on a piece of gum.

The soldier, Sgt. Dias, exited the bus, and we followed his vehicle to another building. When we stopped again, he instructed the tour group to get off and enter, where a different soldier handed us forms to sign, releasing the military of any liability in the unlikely case that actual shooting broke out and we all were killed. Sgt. Dias then made a small speech—by rote—briefing us on the basic rules for visiting the Joint Security Area. Topping the list of taboos was "pointing or gesturing to the North Korean soldiers." After the speech, the lights were dimmed and a quick film on the history and function of the site was blazed onto the white screen in front. We then re-boarded the bus and pulled off into the JSA.

The passengers were silent as the bus ground down the narrow road. What I noticed first was the wildlife: the place was lush with birds. This is one of the only cases where a protracted state of war has benefited animal populations: the DMZ—a four-kilometer-wide swath that bisects the whole Peninsula—is now one of the richest nature reserves in all of East Asia. Hopefully it will be preserved as such, long after reunification—though I'm sure the conglomerates of the South already have designs on this precious land.

The tour guide pointed to the spur road on our left which led to the South Korean "peace village" of Daeseong-dong. A massive *taegukgi* (South Korean flag) flew over the village, which is home to over one hundred farmers heavily subsidized by the government. They're said to be the best-paid rice growers on the peninsula. Daeseong-dong's counterpart in North, Kijong-dong, came into view moments later. According to both the representative from the US Army, as well as our guide, the village is actually uninhabited; the whole thing is just for show. A gargantuan North Korean flag loomed over the propaganda village, menacing the landscape from atop a high tower. It is, in fact, the largest flag in the world. There it was: *North Korea.* I could see buildings, a road, and, in the distance, the city of Kaesong, where companies from the South maintain an industrial park manned by North Korean workers, one of the dividends of the South's Sunshine Policy.

The bus turned the corner and pulled into the JSA parking lot. A large grey building stood in front of us: the South's Freedom House. Directly opposite was the North's own structure, a Stalinist-behemoth called Panmun Pavilion. We exited the bus, formed two lines, and were led into Freedom House by Sgt. Dias, along with Sgt. Morrison, a young blond-haired soldier from California. They were disarmingly relaxed for just having entered one of the tensest places on the planet. They quietly joked and even laughed as we went upstairs and entered the structure—just another day's work, it seemed. Inside of the building were a number of South Korean guards, in olive-green helmets and mirrored sunglasses. Unlike their American counterparts, these guys were all business; I couldn't detect even a hint of a smile. They played their roles like committed actors, part of the theatre that is the JSA.

We shuffled through the Freedom House and out the front doors, right to the edge of the Southern border. Three sky-blue buildings straddled the demarcation line—a slightly elevated concrete slab—that ran straight into the middle of the structures. Southern soldiers occupied positions on their end of the buildings, facing the imposing Panmun Pavilion in the North. At the top of the building's front steps stood a solitary North Korean soldier, who periodically spied us through a pair of binoculars. He was noticeably smaller than his beefy Southern brethren, almost swimming in the khaki-green uniform. The gum-chewing US soldiers told us—encouraged us, even—to snap photos. I latched onto my Olympus digital and zoomed in for all it was worth, capturing photographic evidence of this other human being. For a moment, a wave of shame crept up from inside: I felt cheap and exploitative, like a visitor to the zoo. I quickly extinguished this sense of guilt, however, when I gazed at the buildings, at the soldiers on "our side," at the thirty-or-so other camera-wielding tourists who were attempting to glean the same thrill as me. Here we were, at the money shot of the

DMZ tour, and it wasn't really thrilling at all. There certainly was no overt sense of danger. Instead it felt hollow and strangely routine, even.

We were then led into the middle blue building. It was narrow and long, with a table directly in the middle. Two South Korean guards accompanied us, blocking one of the windows and the exit to the North, respectively. They clenched their fists and assumed rigid Taekwondo stances.

"You're welcome to take photos with these guys, but don't stand too close, 'cuz they *will* hit you," Sgt. Morrison warned us. I posed, assuming my dourest face while our Korean guide pushed the button on my camera.

I then casually walked to the other side of the room, near the soldier guarding the opposite door. As I passed by the middle of the negotiating table, I entered into Northern territory. I had literally crossed the line, which was painted across the floor and table. I was in North Korea. This was it, what we all had really paid for.

We made it out of North Korea and the JSA without incident, just another busload of the one hundred thousand or so folks that make the trip annually. (*Get 'em in and get 'em out.* Isn't that what the tourist industry is all about?) We had our proof that North Korea is a real place, that it's not some realm invented by our governments to keep us up at night. We snapped our photos and crossed the line and saw the big flag with its blood-red star. In one sense it was entirely unimpressive—boring, even. But when I think about the greater context, about the millions butchered in that terrible war, and how the ember that still smolders could reignite at any time, then, yes, I do feel a thrill… or is it dread?

As we drove out of the Joint Security Area, the passengers of the bus were palpably more relaxed. People chatted and laughed and put their minds on more immediately pressing matters, like what to eat for dinner or what souvenirs to pick up before going home. I think I was one of the only folks on the bus who actually lived in Korea full-time, outside of the protective womb of the army base. Behind me were a father and his daughter. He was an American soldier and she must have been about ten, with bobbed brown hair and round glasses. The girl was fascinated by what she had just absorbed, though the experience threatened to overwhelm.

"Is there going to be a war?"

"I don't know. It might happen, darling."

"Will you fight?"

"If I have to."

"Why does North Korea hate South Korea?"

"Because of the war."

"Why do they hate America?"

"Same reason."

"If America fights North Korea, what will China do?"

"They may help North Korea like they did last time."

"Why did they even have the war last time?"

We ate an overpriced dinner at a canteen inside the Dorasan train station. Most of the tour members opted for the bulgogi (with tater tots, bizarrely); I chose the bibimbap (mixed rice), because I know it's hard to fuck up. I sat with the soldier and his daughter, along with his wife and son. They seemed confused by some of the food on their aluminum cafeteria platter, so I explained a couple of things:

"Those are mushrooms in the bulgogi. And that—*there*—is lotus root soaked in sweetened soy sauce. It's one of my favorites."

"Wow," the wife said. "You know a lot about Korean food."

"Yeah, well… I live here."

"Really? Why?"

I paused for a second. Her question had tripped me up. My right hand—which gripped a heaping spoonful of mixed rice—stopped cold between the metal bowl below and my mouth.

"I… I don't know, really. I just came here and… stayed. Expat life suits me, I guess."

The woman gave me a slight smile. I shrugged and stuffed the spoon into my mouth, leaving it at that.

The Cost of Doing Business?

One Tuesday afternoon I was teaching my usual interminable two-hour slog to the same three listless college boys—retreading a lesson from a book that I have squeezed dry for the last five years—when my phone buzzed. I glanced at the screen and saw that it was a text message from my girlfriend:

Ah... North Korea, it read, in terse Korean.

Minhee, my girl, usually eschews politics in her frequent text messages. These missives most often deal instead with when or where we shall meet, what we'll have for dinner, or more simple and heartfelt expressions, such as *I miss you* and *kiss*. The shuttered state to the North had never entered into our texting dialogues, and I knew right then that something was up.

What do you mean? I tapped back.

Check the internet. I'm on the subway and some guy turned up the news loudly...

"Ten-minute break," I told my students, and dashed to the nearby faculty office, where I commandeered the first computer I could find. The homepage was set to Naver, a popular Korean portal. Usually Naver is filled with photographs of leggy girl groups and famous soccer players. What I saw instead was a vivid photo of an island, with several columns of black smoke billowing into the sky.

I gleaned what I could from the Korean headlines and quickly jumped over to the *New York Times* for an English-language version of the shit that obviously had just gone down. The story was short and sketchy on specifics, other than that North Korea had attacked the South's Yeonpyeong Island with artillery, killing a couple of marines and wounding several more. (It wasn't until the next day that we learned that two civilians had been killed as well.) The article quoted the time of the attack as two thirty-six in the afternoon. It was now four, less than ninety minutes after the first shell had fallen. Was the South going to hit back? Would the North bomb more targets? Was this it—the awakening of the specter that lurks in the room every day on the peninsula—the real resumption of the Korean War, in all of its catastrophic, shitstorm glory?

I told my three students, all recently out of the army, to close their books and get out of class; that their country was under attack. I then headed home and proceeded to have about six different hurried and sweat-inducing phone conversations with some of my expat buddies, as well as my girlfriend. We felt a bit safer as each moment went by and the air raid sirens didn't blare, but one thing was for sure: North Korea had deliberately attacked the South, raining shells down on a civilian-occupied island. This was a brazen act of war, a dangerous and almost unthinkable provocation coming on the heels of the sinking of the *Cheonan* (which sent 46 young sailors to their watery deaths). But was I surprised? Could I be surprised by such a thing? After all, North and South Korea have technically been at war since 1950: an armistice ended the first round of the Korean War, but a peace treaty never followed. That Tuesday's attack was a startling reminder of this fact.

Within a couple of hours I joined Sam, our friend Nick, and David Scraggs for some pints down at the Rock and Roll Bar, where we watched the grim newscasters read from teleprompters, the usual backdrop of nighttime Seoul replaced by a massive photo of Yeonpyeong's burning buildings. This wasn't like before. Images of war were being splashed across the TV sets of an otherwise passive nation. This would be sure to inflame public opinion, which can be a dangerous business in a nation so susceptible to groupthink. As of writing this, 70% of South Koreans polled favored some kind of military action against the North. This was up from just 30% after the *Cheonan* disaster. Are they finally sick of eating shit?

"This is serious stuff, mate. The worst I've seen in eight years here," said David, staring at the crimson-and-amber colors on the screen.

* * * *

That night, I had a long conversation with Angry Steve, who is always good counsel during such times of strife and political instability.

Angry's up on the issues: he's a thinker and a reader and his opinion matters. I have some smart friends, and he just may top the heap. We talked through some scenarios, trying to predict which way this thing really could go, but in the end were left with no real answers. It's fun to play at pundit, but in reality no one knows what will transpire. Steve, as a reasonably cautious and practical man, predicted nothing would come of it:

"I don't know, but the South just has too much to lose. Are they going to risk it all with some sort of revenge attack? Or is living with these provocations just the cost of doing business? I think the latter is much more likely."

Most people seem to agree with Steve—that the South will suck it up yet again, keep making steel, cell phones, cars, and semiconductors, and brush off world perception that they are weak when it comes to facing down their bellicose Northern brethren. But hey, who cares what others think, as long as the money's flowing? Right?

"You know the world is laughing at you guys?" I told my girlfriend during a late night chat. I was a bit boozed-up and feeling candid. "How long are you gonna let them pull this shit?"

"You may think that, but this is different," she said. "We are carefully weighing our options and will act as we must."

South Korea is kind of like a nouveau-riche family that recently bought a mansion in one of the nice parts of town and has finally come to be accepted by their wealthy neighbors. The South knows that it's new to the club and is desperate to keep up appearances. North Korea is the South's poor, pissed-off, white-trash cousin that lives in a trailer park on the crappy side of the tracks. Sometimes North Korea gets drunk and ornery and drives over to their snooty cousins' house at three a.m. They blast loud music, throw beer bottles out of their pickup, and do donuts in the front yard. Sometimes they even take out a stop sign with their twelve-gauge shotgun. They're a pain in the ass and an embarrassment, but, in the end, they are *family*.

However, even family members are capable of killing each other.

****

Should I stay or should I go? That is the question. In the event of a breakout of open hostilities, do I stick it out or skedaddle? Will I even have a choice, or just be rounded up and shipped out? I do know that there are evacuation plans for American nationals in the event (I would say *unlikely event* but I don't really believe that anymore) of war. There are several collection points around the country. The nearest one to Busan is at the Korean naval base in Jinhae, about 45 minutes away, providing that traffic isn't totally evil.

I've decided that I would, or will, stay. This is my home now. This is where my life is. My parents are gone. My girl is here, as are many friends, my house, most of my possessions, and two adorable, naughty cats. Busan is far from the DMZ and cut off by a big-ass river. It was the only big city not to fall to the North the first time around; I doubt that they could make it here this time, if there is a *this time*. Also, as a writer, it'd be too good a story to walk away from. Whether this is a ridiculous romantic notion, selfishness, or the height of naiveté is for you to decide, but if the shit goes down, I'm staying put.

But will it go down? Will it come to that?

I don't know the answer. No one does. But my hunch is that something will break along the way. Small bouts of war may very well be the cost of doing business, but at some point that cost will be too high, more emotionally exorbitant than anything else, and that'll be enough. When that happens, there will be no going back. I'd like to bank on peace winning out, but history gives us pretty shitty odds as far as that's concerned.

In the meantime I'll continue trudging along on the peninsula, as I have done for the past six years; I'll don my jacket and teach, attempting to entertain my students and guide them along the endless path that is language acquisition; I'll meet my international pack of friends for long dinners and many drinks, grateful for the fact that expat life is indeed a true equalizer; I'll continue to explore the rural roads by motorcycle and trekking the bare ridges that are the bones of this land; I'll spelunk the alleys that twist through Korea's cities and towns, wander the old-time markets and dive into savory dishes at tiny, family-run restaurants; I'll continue to marvel at the people—where they've come from and where they're going—and keep trying to negotiate my own place within their ranks; I'll continue to live in Korea, come catastrophe or boon, because this where I am. This is where I ended up, and guess what? It's been good to me.

ACKNOWLEDGMENTS

THIS book is the culmination of over six years of living and working in Korea. In that time I've met countless people who have taught and inspired me, made me laugh, fed me, and generally fed the fire that has fueled me to where I am today. So, a big *cheers* to everyone I've come across along the way. This has indeed been a group effort.

Let me begin by thanking my editor and publisher, Marshall Moore, as well as the whole team at Signal 8 Press. This book wouldn't have happened without him. Such opportunities don't fall into an unproven writer's lap too often and I am deeply grateful. Here's to the success of new presses such as Signal 8, reinventing the way to publish books in this digital age.

Next I'd like to thank Will Jackson for the photos, and Lawrence Krauser for lending me his 3rd eye.

I'd like also to thank a whole heap of expatriates and citizens here in Korea, especially Scott Evans, Sam Hazelton, Angry Steve Feldman, Sir David Scraggs, BC Jay Haaf, Chris Peters, Brian Aylward (for the quotes), Craig Nichol, Bobby McGill and everyone at Busan Haps, Kim Dong-ha, John Bosckay, Kim Jeon-gil, Choe Se-ji, Mike Laveck, Jeff Lebow and koreabridge.com, B.R Myers, Cho Nam-in, Kenneth "K" May, Eddie Bae, Park Gu-pyo, Patrick Cole, and Kevin Hockmouth. Thanks also to all my great musician and artist friends in PNU and Kyungdae (you know who you are), as well as Roy Early and all the comics from the Ha-Ha Hole and Standup Seoul. The scene we've got going on in Busan and the rest of Korea is simply amazing.

In addition, I'd like to give a hearty thanks to all the folks who I met in Korea but who have since moved on, including the one and only Nick Bibby, Andrew Tenent (for all the great pours, as well as the job), Eric

Bravo (author of *Culturebook*; read it!), "Scouser Stu" Driscoll, and Brian "The Caf" McCaffrey.

I also owe a great debt to my friends back home, for putting me up and putting up with me during my many visits. This especially goes for Ken and Maravick Cohen, Elizabeth Yeager and Scott Taylor, as well Jason Maniccia and Christie Drogosch. Also thanks to Liberty and Ray Conboy in L.A. for opening your home and subsequently forgiving me for fighting in it. Thanks to David Wahl and Geoff Carter at *Monkeygoggles* for publishing excerpts from this book and paying your writers, as well as everyone down at Unexpected Productions for all the great years of improv. I'd also like to acknowledge my former colleagues from *Piece of Meat Theatre*: John Q. Smith, Eric Layer, and Christopher Goodson. The ten years we spent making theater gave me the tools I needed to eventually make this book.

I would be remiss without thanking my two cats, Motgol and Myeolchi, for never once eating the manuscript, even though it was locked safe inside of my hard drive. That would have been lame.

Thanks to the nation of South Korea, for inviting so many of us in and letting us stay, even when we manage, at times, to piss you off. What you have achieved as a people is nothing short of astounding; you have every right to be proud, and I, for one, feel privileged to live among you.

Thank you, Kim Min-hee, my love and 자기, for holding me up during the last nine months of this effort. Consider this book our first child.

Finally, I'd like to thank my brothers, Mark and Glen Tharp; my sister, Molly Crowley; my grandmother, Marion Christiansen, and the rest of the Tharp and Coates clan. My gratitude to all of you is without measure. This especially goes for my parents, John and Gloria Tharp, to whose memory this book is dedicated.

CPSIA information can be obtained at www.ICGtesting.com
Printed in the USA
LVOW031753261111

256561LV00003B/176/P